P9-DHL-767

The Bastard on the Couch

The Bastard on the Couch

27 MEN TRY REALLY HARD
TO EXPLAIN THEIR FEELINGS
ABOUT LOVE, LOSS, FATHERHOOD,
AND FREEDOM

Edited by Daniel Jones

wm

WILLIAM MORROW
An Imprint of HarperCollins*Publishers*

FIRST EDITION

Designed by Fearn Cutler deVicq

Printed on acid-free paper

Library of Congress Cataloging-in-Publication Data

The bastard on the couch : 27 men try really hard to explain their feelings about love, loss, fatherhood, and freedom / edited by Daniel Jones.
    p. cm.
   ISBN 0-06-056534-9
    1. Men—United States—Social conditions—Case studies.
  2. Interpersonal relations—United States—Case studies.   I. Jones, Daniel, 1962–

HQ1090.3.B38   2004
305.31'0973—dc22   2003064936

04 05 06 07 08 WBC/QWF 10 9 8 7 6 5 4 3 2 1

For Cathi

If the world were a logical place, men would ride side-saddle.

—Rita Mae Brown

Contents

III. Bicycles for Fish

IV. All I Need

Contents / xi

Foreword

want to know what's going on in men's minds," announced a friend of mine one day over lunch—a married mother who outearns her husband and has had
her share of marital strife. We'd been talking about my
book, *The Bitch in the House*—a collection of essays by women that
I'd conceived and edited—when the talk turned to men. "How do
they feel about their marriages?" she asked. "Have they had affairs?
Would they rather be at work than at home parenting? What would
they like to be completely different? Do they feel trapped? Pushed
around? I have so many questions."

My ears perked up. I'd spent the previous few months traveling
around doing readings and panels for *Bitch*; the topic inevitably led
to discussions about men, though the questions tended more toward
mild talk-show-style fodder:

*What is he thinking when the baby calls in the night and I get up for
the third time to go in, even though I have a job too?*

Why does he still not know our son's nursery school schedule?

*How does he feel when I'm too tired to have sex? Is he hurt, is he
pissed, or does he understand that sometimes I just can't add one more
thing to the list of Things to Do?*

I was, I confess, not above wondering some of these same things myself. But like my friend, I also had some deeper questions. How did men feel about their diminishing role in financially supporting the family? Or about the fact that the number of women committing adultery was creeping up on the number of men? How did they feel about working as hard as their fathers had but without the perks of a stay-at-home wife—from the slippers-and-martini greeting at the door to having their home and kids cared for Stepford Wife–style? How did they feel when, in fact, we often *resented* them for doing what their own fathers did (working really hard) if it left them unable to help *us* do what our *mothers* did (cook, clean, fold the laundry, feed the hamster), since most of us were now also working and didn't have time? Seventy-two percent of the mothers in this country have jobs; 30 percent of American working women outearn their husbands. Did men think they were picking up the domestic slack? And if not, *why* not? How did they feel when their wives were "the bitch in the house"?

And so, when talk of a sequel to my book began to be tossed around, to me the obvious successor—in fact, the one I myself was dying to read—was the men's response to our questions, our predicaments, our anger . . . everything we'd laid out in *Bitch*, and maybe then some. Not just any men, mind you, but smart, articulate men who could be funny and witty and charming but could also delve deep. Men who would say the things most men are too loyal or afraid to reveal. Men who, like the twenty-six women in *The Bitch in the House*, would tell the *truth* about their lives.

I floated the idea. I was told, "It'll never work." "Men don't think." "Men don't feel things." "Men have no interest in self-exploration or revelation." "Men won't say anything negative about their wives." "Men are boring." "Men have no interior lives." "Men just want to watch TV and read the paper." I didn't believe it. Okay, I believed some of it. But not all of it, not *really*. My husband, for one, knows how to articulate how he feels. Granted, he may not spend quite as much time exploring his psyche or analyzing his state of mind or going to therapy as I do, but he's no caveman. (In fact, I fell in love with him while reading a short story he wrote.) And neither are the other men we associate with. These are smart guys. Enlightened. Sensitive, even. I didn't believe they never thought about any of this, or that they couldn't talk about it wisely and well, if they tried.

I wanted this book to happen. My husband, Dan, and I both knew it was the logical next step. But I was not, we both realized, the right person to do it. *He* was. After all, it takes one to know one (a man, that is)—and especially to get one, or twenty-seven in this case, talking.

I won't say a lot more, except that the sequel, or companion, to *Bitch* is right here in your hands—and those who said men "don't think," "can't articulate," "are completely clueless" may find themselves eating their words as they turn these pages. I myself was moved beyond what I'd imagined—not to mention saddened, enlightened, refreshed, and howling with laughter—over what these smart, uninhibited, and sometimes utterly hilarious men had to say. But why trust me? I'm the editor's wife. Read on and see for yourself.

—*Cathi Hanauer*

Introduction

n September 2002, my wife published a book called *The Bitch in the House: 26 Women Tell the Truth About Sex, Solitude, Work, Motherhood, and Marriage.* The original essays she collected in the book were uniformly smart and penetrating, the truths of the contributors' lives were laid startlingly bare, and *The Bitch in the House* immediately struck a nerve and became a surprise national best-seller. The essays ranged in perspective from young women warily negotiating their first serious relationships to those in their sixties looking back with understanding and acceptance. But the main thrust of the book, and the aspect that garnered the most attention, was the anger and frustration of working mothers who ostensibly wanted to "have it all"— that is, a harmonious and satisfying blend of career, children, and marriage. The victories of feminism in the sixties and seventies had led the women and men of my generation to expect that our marriages would be different from those of our parents and grandparents. Our generation would feature ambitious working mothers finding fulfillment both on the job and at home, and enlightened husbands who cooked and cleaned and changed diapers—modern parents who were equal partners in the raising of children, the paying of bills, the buying of groceries, the folding of laundry, and so on.

The egalitarian marriage. That was the goal. And why not? Who could argue with the perfect equality of a husband and wife splitting everything down the middle—income, chores, child care? Neither partner would be dependent on the other, and they would complement each other in exactly the right ways. And what a great example for the children! No longer would little Jason and Jennifer be raised seeing only their mommy serving and cleaning up after everyone—now Daddy would serve and clean up after everyone half of the time too. And it wouldn't just be the wage-earning and the grunt work that would be fairly divided. The joys of family life also would rain down equally on husband and wife. Because why should Daddy always be the one to miss out on those precious Kodak moments—the school plays and soccer games and parent-teacher conferences? He shouldn't! With his wife bringing home half of the income, he wouldn't have to spend so much time at the office, right? He'd get some relief from the daily grind as well. It was going to be a "win-win" for everyone.

At least that was the idea.

Turns out that for many couples this arrangement has not been a win-win after all. For the women in *The Bitch in the House*, new conflicts reared their heads at every turn. Some of these women liked or even loved their work, but their kids were being raised by strangers, and this tortured them. Others felt they could never get the balance right. The added responsibilities of trying to combine work and family, without giving anything up, threatened to drown them in Too Much to Do and Not Enough Time. And although their husbands or partners were doing their part to spend more time with the kids and in the house, their contribution was often deemed ineffectual, insufficient, or both. No, what modern women really needed in order to pursue professional lives, they joked, were not husbands but *wives*.

So what happened? How did such high expectations and careful planning lead to this degree of widespread frustration and disappointment, turning otherwise smart, caring wives into shrill "bitches" and their husbands into cowering oafs who could only seek refuge behind their newspapers, waiting for the storm to pass?

Parents of previous generations—mothers and fathers alike—often claim that things were easier in the good old days. Back then, they say, husbands and wives knew their roles and there wasn't constant negotiation about time and responsibilities. All this negotiation, they say, leads to conflict. And there's enough to worry about in raising a family and earning a good living without injecting unnecessary conflict into the mix.

That may be true. But it's also true that negotiation and conflict can lead to progress—in fact, it's usually the first step toward progress—which is why we signed up for the Egalitarian Marriage Plan in the first place; after all, if things were so great back then, why did so many people (particularly women) want change? And so here we are, muddling forward, trying to forge something "better" out of this creaky institution called marriage. We may not be there yet, but projects like *The Bitch in the House* are a healthy contribution to the progress. The twenty-six female voices in that book break down myths about sex and marriage and parenthood; they fuel a frank dialogue about women's changing roles in the home, the office, and the bedroom. As a whole, they paint a compelling, unvarnished portrait of much of modern family life.

But *The Bitch in the House* is only half of the story. It's *her* story. What about *his* story? What's with the yawning silence on the other side? Don't men care about these issues? Are they just hoping to tune it out? Or is it that even now, in this age of dime-store therapy and Dr. Phil and self-actualization, most men are *still* unwilling to say what they think and feel and hope about the things they hold most dear?

I served as a second editorial eye for my wife's book, and as I read what these women had to say I was grateful for their eloquence and brutal honesty. At the same time, I found myself feeling sorry for some of the men, who seemed so hapless and bumbling, albeit good-natured, and who, in any event, couldn't speak for themselves. One book reviewer, in describing one of the working-mother essays in *Bitch,* wrote the following line summarizing the feelings of the author, a hard-charging professional woman: "Her husband can't be trusted with simple tasks." And I had to cringe, wondering what this particular man, whom I have known for more than a decade, would say to that. We are talking about an Ivy League–educated man who is at the pinnacle of his profession, who coaches his son's Little League team and works full-time-plus while tending to the household as best he can. How, I thought, would he respond to the charge that he can't be trusted with simple tasks?

But also I was wondering, *Is this really what we've come to? Is this really the way many women view their men?* Granted, some of the essays were intended to be funny, and what's funnier than men lazing around on couches while their wives or girlfriends browbeat them? (All you have to do is watch a few television ads to realize the marketing popularity of the doltish husband, as commercial after commercial features men acting like Neanderthals and being treated as such by their wives and kids. And these ads are for products being marketed not just to women but to men! Apparently we all feel great about ourselves, and are even invigorated to go out and do some shopping, after watching a dumb man being ridiculed on TV.)

To be fair, I should say that the women contributors to *The Bitch in the House* were generally kind to their boyfriends and husbands, and in some cases (including my wife in her introduction) they went to great lengths to profess how much they loved them and wouldn't trade them for the world. Even if they felt their partners were ineffectual or lazy or absent or simply oblivious, they usually gave them credit for trying hard to act in ways that pleased or satisfied.

Grateful though she may have claimed to be for my presence in her life, my wife also gave me a slight drubbing in her introduction, accusing me of failing to put items we'd run out of on the shopping list and of sneaking a few glances at the newspaper when there were other duties that needed to be performed. But these were minor infractions, really, when compared with what some of the other husbands were blasted for. Maybe Cathi figured that her creating the book in the first place, and immersing herself in it for nearly two years, was enough punishment for me. Because *The Bitch in the House,* after all, was not conceived in a vacuum. It grew organically out of Cathi's own anger and frustration and hopes for the future, and it consumed her every waking thought. For about twenty months, she lived and breathed *The Bitch in the House.* And so did I.

During this time, the essays streamed in—more essays than were ultimately published in the book—and although I read the pieces with excitement and offered advice along the way and enjoyed being involved in the nuts and bolts of producing such a strong compilation of literature, the process also wore me down. With each essay I'd finish, my wife inevitably would say to me, only partially joking, "See, all women are like this. I'm not the only one who feels this way." And evidently this is true, if the responses Cathi has received to the book are any indication. It is comforting for women to share these feelings and know they are not alone in their struggles.

For men, however, it is decidedly *not* comforting to be told that so many women share these feelings of frustration and anger and sexual ennui in their marriages and relationships. In fact, it's a little scary.

And this news comes amid a barrage of troubling developments for men. A burgeoning body of research and literature documents a great cultural shift in the balance of power in Western societies, and this shift decidedly favors the ascension of women and the decline of men. In *The First Sex: The Natural Talents of Women and How They Are Changing the World,* anthropologist and author Helen Fisher argues that women are more capable than men in many areas of business and politics because their "natural talents" (building consensus, multitasking, patience, cooperation, long-term planning) are what the modern workplace demands. Another anthropologist, Lionel Tiger, in his recent book *The Decline of Males: The First Look at an Unexpected New World for Men and Women,* describes how modern reproductive technology has taken away from men their one true biological power—the ability to control the production of offspring—and how this single development, combined with a work and education environment that is increasingly suited to the abilities of women, is heralding the decline of males, possibly into obsolescence. Seems like the line Gloria Steinem popularized—"A woman needs a man like a fish needs a bicycle"—has become suddenly, demonstrably true.

Increasing numbers of women are happily supporting themselves and having their own families without a man or a father anywhere in sight. Conservatives decry this development and commission study after study to prove how important it is for children to have a father and for the nuclear family to stay intact. But still, when it comes to modern family life, Lionel Tiger points out that women can have children without a man, but men can't have children without a woman. And he suggests that men are so confused and rattled and emasculated by this shift of power that they hardly even know what to make of it.

Oh, there have been some attempts to rally the troops. We've had the Promise Keepers, the Christian men's organization that asks its members to "promise" to be better husbands and fathers, an organization seemingly founded on shame. Remember the Million Man March? More public shaming, this time of African-American fathers who weren't living up to their obligations. (With an appealing theme like that, it's no wonder the organizers couldn't get the suggested million men to attend). And I won't even go into the male-bonding stuff, the naked drumming in the woods, the primal yells. At least those events are ostensibly celebratory, but please. This is really the best we can come up with?

If we men want to keep ourselves in the game, I say we had better be more charming. If we can't make ourselves indispensable to family life, we had better find a way to be useful or at least amusing. Because, like it or not, many women are doing just fine without men in their lives. And so much for the stigma of the old maid; these days, according to Tiger, women are more likely to be embarrassed about admitting they're unemployed than unmarried. The old maids of yesterday are today's corporate CEOs. Now it's men who are freaked out about being unmarried. In fact, according to one well-known study, unmarried men are the most depressed people in society, ranking just one spot below—you got it—married women.

Ah, but at least men still have control of the TV remote, one of their last bastions of power—that and the presidency. At least they can be the masters of their couches and entertainment centers and still try, in this limited way, to hunt and gather as best they can. But as they sit back, prop their feet on the coffee table, and channel-surf from *Cops* to *NFL Today* to the History Channel, they'd be well advised not to ignore how the world is changing around them. Beyond men's diminishing role in family life as more families carry on without fathers, it is a matter of record that men's wages and work hours have been falling steadily as women's work hours and wages continue to rise. And this trend is unlikely to reverse itself, as today's colleges and universities are graduating far more women than men, and of course it's the same story with high school graduates. As my eight-year-old daughter, Phoebe, was already sing-songing with her friends at age five, "Girls go to college to get more knowledge—boys go to Jupiter to get more stupider." (Everything we need to know we learned in kindergarten, right?)

Increasingly, men are dropping out and tuning in—to television and the Internet, in particular, where they find themselves depressed, isolated, and sedentary. And as they sit there, growing more obese than any generation in human history, they are fueling a spectacular growth in the pornography and sports industries. It is not, shall we say, a pretty picture.

So, men . . . hello? Agree? Disagree? Anything to say for yourselves?

(Cue soundtrack of deafening silence.)

Okay, I'll say something. As alarming as these trends may sound, I, for one, don't feel like my life is in a steep decline or even in a downward trajectory. The fact that women are in charge of their own birth control and reproduction may be a gigantic cultural shift, but I've yet to hear a single man complain about it. (On the contrary, I've heard only applause.) In general, the men I know *love* the fact that their wives work and make money—the more the better, as far as they're concerned (though there are plenty of men out there, I know, who prefer their wives stay at home). In terms of helping out around the house and with the kids . . . well, I'm sure men differ on this as well. But there is a species referred to as the "enlightened" man who absolutely grooves on this new role. You see him everywhere—on playgrounds, in the supermarket, at PTA meetings. He can't get enough. He's doing it all with gusto—working, parenting, husbanding—and the phrase "in decline" is probably not how he would describe himself.

Of course, it's difficult for people to recognize a social trend they're in the midst of, and the conventional wisdom is that it may well be impossible for men. As Susan Faludi argues in *Stiffed: The Betrayal of the American Man,* men have been "mythologized as the ones who make things happen," so "how can they begin to analyze what is happening to them?"

Well, I believe we *can*—despite the fact that men and women alike continue to claim that men don't talk honestly about their insecurities. Supposedly, we don't talk about our sex lives, our marriages, or our fears in any meaningful way. People love to say it's how we're "wired." We're wired to keep our emotions to ourselves, to soldier on in silence, to say things like "What's happened is in the past. There's nothing you can do about it." Or we're wired to just want to make everything all better, to instantly "solve" problems rather than—God forbid—talk about them.

Thankfully, the twenty-seven men who agreed to write about their lives for this book are not wired those ways. True, these men are still men, and men are not women. Confession and soul searching is perhaps not their natural modus operandi. In fact, countless times in pursuing the topics contained herein I was nearly laughed off the phone and out of my e-mail in box:

"You want me to write about *what?*"

"I'm not touching that one."

"Yeah, maybe in *ten years* I'd think about going there."

And then someone would volunteer a topic that was richer and more explosive than anything I'd come up with myself, and off we'd go.

Still, there's a vast, shark-infested gulf between wanting to explore something intensely personal and actually pulling it off, and each time I'd wait with trepidation, anxious to see the result. My hopes were high—they had to be—but even I didn't expect the degree of outpouring I received. Sure, I expected these guys to strip down and maybe dance around a little on the page, so to speak, but I figured they'd at least keep their G-strings on. I didn't expect them to perform the literary equivalent of *The Full Monty*.

But these smart, thoughtful, literate men lay it bare when it comes to their marriages, relationships, desires, and fears. From the no-holds-barred sexual adventurism and partner-hopping exploits of the opening essays to the devastating indictments of marriages gone horribly wrong at the book's close, the bastards on these couches are not afraid to analyze, confess, or admit *anything*.

I should say up front that this collection does not pretend to reflect the state of *all* men. It is not a mirror image of contemporary family life, where the average meat-and-potatoes working father may still rule the roost. In this book, the majority of the men are dealing with *new* ideas of manhood—some of which they are going after and grabbing, others of which are being thrust upon them by a changing world. They are struggling to define themselves as the first generation of husbands and boyfriends and fathers who are, in many cases, less powerful than their wives or girlfriends in earning, influence, education, and ambition. And unlike women (who have already explored and dissected these new conflicts ad nauseum), we men are just beginning to face our confusion at the surprising roles we're playing both in our marriages and out of them.

As Vince Passaro states so eloquently at the start of his devastating exploration of why men lie in relationships: "I can see now that the long pondering I'd been doing on the subject of men and lies was a circling-the-airport approach to where I might land, which was my own conscience." And this is exactly the course charted by writer after writer—who range in age from twenty-eight to sixty-four—as they seek to explore the reasons for their not-always-preferred marital status, for the disarray of their personal lives, for the unexpected joys and stresses of fatherhood, for the desire to cheat on those they presumably love with those they can't stop themselves from lusting after. They drill deeper and deeper into themselves, trying to figure out why they've arrived at this particular destination and whether or not it's a good place for them to stay. Or perhaps they've already moved on from that place but are looking back, trying to understand what it meant.

And some men, like those in the book's opening section, "Hunting and Gathering," are looking ahead—walking upright and scanning the horizon in search of sex or love or companionship. Panio Gianopoulos, who at twenty-eight is the book's youngest contributor, reveals in "Confessions of a Boy Toy" how he and his recent college-grad friends sought out successful and sophisticated (and sometimes famous) older women to date in the wilds of Manhattan, and how these independent women—with their money, swanky apartments, refined tastes, and active libidos—felt free to behave with these "boy toys" exactly as older men used to behave with younger women, having "unshy sex" according to their own desires and agenda while the boys on their arms got to attend fancy parties and be whisked off to exotic locales. Two writers, *Rolling Stone* contributing editor Touré and Arizona poet and novelist Jim Paul, recount times in their lives when they pinballed from woman to woman (in Touré's case, with cheating as the lure), but one man emerges from this experience with a sense of shame and the other with unabashed endorsement. And Hank Pine, husband of *Bitch in the House* contributor Hannah Pine, is someone who *has* found the right woman to share his life with, but he still—with his wife's permission—seeks out new lovers to keep himself engaged in the world of women, to, as he describes it, "feel more alive in my bones." Yes, it's an open marriage, wherein his wife is entitled to (and takes advantage of) the same benefit.

As we know, first comes love, then comes marriage . . . and not long after the honeymoon the hopeful, doe-eyed couple often find themselves stumbling through the awkward waltz of trying to maintain their individuality, while also holding on to each other for dear life, as they are blasted across the dance floor by blistering conflict and an endless barrage of shared responsibilities.

Sorry—didn't mean that to sound quite so negative. Let me try again.

After the honeymoon, the hopeful, doe-eyed couple often find themselves in a place of wonder and opportunity. But once the whirlwind of those early days spins to a stop, what will they make of their lives together? Who will do what? How will men and women manage when both are working and taking care of children? How will men manage in the home when they haven't been raised with domestic skills?

Welcome to the reality of marriage and parenthood, and to the book's second section—"Can't Be Trusted with Simple Tasks"—where the same man who was so dashing, reliable, funny, and smart before marriage and parenthood suddenly, as if stricken with some paralyzing malady, becomes a burdensome lout who can't even seem to carry his own weight around the house much less help his wife. These men, my brothers in arms, routinely take it on the chin from their occasionally overbearing (I mean, "detail-oriented") wives; they are men who, despite their substantial efforts, can't seem to deliver (to their wives' satisfaction) on their end of the egalitarian promise. Christopher Russell, a ceramic artist married to a corporate executive, writes hilariously about his daily "list of chores," a list his wife "aggressively" writes for him each morning and that he "passive-aggressively" doesn't complete. Sean Elder, also married to an executive wife, describes how he feels when she's too stressed-out and distracted to want to have sex as often as he (or any man) does, and wonders aloud what his marriage would be like if he didn't press for some action every now and then—"A book club?" Fred Leebron, in his essay "I Am Man, Hear Me Bleat," questions our generation's heavily hyped ideal that fathers should embrace their feminine side, a vague and perhaps mistaken goal that has left him unsure of how he's supposed to act as a man and a father. (One word of caution in this section: don't let the title of Lewis Nordan's essay, "Quality Time Keeps Love Fresh," mislead you into thinking he has *any* advice about how to keep love fresh.)

But of course some marriages also work well (to a degree), and in such marriages men are appreciated and even needed by their wives. The book's third section, "Bicycles for Fish," tells the stories of trophy husbands like Rob Jackson, who details his fifteen years as a self-described "housewife," when he took care of his four stepchildren full-time, from grade school to college—as well as cleaned the house, renovated it, and cooked the meals—while his wife worked full-time. Manny Howard, after being stung by how the supposed "equality" of his first marriage devolved into distrustful (and destructive) competitiveness, gets remarried to a woman who outearns him and controls their marriage to such an extent that he feels like he's been handed a Fisher Price toy steering wheel to play with. Although he tries to embrace the little steering wheel, and even sees this inequality as the key to a successful marriage, he's also haunted by the image of a man in a similar position, the boyfriend of a friend of his, whom he sees as being "a clearly adoring, sensually attuned, respectful and responsible man crouched inside of [his girlfriend's] Louis Vuitton carry-on." Rob Spillman, husband of *The Bitch in the House* contributor Elissa Schappell, explains their startling decision to scrap their feuding egalitarian arrangement and embrace their inner Ward and June Cleaver. But as Rob explains in his smart, funny, and unsettling (for many men) "Ward and June R Us," they've agreed to alternate from week to week who is Ward and who is June.

And, naturally, sadly, inevitably, relationships fall apart. Men want their freedom. Or, more likely these days, women want their freedom. Conflicts rage. Deals are brokered. Peace simmers. In the book's final section, "All I Need," men who are in the midst of divorce and those far removed attempt to make sense of what went wrong and why. In the cases where children are involved, the men in these pages, like many men, assume the children should be primarily with their mothers and don't even challenge it, but being exiled and without control tears them apart. As Robert Skates laments in his heartbreaking essay, "The Hole in the Window: A View of Divorce," "I knew that my son would soon be moving in with yet another guy I'd never met, and that this man would greatly influence his life. This man would be able to watch my son sleep; he would advise my son about girls; he would push certain sports over others. . . . But my biggest worry was of course that they'd move. And if that happened, then what would I do? Tag along?"

Even in divorces where the father retains primary custody—when it's the *wife* who walks away—fathers have been surprised to discover that the rules may not be applied evenly. This is what happened to celebrated poet and essayist Thomas Lynch, who describes how the judge in his case—wherein he assumed primary responsibility for his four children after his wife left—deemed alimony to be something only men were expected to provide for women and advised him to wise up and stop pursuing it. And finally there are cases of men trying to figure out why they can't stay married, can't stay in relationships—the serial freedom-seekers who find themselves inevitably but puzzlingly alone, a loneliness that *Jarhead* author Anthony Swofford decides is a necessary, albeit costly, fact of his life.

Among the men in this book are professors and poets, an ex–football player and a Hollywood screenwriter, an inmate and a software executive, an artist and an undertaker. These men fight, fish, and fold laundry. They yell, sulk, cry, and comfort. They make love and war and pancakes. And, when asked, they are even able to explain—on the side—how they feel about love, loss, fatherhood, and freedom.

So without further ado, may I present, in their own words—the twenty-seven men of *The Bastard on the Couch*. (Please, no video cameras or flash photography.)

—*Daniel Jones*

PART I

Hunting and Gathering

The man who has "sown his wild oats" . . . is most liable to have acquired . . . loathsome diseases, habits of drinking, and of self-indulgence. It is dangerous to his wife and children for him to become a father until all of these have been overcome. A woman who contemplates marrying such a man to reform him is inviting disease and destruction upon herself and her children.

—*The Mothercraft Manual,* published in 1916

Median percentage increase in penile blood flow among men exposed to the scent of roses: 4

Median percentage increase in penile blood flow among men exposed to the combined scents of doughnuts and cola: 13

—*Harper's* Index

Confessions of a Boy Toy

PANIO GIANOPOULOS

I've always loved older women. Though she looked a little like a canary, for years Benjamin Hunt's mother was the most desirable woman I knew. Animated and attentive, with an amused trill to her high-pitched voice, she was endlessly fighting off Ben's attempts to draw a mustache on her face. It was as if he hoped, with one cartoonish black curl, to disguise just how extraordinary she was. But there was no disguising it. None of my other friends' mothers were tiny and blond and thin-waisted; none of my bland elementary school teachers preened prettily in the mirror of their Saab convertible before zipping out of the garage; and certainly no girl in my sixth-grade class ever did anything as oddly beguiling as cooing "Blame It on the Bossa Nova"—and even dancing a few of the steps, until her husband got annoyed—in the parking lot of Super Scoops, the local ice cream shop.

Glorious Mrs. Hunt was soon followed by elegant Ms. Eleanor, the thirty-something dental technician at the orthodontist's office. You never forget your first crush, but you ought to take a picture of your second, because all I can recall about Ms. Eleanor is that when she gave me my complimentary toothbrush at the end of the appointment, sometimes our hands would touch, and rather than immediately releasing, we would both let the contact linger. It was a moment that, even at fourteen, I could recognize as illicit: the light joining of our thumbs on the studded plastic handle. Why she bothered with such a flirtation still astonishes me; I had some precocious charm—the insecure child's manic overcompensation—but I also had pimples, a bowl cut, and the reedy muscle tone of a chipmunk.

The hopeless crushes continued even after a respectable growth spurt: the girls' varsity field hockey coach; friends of my big sister, whose math homework I unsexily volunteered to complete; the saleswoman in the vacuum-repair store; Morgan Fairchild; Ms. Morraine, a bow-lipped French teacher who accidentally sat on my hand after hopping onto my desk to teach us the conditional tense. (I kept my hand so still that there was barely a pulse in the crisscrossing veins; if she had sat there for the entire class, I would've ended up being amputated at the wrist.) While other sixteen-year-olds were cruising the high school freshmen, my friend Aaron and I concealed ourselves in the Haymarket Café in Northampton, trying to pick up Smith College girls. They were dismissive of us at first—we smiled too often, and our pronunciation of Sartre rhymed with "harder"—but one evening boredom and perversity convinced a pair of roommates to invite us to their apartment. Aaron slept with one of the girls, while I learned an important truth that night: discount tequila has no respect for the human body.

In all this time, I hadn't entirely dismissed girls my own age; at school I was surrounded by them, cute and flouncy, their ponytails trailing out the backs of their white baseball caps; but just as I was beginning to attain some minor success with a girl in my sophomore English class, I slept over at a friend's house and lost my virginity to his older sister's twenty-year-old best friend. After that flash of erotic insight, there was no going back to the timidity of youth. That arduous struggle for sexual purchase—I put my hand *here,* and you move it away; kiss for thirty minutes; I put my hand back, and you leave it

for thirty seconds . . . then you move it away again—it was such a tedious dance that at times I considered just forgetting the whole
thing. Why did I have to talk a girl into letting me remove her bra,
when Helen, the twenty-year-old, had pulled off my boxers with one
foot while twining against me? I didn't want to have to persuade or
coerce girls. I didn't want to verbally champion sex. I was sixteen
years old; there were enough hormones in my bloodstream to kill an
adult rhinoceros. I just wanted to get laid.

A few years later, when I moved to New York City, that sense of
impatience and frustration was gone. College had bled some of it out
of me; like it did for many people, the four years satisfied a lot of de-
ferred adolescent longings. Falling in love and then messily falling
out of love had also gone a long way to exacting a little emotional development. All of that strange and deadly seriousness of young ardor,
the juvenile earnestness, the heartfelt silliness . . . it had thoroughly
worn me out. So once the heartache had subsided, and I was ready to
begin dating again, I found that, given the choice, I now preferred the
company of older women.

Luckily, I was living in a city with perhaps the most beautiful and
sophisticated women in the world. And as I started to meet some of
them, I discovered what seemed to be a charming, relatively new phenomenon: as much as I and my friends were attracted to older
women, they were also attracted to *us*. It was a little hard to believe.
We were broke, we had annoying roommates and incriminating
video-game consoles, we needed better haircuts, better jobs, better
facial hair—and just out of mercy someone should have carried our
wardrobes into a field and burned them. But the older, richer, more
worldly women we were dating weren't complaining. Complaining?
They enjoyed the eroticism of slumming it. In the morning, they'd
step over the passed-out friend of a friend on the couch and tactfully
ignore the copy of *The Onion* in the bathroom.

Of course, "older" is a relative term. When you're twenty-two, who isn't older? The women I was meeting were in their late twenties or early thirties, hardly *Harold and Maude* territory. Now that I'm twenty-eight, they don't seem old to me at all. But at the time, they were in another league. These weren't college girls with their summer-camp counselor jobs and guitar-playing ex-boyfriends; they had tremendous life experience. They had lived overseas, started their own businesses, read all the great books. They had seen the Woody Allen movies I'd watched on video *in the movie theater.* When we went out, they knew the entrances to secret, exclusive bars, and at the parties they took me to the drinks came in glasses instead of plastic cups. In the summer, while I boiled on Eighty-fifth Street, they escaped to the Hamptons, or L.A., or some island that sounded like Japanese candy—Bora Bora, Aruba, Fiji—and came back with expensive, catered tans.

Once or twice they brought me along on their escapes from the city, but mostly we went out to extravagant dinners and then had vigorous, unshy sex in their much better downtown apartments. They were confident and passionate and had already wasted enough time pretending to be inhibited or genteel. And though I also continued to date younger girls, it was a disconcerting switch. Nineteen-year-olds had their obvious charms, and they were easily impressed—"Check it out, the Brooklyn Bridge!"—but they were just so *new.* When you're forty years old, reliable wonder is probably a stimulating trait in a partner. But for a twenty-five-year-old guy staggering toward adulthood, it gets a little tedious. *I* wanted to be the astonished person in the relationship.

It made me cringe to hear nineteen-year-olds start a sentence with "Today, in class, we learned . . ." The last thing I wanted was a reminder of their lack of knowledge. That was part of the attraction of older women: they *already* knew things—things I assumed I'd learn too, just from being around them. Age is no guarantee of culture, of course, but this was Manhattan, and the odds were good that simply from prolonged exposure, if not professional affiliation, the woman I was seeing was familiar with architecture, or dance, or photography, or art history . . . each of them a fine match with my areas of expertise: martial arts, air hockey, and Ms. Pac-Man.

I wasn't the only guy who thrilled at the instructional possibilities of dating an older woman, and I was far from the only one doing it. At some point, every single one of my male friends was involved with an older woman. Garret, twenty-three, dated Gina, a twenty-nine-year-old advertising executive—suitably blond, unsuitably high-maintenance—until his contempt for her dachshund, which he was forced to walk every night, finally exceeded a degree considered justifiable. By the end of their relationship, he'd mastered the resentful "use the child to get back at each other" technique, raising it to a level far beyond his years. Now, *that's* an education. Jason, twenty-five, dated Maria, a thirty-two-year-old divorcée, for a few months until she moved back to her family in Spain. She had been the assistant marketing director of a pharmaceutical company, as well as an extraordinary drinker. They used to have cocktails on her enormous terrace almost every night—years later, Jason still couldn't stop talking about how incredible her apartment was. On the day of Aaron's graduation from NYU, he met Karen, a twenty-eight-year-old graphic designer whom he dated for two years. At the time, Aaron and I were both living on $120 a week, after rent. A girlfriend who could take you to Nobu—a clever, affectionate, large-breasted girlfriend in possession of a master's in sexology and an apartment off of Washington Square—was maybe the best graduation present anyone I know has ever gotten.

I worked with a bartender, Joe Scipio, who was perpetually on the hunt for a sugar mama. Joe was a twenty-three-year-old black-haired Italian-American kid, as good-looking as he was vain, and his seduction anecdotes were seemingly endless. So his failure to snare a provider always bewildered me. Looking back, I imagine it may have had something to do with his feverish insistence on sex in public bathrooms, or maybe it was just a result of his unfailing misogyny. (If he ever wrote a memoir, he could title it *Joe Versus the Vagina*.) That the bad behavior he used to charm younger girls failed to succeed with older women shouldn't have surprised me. A couple of the women I dated had been married before; many had gotten close and then prudently backed out. Whatever their amorous histories, almost all had, by now, enough romantic experience to have overcome the girlish draw toward being treated badly.

Still, though we had pleasant times, the relationships didn't always last long. But then, endurance wasn't really the point. These were modern women. They were successful, intelligent adults, with lucrative careers of their own. They didn't have to rely on men for financial support, so they could just enjoy themselves, dating whomever they wanted—without surrendering thrills or personality for long-term compatibility. Basically, they could now act like men used to: picking lovers who were young, entertaining, and a little enthralled. Forget the future. Forget forecasts. Forget promises.

It was with this reassuring romantic levity in mind that, at twenty-five, I met a thirty-three-year-old woman. We had been introduced through a common friend via e-mail, and after a flirtatious correspondence, we decided to meet in person. Ordinarily this is a stupid thing to do—people never live up to expectations—but in this case I wasn't dealing with high expectations. Her expectations were dismally, even insultingly, low. From my name, she had imagined a swarthy, hairy, squat Greek man with eyebrows bushy enough to shelter small birds from predators. I am, in fact, about as swarthy as a banana cream pie.

On my side, I had a rare premeeting advantage. She's a famous screen and stage actress, so I already knew what she looked like. We met and hit it off in that giddy, slightly incredulous manner of genuine romantic excitement, and soon we were casually dating. Casual because I had recently ended a fling with a twenty-eight-year-old who was dangerously close to declaring squatter's rights to my apartment—defying my easy-natured theories about seeing older women—and the last thing I wanted after that was something serious.

And neither did the thirty-three-year-old. She had never dated anyone younger than she was, and the age difference troubled her. "You're twenty-*five*," she would marvel early on. "Can you even rent a car yet?"

"I can *totally* rent a car," I'd bleat.

Just as my age occasionally perplexed her, her fame occasionally perplexed me. I was accustomed to being the younger one in the relationship, and even being the less successful one didn't sting anymore, but being the anonymous one was bizarre. I like to think I'm not a particularly proud person, yet the cloak of invisibility I'd feel draped in when going out to a movie premiere with her, or to a fashion show, or to any flash-happy publicity event was, at times, oddly emasculating. This feeling was maybe an arrogant response to the ridiculous phenomenon of fame in America, and luckily one that I outgrew—just as every man involved with a celebrated, successful woman must. But for a while, as people edged past me to get to her with rarely a glance of acknowledgment, I regretted ever having said that I wanted to be a fly on the wall. A fly's life is actually quite demoralizing. Especially a little boy fly.

I never expected, however, having to get over *anything*. This was supposed to be casual. But as any boxing trainer will tell you, it's always the punch you don't see that knocks you out. Nine months later, we were still together. Happy? Yes. Perfect? Hardly. Our relationship was beset by some of the same earnestness and insecurity that had so infuriated me as a nineteen-year-old. Yet I was beginning to realize that maybe love couldn't help but be a little infuriating on occasion. Everything has a price, and I was getting old enough—God forbid—to appreciate the rare occurrence of mutual respect paired with physical attraction. Not that we talked about the relationship very much. We had yet to really discuss its official trajectory. Whether *she* was secretly harboring thoughts about our future, I didn't know. Maybe. This was courtship, after all, and courtship without misdirection is like Las Vegas without gambling—no one would ever bother with it.

Regardless, I didn't need to worry about secret thoughts. We were both adults, both optimistic, both with plenty of time to grow and learn about each other. If things worked out, as it seemed that they would, then great. But there was no need to rush. We would simply take it one day at a time.

At least, that was the plan.

I was sitting in Union Square Park the day that I was told I could no longer date my girlfriend. It was just around noon, a breezy April weekday, and I was trying not to notice how similar being a freelance writer is to being unemployed. All around me were men with sodas pinned between their thighs and ties flung over their shoulders, and women in their lunch-hour sneakers. Beside me on the bench, a man had a copy of *Time* magazine on his lap, and he was flipping through it a little distractedly, as if hunting for cartoons. When he left, he abandoned the issue face-up on the bench.

On the cover was a picture of a plump baby in an office in box, and beneath the innocuous title—"Making Time for a Baby"—was the alarming subtitle: "For years, women have been told they could wait until 40 or later to have babies. But a new book argues that's way too late."

I snatched up the magazine in terror, staring hard at the ominous cover. It looked like the baby was crawling right for my throat. I could almost hear its soft fleshy knees thumping against the desk, and the tiny assassin drag of its diaper.

Exhaling, I flipped to the cover article and started reading about Sylvia Ann Hewlett's new book, *Creating a Life: Professional Women and the Quest for Children.* According to Hewlett, it said, women had been misled by the medical industry regarding their fertility chances. Census data revealed that childlessness for women over forty had doubled in the past two years, and a national survey of 1,647 "high-achieving women" showed that over 42 percent were childless. Hewlett was here to set the record straight. Women don't have until they're forty to start thinking about kids; fertility rates start decreasing at *twenty-seven.* "By the time a woman is married and settled enough in her career to think of starting a family, it is all too often too late," the article asserted. A couple of outraged feminists were quoted—"The subliminal message is, 'Don't get too educated; don't get too success-ful or too ambitious,' "—but no matter how intelligent and insightful Caryl Rivers's response was (which I agreed with), for sheer emo-tional manipulation it simply couldn't match the reproductive en-docrinologist describing the heartbroken never-to-be mothers who visit him, and his glib conclusion: "I go through Kleenex in my office like it's going out of style."

A few months earlier, I had finally sublet my rent-stabilized apartment on Eighty-fifth Street to move in with my girlfriend. I was tired of riding the number 6 train back and forth three or four times a day, tired of rushing home to feed my cat and of dumping out yet another half gallon of spoiled milk in my neglected refrigerator. These were all nothing more than nuisances, however; really I was tired of that feeling you have, when you love someone but don't live with her, that as soon as you show up you're leaving again.

My girlfriend had just turned thirty-four. Baby talk had surfaced, vaguely—"Sure, I like kids," I'd said. "I mean . . . very abstract, quiet kids"—but mostly we'd pushed the issue off. She wasn't in a hurry, and I didn't want to think seriously about having children yet. Pro-fessionally, I felt too unaccomplished. It seemed like the step from being a hopeful to being a never-made-it was just one cigar away. When would I have the time to write, with a day job *and* a kid? Kids need things like sandwiches and clean clothing and loving yet firm theories of portion control. They can chain questions together all day, like little lunatic Socrateses—"Where do quarters come from? Can animals use them?"—and they're so cute that you can't help but neglect your creative aspirations for them. It's like they were invented by the Republicans who figured that, in the end, the best way to get rid of federal funding for artists is to make all the artists so distracted and sleep-deprived that they'll just give up.

And sitting in Union Square Park that day—a place that despite the landscaping and the fountain and the Mahatma Gandhi statue wants nothing more, in its little concrete heart, than to be left alone so that people can sell drugs there again—I knew that it was over for me, just as it was for every other young man dating a woman in her thirties or early forties. I had previously—and a little smugly, I'll admit—watched older men be labeled selfish for courting much younger women. They were chicken hawks, predators employing power disparity for sexual and egotistical gratification. But now, overnight, *I* had become the selfish one. *I* was the one vainly, carelessly getting in the way of a woman's chance to have a family, and it was actually the older men with younger women who'd had it right all along.

A little dazed, I stood up and dropped the magazine onto the bench. I thought about my friends who were dating older women, and about my thirty-one-year-old sister (Where was she on that oppressive fertility graph? I'd forgotten to check), and I worried about my girlfriend's best friend, Moira, who was soon going to turn forty. She wanted children with the kind of biological desperation ordinarily reserved for emergency bathroom breaks on the highway. What would Moira do now, after reading this? She was already only a wolf whistle away from sexually assaulting the first unmarried fireman who crossed her path.

But once the competing surges of self-incrimination, anxiety, and melancholy had passed, I was faced with the considerable fact that I loved my girlfriend very much. I loved her talent for saying the precise thing that would embarrass me, despite my continuing insistence that I was unflappable. I loved her intelligent eyes, and her guilty laugh, and the way she read in bed, with her right hand straying up and out of the covers to touch the side of her neck, before dipping to turn the page. There was a long list of adorable things she did (and still does), and a much shorter list of annoying things, and I thought that happiness might just be right there, held in that exquisite differential.

.   .   .

It's been a year and a half since that startling day in the park, and though all my friends eventually ended their relationships with their older girlfriends, I was wrong to so recklessly write off the giddy conspiracy of younger men and older women. Hewlett's book bombed. Moira is dating a thirty-three-year-old. My sister is dating a twenty-five-year-old. And I won't even bother with the latest tabloid stories of older women celebrity boy-hunts.

"There are three kinds of women," explained a friend of mine, when the issue came up last week. "Women who want to be taken care of. Women who want to be in charge. And then there's a third, *new* kind: women who want to shape the guy who's going to take care of them."

"That sounds kind of manipulative."

"No, it's flattering. They pick intelligent, promising young guys. Like us."

"Like you," I said.

"Come on. *You* can hardly count yourself out of this."

Oh, but I can.

In the past six months, I've developed a crush on a girl much younger than me. I haven't met her yet, but I've seen a few black-and-white pictures, and she's gorgeous. Her nose is tiny and slightly upturned, and she has slim, delicate fingers. When I do finally meet her—her due date is in ten weeks—I can only hope that, unlike her mother, she prefers the company of older men.

An Invitation
to Carnal Russian Roulette

Touré

 t is perhaps the greatest game ever created. It blends seduction, deception, danger, and electric, illicit sex. It demands a gambler's heart and a cat burglar's cool. The Game can be expensive emotionally, financially, and, if the other member of the threesome catches you, physically. People have played carnal Russian roulette for thousands of years, and many have been killed because of it. I am not necessarily proud of my behavior, but this is no cautionary tale. Consider it a recommendation. The Game is among the great, rare pleasures in life. Imagine the cactus with milk so sweet it's worth the needles.

I've heard of bank robbers who continued their career after becoming filthy rich because the thrill of stealing was a greater pleasure than even the money. Those sensitive artists are my brothers. They'll understand me if no one else does. You see, the Game is not about love on any level. It's about trying to touch fire without getting burned. It's about embracing your inner bad guy and being a slave to your id. It's about gambling with life and love. I once saw a Hitchcock tale about a gambler who'd bet young men he met in bars that they couldn't light a lighter ten consecutive times. That's a boring proposition until you hear the wager: if you succeed, you get his beautiful Cadillac. If you fail, he gets to cut off your pinky. Now, that's excitement. If big risk can supercharge the most boring little contest, imagine what it can do to sex.

I've always found the word *cheating* to be a simplistic, flaccid, and overall pathetic choice to describe the complex missions I've completed. Besides, they say all's fair in love and war. Is it cheating because I combined love and war? Why don't you decide. Sit awhile and listen to the memoirs of a twisted young man who believed the only good sex was forbidden sex, a man who could enjoy sex only when served with a side dish of danger. Names have not been changed to protect the innocent because no one in this sordid tale is innocent. We have lied, deceived, and committed sexual theft (translation: cheated). Of course, the lying and deceit came mostly at my urging. I was a carnal cat burglar, a sexual desperado, one of those little devils willing to risk life and limb for forbidden fruit. Sure, I made a mess of my life, but I had fun. What happened exactly? As Humbert Humbert said at the outset of his sordid tale, Look at this tangle of thorns.

The trouble began long ago. I once thought it started with the trauma I experienced after a bizarre three-way involving a restaurateur, a waitress, and a handgun, but no, it starts much, much earlier than that. You see, as a child I had a bad habit. I liked to steal. As early as age seven I was developing sticky fingers and a flexible moral compass. I did it for the adrenaline, the outfoxing, the conquering of fear, and the excitement of getting over. There is no rush quite like opening a wallet you've liberated.

But all that came to an end one horrid afternoon when Dad caught me committing a relatively harmless theft (from his wallet) and punished me cruelly. (That was not when my conversion came.) That evening we went to Grandma's house and he trumpeted the story to her, casting himself as the self-righteous sheriff collaring a jailbird in training. Such vulgar fiction. Grandma pulled me aside and exposed me to the cold truth. "It's not bad that you did it," that sage said. "It's bad that you got caught." That old angel, a professor of moral relativism, showed me the light.

Many years later the second of the three moments that transformed me from an ordinary citizen into one who hungered for the Game arrived in the form of a brief, wordless invitation from a player. It was the beginning of a summer during my college days. I was hired to do menial tasks at a hip and romantic little restaurant on the eastern seaboard. As the youngest member of the staff, I was apparently seen as something of a tasty morsel, for no fewer than three members of the staff moved in to have a bite of me.

The first made her move within the first week of my employment there. We went for a drink after work, and before I knew it her tongue was down my throat and her wedding ring was in her pocket. It lasted just a moment—then she ran—but her danger-charged kiss was more electric than anything I'd ever felt. Still, I was not ready. There was one last incident that completed my transformation into a monster. The bizarre three-way. It took place at the end of the summer.

Long before I arrived at that little shop of sexual horrors it'd been widely rumored among the staff that a particular sexy waitress was dating the owner, but despite plenty of circumstantial evidence, both of them denied the relationship. This threw a strange shroud over the story, for there was no reason for them to lie. I had not yet discovered the Game but was attracted to the supposedly single waitress all summer long. At the end of the summer, since they both refused to admit to a relationship, I made a play for her. And thus one night during my last week there I found myself alone with her in the restaurant after closing, with her tongue down my throat. Then the owner walked in on us. Without a word from anyone he put his gun on the table, took off her dress, and initiated a three-way in which he never acknowledged me. It was as if we were having independent encounters with her at the same time: even when we were both touching her he never even grazed my soft fingertips as he manhandled her. It was a moment injected with danger on so many levels, a moment so bizarre that while it was happening I wondered if I would one day discuss it in front of a jury. But hours later, after I caught my emotional breath, I realized I'd stumbled onto another level.

That night left me so scarred I needed all my sex to have some sort of danger, and I began playing the Game. My sexual war games are, of course, threesomes. The third member isn't consenting and usually isn't fully aware of the threesome in which he or she is participating. But it's that other person, the one who's getting screwed without getting sex, who we can thank for the sense of risk that gives the Game its supercharge.

In the following years I had a few brief conquests (I once lured a lesbian away from her girlfriend and twice had actual threesomes) but was unable to play the Game robustly until I met, let's call her Debbie (because that's her name). Debbie was a beautiful modern dancer who didn't know she wanted to play, but even though she'd been living with her boyfriend for three years, she neglected to mention him until forty-five minutes into our first date. She spoke of him in passing and with a minimum of feeling, as if he were a small chore she had to do later that evening but didn't know why. Clearly, this was a difficult moment in their relationship. A greater man would've walked away, respectful of the challenge of making any relationship work. But I'm not that type of guy.

Over the next two weeks, as we went to dinners and out dancing and to the movies, she told me repeatedly that she wasn't going to sleep with me. She told me every day. In those days she was staying in New York, where her dance company was rehearsing. The boyfriend (and she) lived in another city. She was borrowing a gorgeous apartment on Riverside Drive from some Columbia professor on leave (off in Italy playing the Game, no doubt). It was a cavernous place, a romantic fantasy with majestic views and a giant bed with four engraved mahogany posts, the sort of apartment only Hollywood would envision as a plausible place for two young, black, largely penniless artists to find themselves alone and horny late one morning. We ripped each other apart in a lust frenzy. But if that wasn't enough, either fate or the great director in the sky cued the phone to cry out for attention just a moment after we finished. It was her freshly cuckolded boyfriend. She spoke to him briefly while wearing nothing and struggling to hide her labored breathing. As the light from the window pointed out a small dimple on her ass that I hadn't noticed during our strenuous workout, she told him, "I love you." I could tell he knew something was awry but didn't know what. I loved it.

For the next year Debbie lied and deceived while I aided and abetted and her boyfriend played the perfect foil, chasing after us in the shadows, quick enough to smell the smoke but too slow to find the fire. It was dramatic and messy and occasionally called for the cloak-and-dagger work of a cold-war spy. (He almost caught us together once, unwittingly of course.) Every time we had sex she said it was the last time. Every moment together was stolen and thus precious. (So twisted.)

After a year of our ongoing fiasco Debbie left him for me and we began seeing each other on more conventional terms. This went bad quickly. It wasn't nearly as much fun without the Game. But she was beautiful and I didn't want to leave her. Then one night a friend of mine introduced me to Keisha and mentioned that it didn't matter to her that I had a girlfriend.

Keisha was a sexy little buppie with big tits from upper-crust Connecticut who rebelled against her privileged upbringing through deviant sex. She loved the Game. Thus began a new threesome. It seemed like the right thing to do because at that point the entire country was talking about a presidential intern named Monica Lewinsky.

Now, I understand that the intrusion of that name into this tale is overtly self-mocking and caricaturish. If this were fiction, this subplot would be too easy, too pat, too hokey. But in some way, knowing that the president of the United States was still one of us, one of that band of crazies who just love the Game, made me feel I should be playing, if for no other reason than to support my leader. Keisha was more than happy to second my motion, sharing my vitriol toward the evil Ken Starr and showing up for our trysts with her hair bobbed and peeking out from under a beret, a blatant copy of Monica's famous look, an appropriately twisted little joke.

For months there was lying and deceit and a shadowy three-way transfixing Keisha and Debbie and me. But this time the stakes were higher. I hadn't cared about Debbie's boyfriend's feelings and I wasn't scared of him. I enjoyed stealing from him. But in the new three-way I was gambling with Debbie's feelings. This level of danger made things with Keisha not electric but explosive. But if Debbie ever found out what I was doing, it'd break her heart. I couldn't have that. So I dumped Debbie and started seeing Keisha exclusively. That was stupid. As any good west coast rapper will tell you, Ya can't turn a ho into a housewife.

I really tried to leave the Game alone then. For the first year of my relationship with Keisha, I stayed away. But for some reason Keisha never trusted me. A lack of evidence only fed her suspicion, made her think she wasn't looking hard enough. Eventually it didn't make any sense not to play because she was already acting like a bitter, jealous cuckold. So I had brief flings with Debbie, a couple of tenderonis in L.A., a good friend of Keisha's, and the sitter for the baby downstairs, a low-level model from eastern Europe. Through it all Keisha played the perfect foil, chasing after me and my cuties with the competence of Inspector Clouseau.

One day around this time I went to visit an old, old girlfriend of mine who had had twins. When she started to breast-feed in front of me her boyfriend flew into a jealous rage and threw me out of their house. I couldn't be too mad. It was a bit like being accused of a crime you didn't commit when you've already committed that same crime on other occasions. I guess I'd acquired the look of a criminal.

Three years ago I retired undefeated. Never once was I caught by any of them. I don't think I've ever been the cuckolded member of a threesome, but you can never be sure. Alas, all that's behind me now. I leave this as a testament for those who will play in the future. Hopefully my story will reach some young people at the beginning of their romantic careers and let them know there is another path. There is an electricity that comes from illicit, ill-begotten, stolen sex that is unlike any other feeling. The Game is a roller-coaster everyone should know once.

How does my current flame keep me happy all by herself? Let's just say that public sex has quite a high degree of danger. But more, I've found that being able to share my danger with a single rare angel like her can be more intense than the chaos of the Game. She also has a collection of wigs and speaks three languages, but I digress. The bottom line is she's the best thing that's ever happened to me. It's cool to go to Vegas and get into a little trouble, blow your funny money, and have the time of your life, but the guy at the craps table gambling with his rent money is an idiot. I might be crazy, but I'm not stupid.

In Search of
a Female John Wayne

STEPHEN ELLIOTT

was engaged once, to a modern woman. I proposed to Rachel on a mobile phone while running errands for Matador Records. The call went like this. "Wouldn't it be funny if we got married?"

"Oh my God, people would freak out."

Back then cell phones were rare and airtime was a dollar a minute. When Madonna's label tried to charge me for that call, I denied ever having made it.

I met Rachel while I was waiting tables at the restaurant where she worked in her final year of college. She was a Democrat from Texas. Her mother was a professor and her father a doctor; her mother ruled that roost, loving but iron-fisted, and there was never any doubt who was in charge. Her father was a large, kind man, who liked to eat and sleep and who never tired of professing his love for his wife.

What I loved most about Rachel was that she didn't need me. Rachel was popular, full of confidence. She was utterly self-sufficient and didn't rely on her relationships to give her life value. Virginia Woolf wrote of women who were defined by the needs of those around them, women whose sole purpose was to sublimate their own needs in the service of others. In "Professions for Women," Woolf held up as her hope a time when a woman could define herself by her own needs and desires.

Rachel is the only woman I've ever met who actually embodied this ideal. She was absolutely certain of her worth. I've dated hard-core lesbian feminists who burn through the streets and over the hills of San Francisco naked on their motorcycles, women whose hard exterior melts away in a matter of weeks to reveal the fragile, needy, withered human being that exists inside most of us, the beating heart beneath our social theories. But not Rachel. She could outlast anyone, and as such the world catered to her, and she expected from the world.

"I have a date," she would say.

"Bring me the leftovers," I'd reply. We had an open relationship. People should be told in advance those things don't work. It was my idea mostly; I was afraid of commitment. I tried to outcool her and failed. We had rules. Like not in front of each other, not with each other's friends. Rachel broke those rules, a regular Donald Rumsfeld, secretary of dating. But that's not why we didn't work out.

What I loved least about Rachel was her insistence on having it both ways. She didn't believe in sacrifice; as far as she could see, there was never a conflict between two desires that couldn't be navigated. She walked into a room, straight-backed and smiling, and asked what that room could do for her. She never looked for me first in a crowd. She was a flirt and she loved to meet new people. She wasn't a cheat, per se, but she chose not to see things she didn't want to see. She danced when she wanted to dance. Our downward spiral started when I walked out of a bathroom in Seattle in the summer of 1996 to see her standing by the pool table with her hand in the back pocket of a boy named Doug. Doug had money—his parents had died and left him something. I had arrived in Seattle at Rachel's encouraging, having lost all of my money in a game of poker in West Yellowstone. Rachel was bartending in trendy watering holes and experimenting with expensive drugs. She dressed nice for Doug. I remember black stockings she sent me to buy at the Safeway. I remember Doug sitting in our living room and Rachel coming to meet him in those stockings and a skirt. I remember puncturing the stockings later with a pen and tearing them to hell and finally calling Doug and saying I was going to beat Rachel and it was going to be his fault. It took me years to understand Seattle for what it really was, a drizzly northern city where I came face-to-face with the violence of my own jealousies and insecurity.

From Seattle I went to L.A. to make it in film and Rachel went to detox in Houston. She came out to get me a few months later and convinced me to move back to Chicago with her. I bought her an engagement ring from a gumball machine outside of Wal-Mart. "Let's do it," Rachel said as we drove through Nevada. We had spent the night in a casino parking lot. She had a kind smile. She loved to have a good time. "Let's get married right now. My parents will be so surprised."

"I don't know," I replied, my shirt tightening around my neck as the blinking lights of Las Vegas faded in the rearview mirror.

We didn't work out because she went to law school in Washington, D.C., and expected me to follow.

"Why did you drag me back to Chicago only to leave four months later for Washington?" I asked.

"After this we'll start making decisions together," she promised. I imagined my cuckolded fate in the nation's capital. I'd end up tying a noose around my neck and jumping from the Washington Monument. There would be no friends except the other students Rachel may or may not introduce me to. I decided it would be too much. There was nothing for me there, and I knew it wouldn't take Rachel too long to realize that and leave me stranded in Dupont Circle in exchange for some third-year student with a clerkship. Rachel had never been broken up with before and treated it as a declaration of war, a war she ultimately won by marrying my best friend. But that's another story.

I've always been attracted to strong women. My first girlfriend, Sonja, had her seventh-grade boyfriend's name tattooed across her knuckles. She was Puerto Rican and American Indian, with green eyes, black hair, and sand-colored skin, and I never doubted that she was the most beautiful woman I would ever sleep with. I still have a picture of us. She's holding our black cat in her arms. I have an arm over her shoulders, and my T-shirt reads MY LETTER WAS PUBLISHED IN PENTHOUSE FORUM. We look like Beauty and the Beast. She liked fistfights and rock concerts and mosh pits. When I got too hot with her in an alley one night she punched me in the stomach and I dropped to one knee. She carved SONJA + STEVE on my apartment's wood floor. She liked manly men, and since I rode a big motorcycle and we had met in the parking lot of T.J. Maxx, that's what she thought she was getting. But I got rid of that motorcycle in our first week. When I refused to fight the boyfriend of a girl she had beaten up, she said I was a wimp and incapable of keeping her safe. Both charges were absolutely true, but they stung.

After Rachel there was Abby, a sociology Ph.D. from Northwestern. Then Chrissy, a full-time political activist and part-time German literature lecturer who had recently finished an eight-year relationship with another woman; they had lived in a van shucking corn across the Midwest. Chrissy said she was not a relationship person. Then there was Tammy, an insane, brilliant writer who invited herself to sleep over then told me not to try anything funny; when I didn't she did. All of the women I've ever dated have been smart and, on the surface, fiercely independent. But they have always ended by wanting me to drive them somewhere, to fix their television, to protect them in some way. They have all wanted me in some form of traditional male role. It's disappointing.

Finally I met Wendy. I was living in San Francisco, finishing my first novel and working as an instructor for the Law School Admissions Test. Wendy was a professional dominatrix of some renown. Here, I thought, was the woman for me. And she was great. She made all of the first moves; she took initiative. She took care of me. Instead of walking arm in arm with me, she would hold me by the back of the neck when we walked down the street. If we were both asked a question, Wendy would be the one to answer it. If there were three people in a car, I would sit in the backseat. When I lost a fifty-dollar bet at a pinball game Wendy paid my debt for me, then sent me to buy drinks. She insisted I sit on her lap at parties (Wendy is an Amazon, perfectly proportioned, about six feet tall), which I found embarrassing and erotic. But when I didn't see her for a few days she cried that she had fallen in love with me and I wasn't paying her enough attention, and I knew in her sadness it was over. Her domination wasn't an act, but she was as insecure as the rest of us; she was utterly human, and humanity often presents itself in unbearable ways. The more she wanted my attention, the less I wanted to give it to her, which made me feel like a jerk. She was dominant, wonderful, she made me feel safe; but she was not a self-sufficient woman who would be fine with or without a boyfriend or husband. Beneath everything, her desires were no different from that of a sorority girl, or a mid-American housewife from the fifties. Her pride as a sex worker and a highly educated woman who worked for herself spoke directly to a society that had undergone a transformation. Her need to be in a relationship, her tendency to value her romantic relationship above all other things and to subvert her own personality to that relationship spoke directly to a society that hadn't.

So what is my problem? My father was an old-school sexist who proudly wore a T-shirt that proclaimed MALE CHAUVINIST PIG. He never thought twice about hitting a woman or child. He cheated on my mother often and openly. He told my mother when they got married that they had made a bargain—he'd bring home the money, she'd take care of the children. If what he said was true, they both failed, though not through any fault of my mother's. She became terminally ill when I was eight and was mostly paralyzed for the next five years before dying in her sleep. I left home when I was thirteen and spent the rest of my adolescence in state-run group homes. No one is more a product of society than I am. Because I was a ward of the court, society took custodial duties for my upbringing—the state served as my parents, the state paid for my college. I come from society at large.

The group homes, like much of the world, are violent places, where one is not allowed to be a coward. Inside these understaffed facilities, some with thirty beds to a room and two staff watching it all from behind bulletproof glass, boys are beasts. Female staff members are unattainable prizes in wars of attrition. These are gladiator arenas, and modern thought has yet to filter through. People fight fiercely for the smallest scraps of attention. We were kids. You had to maintain a façade of toughness. Queers and sissies were despised. I had to internalize that, so my guard was mostly up and still is. I didn't win too many fights, but I fought when I had to—there wasn't any choice. And the occasions when I did back down, overwhelmed by my own fear, are the tragedies of my youth.

Wendy once told me that I wanted to be the girl in the relationship. I wanted to be looked after, provided for, and told what to do. Preferably still, I wanted to be the abused girlfriend. I think she is both right and wrong about this. I want to be protected and mothered. I am not a caretaker. In any case, in today's world, neither role exists within the standard. The girl Wendy believes I want to be is not an acceptable choice for the modern educated woman. The man who sits on the couch and yells for his wife to bring him his beer is not acceptable either.

But for me there is something else. Of all the women I have ever dated, only Rachel had the confidence to do it without me. That's why I loved her so deeply. Cruelty and passive aggression aside, she is the only modern woman I have ever known intimately, the only woman I have ever dated who did not define herself by her relationship to a man. For me it is crucial that I not be responsible for the other person's happiness. Rachel was the only woman to relieve me of this duty. Her happiness and unhappiness sprang solely from her own sense of self. Think of the old heroes, Humphrey Bogart and John Wayne, and the women who loved them for their quiet strength. I'm looking for a female John Wayne.

I ran into Rachel for the first time in years last summer. I was boarding a train in Chicago, miles away from any neighborhood we had ever lived in. It was the last car of the train and there was a seat open next to her and she was reading a paperback book with the Oprah Book Club Selection sticker on it. It was a ten-car train, so even on the same train the odds were only ten percent we would share a car. I sat in the seat and said, "Now isn't this the strangest thing." She ignored me at first, thinking I was some crazy person, just like the old days. Then she put her hand over her mouth and laughed.

She was wearing a sleeveless copper-colored shirt. I convinced her to get a drink with me after we got off the train, and she agreed, but not without first calling her husband and telling him who she had run into and where she was going. At the bar the roof was leaking and there were buckets everywhere to catch the water. "Wow," I said. "This bar is like a metaphor." A pipe had burst on the second floor. The bartender kept placing new buckets. A steady stream poured onto the table across from us, and the floor was puddled. None of the old drinkers at the bar were concerned that the roof was certain to collapse at any moment, the final beams of a rotten, sinking ship.

It was chilly in the bar, and I noticed that Rachel didn't have a sweater or jacket with her, so I gave her my sweater to wear. We made a lot of jokes and had a lot of laughs before it got serious. "I never would have left you," she said. "Why did you break up with me anyway?"

It was a good question, and I realized for the first time that I didn't have an answer. I wished we had gotten married when we were in Vegas, like we almost did. That way we could have gotten divorced. But at least we would have done it.

Her husband, Mickey, came by. Mickey and I had hung out all through college; I had holiday meals with his family. I held out my hand, and for a moment I wasn't sure if he would take it, but then he did and he smiled. "How have you been, man?"

"I wish you had told me you were going out instead of me having to find out through other people," I said.

"I was making a choice," he said. "It was you or Rachel and I chose Rachel."

Mickey's an administrator in a nursing home now. They both had to be at work in the morning, so they didn't want to stay out too late. I wanted Mickey to leave so I could bask in Rachel's glow. I didn't have to be at work in the morning, on any morning. I'm a writer. Successful in that I don't have to do anything else, just write. I've made it in this world in some strange way. Rachel said she always knew I would be a writer, and that I would keep wandering.

"I always knew you would turn out fine," Rachel said, smiling, her large cheeks nearly covering her eyes. And of course I knew what would happen to her as well. She's a lawyer now with the National Labor Board. Mickey joked that he'd married ninety thousand dollars in debt. Haw haw. Mickey got a good deal. They want to leave Chicago. Rachel and Mickey want to go to Charlotte, North Carolina, where property is cheaper. They seemed very much in love, but who would they know in North Carolina? They would have each other and that would be enough. I could have had this, I thought. I'm sitting across the table from the closest I ever came. Their lives sounded boring and horrible to me, but I was glad to see them. I realized what every married couple probably already knew—that a few key relationships and the stories behind them make up most of the fabric of your life.

When they got up to leave, Mickey and I shook hands again, and then we did one of those awkward male half hugs. "I care about you," he said.

"That's nice of you to say," I told him.

Rachel took off my sweater to give back to me.

"Keep it," I said, and I really hoped she would, but I knew she wouldn't.

"Don't be silly," she replied. "We're going straight home from here."

A Bachelor's Fear

STEVE FRIEDMAN

I'm forty-seven years old, reasonably articulate, reasonably attractive, neither rich nor poor, heterosexual, and while I've had my share of girlfriends, I have never married. This must be because I'm a selfish and self-centered oaf, a philandering lout in Lout Heaven, a.k.a. Manhattan, a city filled with long-legged and plump-lipped libertines. It's because I'm hopelessly enthralled with the idea of waking up when I want, watching TV when I want, eating when (and what) I want and, in the process, having friendships, romance, and sex when (and with whom) I want.

Or maybe it's because I'm an emotional cripple, driven by terror I barely acknowledge, much less understand, so averse to intimacy that I sprint from it whenever things get too good.

Or perhaps it's because I'm possessed of a rare and precious courage, and while others marry out of fear of sickness, old age, and solitary death, I bravely soldier on—refusing to settle for anything less than revelatory, transformative love, or, absent that, the noble but sometimes difficult business of pizza for one and holidays alone.

Or—sociohistorians and psychobiologists take note—it's not because of anything *I'm* doing. I'm merely an innocent scrap of human flotsam swept up in the tidal wave of history and the concomitant changing nature of reproductive destiny. Now that a woman can have a baby by herself, and now that a woman can make more money than I do, and now that there are very few saber-toothed tigers and misogynistic laws to prevent women from becoming attorneys and doctors and investment bankers, my historically most salient attractive selling points—brawn and ferocious cunning and massive earning power and the ability to protect and provide for and otherwise nurture my helpless and pregnant wife and our mewling offspring—don't matter so much. Nowadays it's a seller's market, and I'm the hapless buyer.

Then again, maybe the females resisting that historical tidal wave—the spiritual heiresses of June Cleaver and Harriet Nelson, the women in their twenties and thirties who, careers and postgraduate degrees notwithstanding, ache to marry and multiply and maybe even whip up a casserole or two—maybe they don't see me as the best person to marry and multiply with. I mean, being funny and sensitive and emotionally supportive and all is nice, but it seems to me that any self-respecting spiritual heiress of June Cleaver wants a man who'll take care of her, who will protect her and the mewling infants from predators and poverty. I'm a freelance writer.

Or maybe I've remained single because I'm the *beneficiary* of the tidal wave. These days a lot of women, wonderfully cognizant of the new reality whereby they don't *need* a man to protect and support them, aren't looking for one. So when they go on a date, they're not seeking commitment, or deep and enduring love, or a lifetime partner. They're looking for a good time. Strike up the bachelor theme song, heavy on saxophones and finger snapping. Which brings us back to the long legs and plump lips. A confession: I'm looking for someone more romantic, a woman who yearns for something more than laughs and sex, who believes at a cellular level in the redemptive power of love. A woman who shuns marriage and who believes she's fine alone frightens me. I'm not fine alone. Why should she be? (And yes, I know there's something weird and possibly pathological about a longtime bachelor only dating women interested in marriage. I'll get to that later.)

Or maybe my single state is just a simple choice, neither dark nor heroic, much like choosing breakfast cereal (which, I must admit, I struggle with). You want Raisin Bran, I go for Special K. You, married guy, opt for companionship and compromise and squabbling over whose turn it is to cook dinner and debating whether your failure to take out the garbage was an unconscious manifestation of laziness, thoughtlessness, or long-repressed hostility to her female power. I choose to see action movies at night instead of going to the in-laws'.

Or maybe it's because I haven't met the right woman.

·　　　·　　　·

I was pondering the alternative causal theories of my bachelorhood the other day, after having slept late, lingered over the sports page, checked my e-mail, called some friends, and made plans to watch a basketball game on television later in the afternoon. Were these activities in which a married man could indulge at his leisure, with impunity? I think not. Then again, this was a good day. There were also those mornings, especially holidays and weekends and times between assignments, when I had no plans, when my buddies were out of town or with their wives or girlfriends, when I wondered if I would die alone, when I wished there was someone next to me, someone sweet and loving and warm and funny and sexy, someone who, even if she might curtail my sports-page reading and sleeping late and e-mail checking, might let me hold her, might hold me, might ask me to help her work the crossword puzzle, might murmur with affection as I worried aloud about a vexing work project, who might bear my children, grow misty-eyed at how I would teach the little rascals to be strong and to shoot baskets and how to be helpful and sensitive to others' feelings while remaining true to their own convictions, who would indulge my sneaking them sweets between meals and telling them scary stories at bedtime, who might agree—exuberantly—to be my partner while we moved through the world, shoulder to shoulder, fingers interlocked, someone who would stroll underneath aged oak trees with me as we turned white and wrinkled, leaning on each other, someone whose fears I might help recognize as puny phantoms compared with our enduring and transcendent bond, someone who might liberate me from the crushing burden of myself.

A few women have volunteered to take on such an assignment. They were sweet women—loving, warm, funny. Some were gentle murmurers. A few were even crossword-puzzle enthusiasts. Any man my age who claims he's single because he hasn't met the right person is more deluded than I am. Exponentially more deluded. By this time in our lives, we've all met at least a couple of "right" women.

So why was I still single? Did asking that question indicate that I wasn't entirely and blessedly content with my bachelor status, that perhaps I was being driven by things I didn't understand? Was caring so deeply about the answer persuasive evidence that the Emotional Cripple Theory (ECT) applied at least in some part to my bachelorhood? (Short answers: yes and yes).

And speaking of emotional cripples, was I single because I felt somehow inadequate, and was I waiting until I was more successful before inflicting upon a woman a lifelong partnership involving me, and did I desperately need to accept that none of us are ever exactly as we should be, that we're all God's creatures, perfect in our own ways, and having had that spiritual awakening, did I then need to bask in the varied and blessed and all-encompassing beauty that love and partnership has to offer? (Short answer: well, yeah, probably.)

I thought about these and related questions while I roller-bladed around Central Park that day (another activity easily undertaken while single, slightly more tricky to pull off when there's a wife to love and children to teach about strength and sensitivity and such). As I bladed, I listened to "Desperado" on my CD player, getting misty-eyed over the mournful closing line, crooned in a decidedly minor key, "You'd better let somebody love you, before it's too late."

I was reveling in the freedom that being single and childless allows, wallowing in the bathos that being single and childless entails. This is common bachelor behavior.

·   ·   ·

"You're sad," a girlfriend once informed me. "You are going to end up sick and old and alone and no one is going to be around to take care of you. I feel sorry for you, because unless you wise up soon, you're going to be alone forever."

"But," I said, "I don't think I'm in love wi—"

"Just shut up," she said. "Just. Shut. Up. We get along, we make each other laugh, sex is good, we share values. You can learn to love. Commitment is about a lot of things, and the thing it's about most is two people promising to take care of each other, because the alternative—being alone—is too terrible. So quit being an idiot and let's get engaged, because otherwise, you're going to have a life of take-out pizza and too much sports on television. And you're getting bald. And your apartment is a mess. You're lucky to have me."

A good friend of mine recently broke things off with his girlfriend. He had been married once and had a son, and he didn't want to do it again. His girlfriend would not stop—and I use the word advisedly—*nagging* him about getting engaged. A week after the breakup, he found a package in his mailbox. Inside the package was the book *Men Who Can't Commit,* with a note from the ex-girlfriend. It said, "Read chapter 8."

When my male friends feel slighted, or hurt, or neglected, or upset by something I've done, they usually express their feelings clearly and succinctly. Language ranges from "I'm feeling slighted" to "You hurt my feelings when you did this or that" to "Fuck you, dickhead." Then we're pals again.

Women, though, at least in my experience, tend to express hurt and rage by telling me what is cracked in my soul, what are certain to be the horrible consequences of my heinously twisted insides. Instead of "I'm hurt and angry" or "I hate that you don't want to spend Easter with my parents" or "Fuck you, dickhead," it's "I feel sorry for you, you pathetic old bachelor" or "Read chapter 8."

To my dismay, there is widespread institutional support for such female behavior.

I have written articles about dating and sex and love for women's magazines, and I learned early on that there must be a moment in every article when the man sees the error of his ways, the emptiness and bleakness inherent in a life of chasing beautiful young women. There must come a time, usually no more than a thousand or so words into the piece, before the jump, when the man renounces his selfish and silly ways, embraces the ECT, and vows to pursue love. (Or, even better, meets a woman, is transformed, and settles down.) I say there had better be such a moment, because I have tried these stories without the moments, and I have been told: Without the moment, "the story doesn't work." When the story doesn't work, I don't get paid.

No moment, no payoff. Story of my bachelor life.

•   •   •

A forty-year-old friend tells me he's single "because there are no worries, no cares. You come and go as you please. Look, having sex with the same woman, no matter how good it is, gets old. Plus, as a bachelor, you get up, you turn the radio on, it doesn't matter how loud it is, no one's going to tell you to turn it down."

A novelist I admire suggests, two months before his wedding, that I be brave. "We all make decisions from a feeling of shortage, from economic insecurity, from fear," he says. "My suggestion is that if you're working to develop your spiritual life, you don't have to make decisions based on those factors. You can—you *should*—make feelings based on abundance, on the sense that everything's going to turn out all right, whatever you choose. Then choose. If you choose being single because it feels right, fine. If you choose marriage, that's fine too."

My younger sister, married and the mother of two, offers advice. "Tell the next woman you go out with that you're divorced instead of that you've never been married. It's less scary."

My older brother merely nods as I blame our parents.

"I think part of the reason I never married," I tell him, "is because Mom and Dad had such a bad marriage. I remember them never being happy. I think I somehow internalized the idea that being married meant being locked together in an angry, disappointed, frustrating dance of constant compromise and eternally squashed dreams."

"Yep," my brother says, monotone, flipping through a camping-supply catalogue. "That's a pretty accurate description of what it's like."

My best friend for the past twenty-five years suggests I stop thinking so much. "For men, true love is just a limbic response anyway," he says. "You see someone, or smell them, you want them. You touch them, you want them more. Then you decide she's incredibly wonderful, or smart, or sensitive, or kind. You *decide*. You're just making stuff up to justify your limbic response. You're a man first and foremost, so stop being a philosopher. Give in to the delusion, make it real, and quit worrying so much."

• • •

I mention my struggles to a thirty-eight-year-old woman I know who has been happily married for ten years. She also tells me that I need to stop worrying so much. "You need to think of marriage not as the finish line, but as the beginning of an adventure." I ask her what she likes best about being part of a couple. "I get to hang out with my best friend," she says.

Visiting a friend in the hospital (a bachelor might be self-involved, but he can also do the right thing), I meet a Russian émigré who happens to be tall and beautiful and blond, also long-legged and plump-lipped, with eyes the green of an old 7-Up bottle. She is visiting the same friend. The émigré is twice married, soon to be twice divorced, possessed of a college-aged daughter, gratitude that she's "done weeth the marriage thing," and a fierce desire to "hof fun."

Not to be forward, but our friend seems to be resting comfortably, and would the émigré like to join me for a cup of coffee at the hospital cafeteria?

There, she tells me that living things are not meant to be together for life, that after mating, the male of the species intuitively and quite naturally seeks other mates. "Thees ees the way it ees," she says, "so why do we pretend it ees not?"

•   •   •

Is my glib bachelor friend doomed, and if so, how come he's so sanguine about it? Is the novelist babbling the secret and short-lived language of the bridegroom-to-be, and will he be talking less about abundance and more about custody schedules and alimony arrangements in a few years? Is my brother, a doting father and Little League basketball coach who just celebrated his sixteenth wedding anniversary, merely expressing the weary worldview of an inveterate grouch? (And is such a worldview the absolutely essential philosophy of any inveterate grou . . . I mean, longtime spouse?) As for the thirty-eight-year-old bride's sentiments, I have a couple of best friends, and I'm perfectly happy with the amount of time we spend together.

During much of the week after my visit to the hospital, I find myself obsessing about shared lives and love that lasts. These are good things, no doubt, and people who think otherwise—people who turn their backs on marriage—are surely missing something life-affirming, an institution that is both astonishing and magnificent. I decide that I must persuade the Russian émigré that not all men are philandering louts, that there is no cynic as bitter as the failed romantic, that love can heal as well as hurt, that I can offer what she has so long been seeking, what she has wrongly and tragically abandoned.

My plan feels so right. I suspect it is very wrong.

•   •   •

There was a time, not so long ago, when I dated mostly married women. Or heavy drinkers. Or women who seemed to have lots of boyfriends. When, a couple of years ago, I hit the trifecta, I started seeing (as in, *paying* to see) another woman—a therapist.

She helped me see that by targeting unavailable women for life-long commitment, I was assuring myself that I would remain single, while telling myself that I wanted a partner. She helped me see that there is nothing wrong with a single life, that if I wanted to date different women at different times (or at the same time, if I was honest and it was okay with them), I should feel perfectly comfortable doing so. She helped me see that volition was the key—that if I was avoiding marriage because of some barely conscious fears, perhaps I might be happier if I overcame those fears.

After a few months—without any explosive epiphanies—I said maybe I should start thinking about marriage as a job. She arched her eyebrows.

"Well, jobs are often a drag," I said. "You have to get up early, you have to sit at a desk when you don't want to, you have to do what someone you might not like tells you to, you can't go home and take a nap whenever you feel like it, and—"

"I'm not sure," she said. "I—"

"But you get a paycheck, and health insurance, and a 401(k), and you get to hang around people who wear nice clothes and smell okay. So maybe I just need to resign myself to the fact that marrying means disappointing someone and getting bored with sex, and her getting bored with me, and having to do things when I don't want to, but focus on the companionship and the walks under the oak trees and—"

"That idea might be fine for your brother," the therapist told me (which I thought was kind of a cheap shot, but I let it pass), "but I think we need to work on figuring out what you really want."

"But—"

"Steve, what do you want?"

•   •   •

I want companionship, intellectual excitement, really good sex, fidelity, incandescent, thrilling love, at least one child, the walks under the old oak trees, naturally, someone kind, sweet, not too bossy, not too rigid, not too easily upset by a partner given to occasional bouts of torpor (it's not clinical, I swear), someone not inclined to express personal hurt with personal attacks. (I don't want to read chapter 8, okay?) I want a woman who sees marriage as neither the definition of her very essence, nor as a patriarchal plot to enslave and oppress her and her sisters worldwide. I want a woman whose hopes and dreams I can cheer and support and who will cheer and support mine. I want it through the sickness and health, good times and bad, of course. I want a gentle murmurer. If it turns out that I make the money and she raises the kid, that's okay. If, instead, we take turns with the money making and kid raising, that's fine by me, so it should be fine by her. I want a woman for whom money is not a big deal, who reads a lot, who's at least a little athletic, who's neater than I am but tends toward bemusement rather than irritation when confronted with towels on the floor.

I'm working on the fears, telling myself that not all marriages are my parents' marriage, that some women in fact will consider free-lance writers as lifetime prospects; and I think I'm ready to seek a life with the appropriate person, if she loves me and I love her.

I decide to abandon my plans to woo the Russian émigré. I'm not sure, but I think this represents progress.

Unsticking the Bodhisattva:
Love, Bad Faith, and a Chance to Change

JIM PAUL

hen I left San Francisco, I found something in my apartment that seemed emblematic of my eighteen years in that city. I was boxing up some items on the hall table, and I came across one item fixed in place with a wad of sticky blue putty. The foot-tall wooden statue of the Buddhist Goddess of Mercy—the Bodhisattva Avalokiteshvara—had been stuck there since 1989. In the big earthquake she had done a little dance, all the way across the table. I had been disturbed by this and had got out the putty, which I used to keep the pictures straight in that shaky town. After that, my Bodhisattva danced no more.

A decade later, as I unstuck her, I considered how odd and stuck I myself had become. It's common to get more idiosyncratic with age, as propensity, circumstance, and luck carve out the shape of each particular life, though one's own idiosyncrasy is not as obvious as others'. Inside our separate oddnesses, we watch as the world seems to diverge from us. I do, anyway.

But now I could see it. I had lived in that town as a single man for those years, not once settling down, not once finding—or letting myself find—a woman I could be with. I'd become supremely, painfully self-sufficient. I'd moved into that small apartment in the Mission District, and within a couple of years I had created a workspace, a writing hut on the roof in a ten-by-ten structure that in the building's early years had held the laundry facility. After that the years seemed to whip by.

I fossilized in my routines. I did the dishes before going to bed. I slept in clean sheets, in one position, wearing earplugs to ward off the city's roar. I had a cat and no other deep attachments. It was all as tight and snug as a boat at sea. Once some guests came over, and one of them, a woman, looked at the immaculate surface of my stove and began to insist, rather angrily, that I had a maid service. I did not. Nor did the Bodhisattva move around on her own.

What had happened to me? And what was about to happen? For me the end of the twentieth century presented a real change. I moved from the density and intensity of the Mission District to the openness and silence of the mountains. More profoundly, I moved from a life of not connecting in the city to a real relationship of integrity and faith with a woman I love. I am still not sure how it happened exactly, though I'm grateful for it. Of this I'm sure: it came about as a surrender, not as an effort.

My relationships in the city had been of two kinds. Most often, I fell into being with someone without letting myself have any deep feelings about her. Such withholding, however self-protective in its origins, ultimately made things worse and made such feelings harder to face in the next round. Occasionally I felt passionately about someone, but I see now that I never fell in love with anyone who was actually available to me. So I remained apart in these instances too, and these relationships too seemed to accelerate the spiral. By the end I had come to the bottom of it, and I felt radioactive, toxic to those I chose to be with. And baffled, so defeated by the process of making a relationship that I determined not to do anything with anyone.

All that time I'd been reacting, actually, to events that had occurred on a specific June day some twenty years earlier and nearly three thousand miles away in Michigan. That summer I had a job at a government fish hatchery—a few offices and a dozen hangarlike bays each holding a big tank filled with trout. They were circular tanks, and the trout all swam in one direction. On my lunch hours I liked to visit the tanks and to toss in a handful of the granular food we gave them, setting off the silver explosion the fish made as they shattered the surface, plunging after the bits.

My wife and I had just celebrated our first anniversary. Katie and I had met five years earlier in college. As sophomores we rented a basement room on Genesee Street in Buffalo. Neither of us had been in a sexual relationship, and we proceeded intently into one. When the snowdrifts darkened the place, covering the ground-level windows, we mostly stayed in bed.

Our life was inner-directed in the fierce way of new lovers. We didn't go out. We cooked canned raviolis on a hot plate. We read a lot, did jigsaw puzzles, played cards, and, though we were barely in our twenties, reminded people of an elderly couple.

And we studied. It was the High Feminist period, and we were both students of the movement. We split domestic chores precisely, with a chart, and she was not interested in pregnancy, in fact would come to consider it a kind of colonization of women by men, one radical argument of the time. I didn't argue. We were impoverished students, and by then I was more interested in writing than in having kids.

Katie was smart and in her way aggressive—in three years she won almost every pinochle hand we ever played. But she was painfully shy about the external world, hating even to have to talk to clerks in the bank. This was no problem for me. I never had a problem chatting up strangers. So I took up those duties.

Katie kept a hope chest at the foot of the bed, in it linens, table-cloths, things married people would need. She was a planner, and getting married was part of her plan. I went along with it, and a week after graduation we did get married, right on schedule. She unpacked that hope chest, and we had a ceremony on Long Island, where her family lived. I got to the church early, in my powder-blue suit, and saw, to my horror, a huge raven sitting atop the spire. I threw acorns at it and shouted, but it would not leave.

We went on to graduate school and moved into married-student housing. That first year was difficult for us. We'd been accepted at the same big university, in different departments, she in psychology, I in English. And both programs put us through boot camps that year. The work was intense, and remained so for five or six years, until we'd both gotten our doctorates.

That spring we made friends with a guy from her program. His name was Jake, and his interest was the psychology of information. He had a lot of surveillance equipment—scanners and recorders and wiring and cages, and he had no room for all this stuff in his small graduate-student apartment, which was not far from ours. We had a basement, and he asked if he could store some of his stuff there. We agreed, and Jake brought over several carloads of boxes.

When the term was over I managed to get that job at the fish hatchery, which was nearby. I rode my bike to work. I was the grounds-keeper. On the job I drove a ride-on mower, cutting the grass and collecting the clippings in a small trailer—just a box on wheels, actually, that I towed along behind me. The box had a big picture of a leaping trout on it.

That June, while I drove this silly vehicle, I was having some seriously bad feelings. I thought I was going crazy, but it turned out I was just being lied to, which at the time was new to me. I was innocent then, so faithful I hadn't even thought about the concept of faithfulness. But now things were not adding up. Something was wrong with this business with Jake. One morning I thought I would feel better if I called Katie, so I got off the tractor and went inside and dialed our number. She wasn't there, and in a horrible moment I knew where she was and what she was doing. I told my boss, Chester the janitor, that I had to go—my wife was having an asthma attack. Then I got on my bike and rode over to Jake's apartment. Even walking up the walk I heard the familiar sounds she made, making love. I was so shocked I could only kick open the door, scream into the dimness— no words, just a wail—and pedal home.

At home I got out the biggest suitcase and starting throwing things into it, stupid things, like the extra piece of cloth that came with my suit jacket. I called a cab, but I could not think what I was going to tell the driver when he asked where I was going. We had no family, no real friends in that town. And then Katie came in, crying hysterically, and I tried to forgive her and stayed with her for seven more years.

Actually, I couldn't forgive her. I wonder now what I would have had to do to reach forgiveness, and I wonder if I can get there now. Certainly I could not get there at twenty-three. I had murderous rage for the guy, Jake. I went down into the basement and smashed all his electronic gear against the concrete floor—this I recall as the only momentarily satisfying part of the whole deal. Then I threw the broken pieces out into the yard, where sometime during the night he took them away. In the morning they were just gone, and their absence seemed to promise that the rest of the mess would just go away as well.

I hoped we'd simply go back. But, though we rarely mentioned the incident, there was no going back, and living in the hope of it just increased my hurt and anger. I plunged into my work, applying myself completely to my studies. I earned a doctorate in English in four years and got a job at a small college in Illinois, where we went together, still living in the outward form of the marriage.

One spring, seven years after the disaster, I took a train trip by myself, to New Orleans, to do some research, but mostly to get away. I stayed in the French Quarter, and in the bar of the hotel I met another guest, who invited me to her room. She too was escaping from a midwestern marriage. We went to bed and had sex, after which she began screaming and weeping, which she continued to do until I had to leave.

Though it was late at night, I couldn't stay in New Orleans a moment longer. I checked out of the hotel and went to the train station and rode northward, through the night, until at dawn I reached the little town where we lived. I got off the train and walked through the quiet streets. The place seemed like a toy town beside the railroad tracks. The whole neighborhood stank of honeysuckle. I let myself quietly into the house and found there Katie and a young woman, asleep in each other's arms. I stood at the foot of the bed, feeling not bitterness but an odd detachment, a numbness, and the sure knowledge that it was finally over. I slipped off my wedding band, put it in the nightstand drawer, and left quietly, without waking them.

In Illinois then, you had to have grounds for divorce. I still didn't want to face things squarely, and yet there were only a few choices for these grounds: drunkenness (no), adultery (yes, but isn't there anything else?), physical cruelty (no), mental cruelty (well, if it had to be something, that sounded okay). Despite this, it was lots easier to get divorced than I'd thought. I found myself in the county courthouse in that midwestern town, claiming mental cruelty. I had no lawyer. I was representing myself and had made some mistakes, but the judge was sympathetic. "I don't like to make these things difficult," he said. "Now why don't you just tell me what your wife did to you that you feel was mentally cruel?"

There was a lot to say. But at the moment I could only summon up one lame fact: "Lately," I told him, "my wife will only listen to music by women." To my amazement, this was enough. The judge raised a hand to indicate he needed to hear no more, then gaveled the bench and told me I was divorced.

·   ·   ·

By then I was thirty. I had to get out of the Midwest. I was innocent no longer, and I longed to be on my own in San Francisco. I loaded a few things into the car and drove there. I found that apartment. And the years passed—two, three, five. I lived there by myself, but I didn't have it in me to be alone. I missed being with a woman, and as a single, heterosexual man in his thirties, I had no trouble meeting women. Sex too was easy in those days. Mostly, all one had to do was have the nerve to ask.

I did, but I wasn't really there. I'd been naïve before, and at this point I was being something just as limited, inhabiting naïveté's antithesis, which is not wisdom but distrust. So I began my odd and isolated existence. I mostly chose to be with women who were like me, I thought, insulated from their own intimacy. Often we bounced off each other like ball bearings in a box. Sometimes a woman would come to hope for something more from me, and then there would be hurt and anger. Sometimes she broke up with me. But more often I found a reason to break it off with her before anything happened.

Usually I searched out something I wouldn't be able to stand in the long run. One woman saved every newspaper she ever bought and stacked them neatly on the floor of her living room, where they became towers of paper you had to walk around. One wanted me to meet her parents and suggested I get some body work done on my car before I met them. Another called me one morning from the psychiatric ward of San Francisco General. Would I pick her up? she asked. She'd been arrested while acting strangely on the Golden Gate Bridge. I did pick her up and then slowly, carefully, as if I were backing away from nitroglycerine, ceased my contact with her.

Another woman simply cleaned my apartment while I was away on a trip. This was meant as a kindness, but I felt violated by it. One was just too young, finally. One—and I mention this with shame—was just too fat. And one greeted me at the doorway of her house, when I had gone there to pick her up for a date, literally falling-down drunk, so drunk she had no idea the next day that she had ever seen me that night or had been supposed to.

Some of these are great reasons to break up with someone, some of them not so great. Some of these difficulties I might have taken up for a time, earlier in my life, thinking that I could help. Maybe I could get her into AA or help her clean up the newspapers or lose weight. Maybe I could have shown more understanding about fixing the dents in my car. But by then I did not trust any situation to improve. Any trouble seemed to be a sign of a deeper disorder that I was not ready to address. And at last I knew there was in fact a deeper disorder, and it was my own.

·   ·   ·

I was acting in bad faith. San Francisco was going through its latest effervescence, the dot-com period, which came in with lots of money and lots of new people around. And I was rudderless in this swirl. And then, all at once, as the nineties came to a close—and coincidentally as the Clinton impeachment got under way in Washington—I woke up. Literally woke up, in the middle of the night, next to someone I did not know and, I realized with a shock, did not much like. Clarity poured in over the next few days, as I went over the women I had been seeing and came to the conclusion that I could be with none of them any longer. And that it was not possible even to begin a relationship again without some profound adjustment in my thinking.

But what that adjustment could consist of, I had no idea. This was a horrible time. I cut off my would-be relationships, without offering much in the way of explanations. My answering machine served up the furies. My old cat got sick and had to be put down. My place didn't seem like my own anymore. City life grated. The dot-com boom had stripped the town of many familiar hangouts. On Valencia Street a crowd of new, young faces replaced the old. I was in no mood anymore to hang out with people in their twenties. Ultimately, I had no faith in my feelings. I wanted to see no one, in any sense.

And then, as if providentially, I was offered a chance to leave town, to take a job out in the vast space of the big West. I jumped at it. By then shorn of certainties, particularly of certainties about relationships, I packed up my stuff, unstuck the Goddess of Mercy, rented a truck, and drove to Arizona.

And so I found myself new in a new town. I knew no one, and I had a chance to do things over again, this time the right way. I moved very carefully, preserving my solitude. As far as women were concerned, I had come to a clear knowledge that I knew only one thing: I would not try to make anything happen. I would not try to compose my fate with a woman. If something happened, I was ready, but if not, I was ready for that too.

This release of determination worked somehow. Within a couple of months I met someone, she too, at that point in her life, unwilling to force something to happen just to be in a relationship. She too had gone through long tribulations and a divorce. Her response had been the opposite of mine, in a way. She had sought the solitude and comfort of wilderness, where she lived. Later, it seemed to me that I too had sought something like this, without finding any comfort, though, in the wilderness of the city. In part because of our sense that we had parallel histories, there was a kind of ease between us I hadn't known before. It was so easy it felt like nothing less than fate.

She's about my age, which I like. There's the commonality of music references, for one thing. And of course the larger connections, of having been through hard times and of sharing a sense of the scale, scope, and moment of a life. Oddly, had we met at twenty, we would not have shared a lot in our backgrounds and upbringing, but by the time we did meet, we found ourselves quite similar, with years of things to talk about and deep interests in common.

Now we live together on a ranch in remote mountains in Arizona, just the two of us and the cats and the dog, and life, like the peaks and the desert around us, seems to get bigger every day. In this context the wilderness seems elemental in every way, especially domestically. It feels as if we are the first man and woman, deciding, not on the basis of some plan or ideology or dream but on who we are and what we need, how we can live together. So after nearly twenty years of living as a single man in a city apartment, I have a second chance at a home. I've taken up fence building, soil breaking, stone masonry, dog wrangling, and other hard work. For six months I renovated a trailer on the property to put in offices for us, work that included carpet laying and crawling around in the dark underneath the structure, which is to trailers what a 1974 Mercury is to cars. I even figured out and redid the big pipes to the septic. I work in the west end of this trailer, beneath a window that looks out onto the long dirt drive that winds up to the house. I am writing this there now. Late in the day she comes back from her work at the university and the dog hears the car and we both get up. I like being home to welcome her.

I moved here three years ago, and each year I've felt a little less strange inside myself, as if a calm old friend has returned to stay. For long periods I don't notice this new self, then all at once there he is, me. I bring to this new life everything I learned—often the hard way—in my old existence. Now I know that I need the truth, above all things, and that nothing is possible without forgiveness. I aspire in this relationship to real compassion, to a love that is not dependent every minute on the attributes, attitudes, and actions of my beloved. As for the gratitude I am carrying around now, I don't even have to try to feel that. I've been rescued. The Bodhisattva, by the way, made the trip safely too. Unstuck, she stands on the mantel here, which is solid stone.

My Marriage, My Affairs—*His* Story

HANK PINE

'm angry at myself and a little ashamed. I've agreed to write this essay, but I can't tell you my real name. I'm actually depressed about that.

I mean, it's pretty ridiculous. My wife and I have had a few *non*illicit affairs. I promise you we're happy and that the "openness" of our relationship has not proved harmful to anyone. So we have affairs that are not betrayals. Yes, we allow each other to do that.

And yet the public disclosure of this in fact small difference would endanger everything from career to friendships to community standing. We'd be disparaged behind our backs and probably also in person. We could never adopt a child, due to the joint unfitness of our character. Of course our parents would be mortified, while parents our own age would keep their children away. A giant *O* would hang above our house, a scarlet letter emblazoned upon the sky for the general protection of the citizenry.

Recently I attended a party where, after a few drinks, the talk turned to sex, as it so often does. A woman who knew nothing of my situation blurted quite out of nowhere that she just couldn't be in an open relationship. Now, this comment is dismissive from a point of nonexperience but not too egregious. (For purposes of instruction I would suggest something along the lines of "Well, I don't think I could be in an open relationship, but I haven't tried it.") Then she went on to say, and everyone seemed to agree, that an inherent pathology lurked at the core of such a relationship, a perverse power dynamic that excluded real happiness. Now, here we have a progressive group of adults who would never denigrate sexual difference in any other form but who felt free to loudly and confidently pathologize a private sexual choice they really knew nothing about.

Which is not to say that such bias rises to the level of homophobia; any burden I might experience, if exposed, would pale dramatically to the historic pains suffered from that prejudice. But the analogy is helpful. If I were to publicly proclaim the agreement my wife and I choose to live by, our lives would take a hard turn for the worse simply because we behave differently in a way that harms no other human being. Sure, feelings are hurt, relationships break up, and new ones form. But this is the stuff of life whether you are married or single or in an open marriage or not.

Still, I know, many people can't handle this, even those from the ranks of the progressively inclined.

Not that long ago, in fact, I couldn't either. I was once a member of that forward-looking though pious group. Probably in my past somewhere, at a party not so different from the one I describe above, I also maligned open relationships as somehow inherently flawed. Or at least I nodded when someone said it was impossible, that the constituent partners were "living a lie." Which is just the kind of thinking—the "closed" kind regarding desire—that too often leads to sexual entropy and the forbidden fruit of an affair.

·　　　·　　　·

This all started when my wife and I were living in the Midwest, happy with each other and acting "normal," when I developed a crush on a coworker. Following the usual script, I "struggled"—using all the metaphors morality and social convention could provide in defense of monogamy—but finally "succumbed" to desire. I kept the affair secret for a while, and then, feeling wrong about such secrecy, I "admitted my betrayal." (Okay, so I was forced to "admit" it since my wife "caught" me—I wasn't in my office much, I'd forgotten our anniversary, I was singing in the shower, et cetera. Hannah confronted me with her suspicions, and because I felt so guilty about lying, I wasn't very good at it. The only models I had were in the movies where "cheaters" acted that way.)

And yes, for a brief time I even thought I was "in love" with the woman I'd been "cheating" on Hannah with—I'll call her K. I figured I had to be in love because we felt intimate in an exciting way, but in fact we were just having good sex and those tiny chemicals of exhilaration were firing off in my head. (Sadly, it's here that many people abandon a more compatible present lover for a "new love," when actually they're just practicing serial monogamy.) And how could I not feel exhilaration? K. was wild, was at the top of a field dominated vastly by men, and had a penchant for skydiving. She had long legs and blond hair. She even liked my wife. They went bra shopping together. And sometimes I'd leave my office at lunch and go to her bleak condominium and key in the password at the little gate and she'd be upstairs waiting for me, on the rug next to the fake-gas fireplace.

Things at home were a little less romantic during this time, and even after Hannah confronted me about my affair and I admitted it, I still wanted to see K. But soon, thankfully, I came to my senses and broke it off with her. The pain I caused my wife just wasn't worth the good sex. I resolved myself to loving just one damn good woman who loved me.

Still, there were a few scenes left in this little morality play of the seventh commandment. I apologized to Hannah for having "cheated" and asked if she could "forgive" me. I felt "ashamed" and promised a "rebirth" into fidelity. And though I had contravened the "sanctity" of our relationship, Hannah "accepted me back into the fold" and "absolved" me of my errant ways.

In turn, her friends struggled to accept her decision to stay with a man who had "betrayed" her—"Once a cheater," they preached at her, "always a cheater." But they also liked me and hoped Hannah and I could "work this thing out." Maybe we could "beat this," they suggested, if I could get "it" out of my system.

·　　　·　　　·

And then an unusual thing happened, for which I have to credit Hannah. We began talking through the human predicament of desire, inquiring after real answers rather than the standard liturgy of convention, and somehow a new door opened. We abandoned the movie scene (tears, recriminations) and forged ahead on our own. Without becoming too philosophical, I'd have to say that we had an existential moment about the body—that there was nothing more than the body, a gift of unimaginable luck, and that as a couple we should allow our little fading-away presences the greatest possible fulfillment in a very short life. In other words, Hannah said she was willing to let me have affairs and, in fact, she wanted to have affairs too.

Without a program, then, and without any semblance of script, we decided to try it, the "open relationship" thing. And after a couple of weeks of talking about the possibilities, Hannah suggested that I go see K. for an evening. I remember the moment exactly. "Just go over and see her," she said. "I don't mind." I peered closely at her. She's the sort of person who can hide nothing. "Really?" I said.

So it would be our first step along a path without direction, through a whole terrain of unmapped hills and valleys, a path upon which we'd make some real mistakes. And for better and for worse, as the saying goes, it was not out of insecurity or some other weakness that she told to me to go. It was out of love. The real kind.

. . .

I did go to K. that night, and she and I sorted out some things. We also had sex unsuffused by the atmosphere of the illicit. (Hey, it was still pretty good, if you were worried about that.) And though we did feel close, there was a certain sadness to the event in that the Love with a capital *L* aspect had fallen away. Sure, we were lovers in a real sense, but the "in love" language had been dropped. A boundary had been marked and not crossed. This was my first lesson in keeping the affair in a certain place, a limiting necessity that can be a little hard to get the hang of.

When I arrived home in the morning, Hannah looked haggard and upset. She'd watched the same movie three times in a row and smoked a zillion cigarettes—and she doesn't even smoke. She was jealous and hurt, and in turn I was upset by what I saw as her contradictory behavior. We both seriously moped around the house, for about a day.

Yet even then, when we were confused and just beginning, there was a clarity about things that drew us closer, a shared feeling commensurate with the significance of being human, of having that body. And it was easier for me; it was my body that had gleefully pressed against someone else's the night before.

We got through that. Hannah and K. remained friends, and sometimes I slept with K. Of course, the three of us didn't hang out anymore as a trio; we weren't sophisticated enough for that at the time, and even though K. and I were past the foolish love stage, things were still a little bit raw. It was a nervous time but sometimes funny. They went out one night and bonded, talking about what a louse I had been. (Hannah couldn't help but tell me, of course, when she got home.) Hell, I was sleeping with K. and in love with my wife—and my wife was cool with that, and *she* was also incredibly sexy to me. I imagined the two of them drunk and talking about me.

It wasn't depressing, to say the least.

•   •   •

Soon afterward we moved to a beautiful city in the Northwest, and it appeared to be Hannah's turn. She met a guy she liked a lot, a musician, and I was the one left alone through a very long night. When she came home I tried to act okay, feigning interest in the sports page I'd already read, but I instinctively drew away as she tried to kiss me. A sudden fury rose in my blood, and I stomped out of the room, slamming the door to my study. Hannah tried to soothe me through the closed door, but I would have none of it. A pretty good yelling match ensued, and I cleared out of the house. Hannah stood crying at the door.

And then, by the afternoon, we were laughing at the absurdity of it all. We'd both acted exactly the same way, as if it was somehow impossible to tell yourself not to be jealous. That day, and for many days after (it's a conversation we occasionally revisit even now), we talked a lot about jealousy—what was it? And settled on the opinion that it was a fairly predictable and inane emotion, a type of primitive reflex response. Actually, I've heard the theory that jealousy is a late arrival to the human emotional landscape—that it evolved to encourage monogamy, because the species proved more successful when two parents were involved in child rearing. Such assumptions regarding our hunter-gatherer ancestors seem facile to me, but even if true, what place does jealous behavior have in the modern world? In addition to the fact that successful parents these days are gay, straight, single, and multiple, what of the simple proposition that the jealous partner doesn't leave out of jealousy? And to us it started to feel like just a stupid emotion, perhaps unavoidable but easily contained when revealed in its crudity.

Jealousy also seemed to have a short half-life, to live in a quick flash of hot-bloodedness like its dumb cousin, anger. While feeling hurt or insecure is complex—and more about this later—jealousy is simple and brutish. So we decided to expect to feel jealous and to give the other person some respectful space when we did. You couldn't force someone not to be jealous by kissing them hello and acting really nice. Neither were you expected not to feel jealous. For a reasonable amount of time, you could mope. Once this was established, jealousy was an easily navigable problem—and the benefits of that are difficult to put into words.

•   •   •

Eventually, I found someone too. N. was younger than I was and had recently broken up with her first serious boyfriend. She had just finished law school and worked long hours at her public-interest job. In a sense it was the perfect arrangement—she didn't want a relationship and so felt willing simply to have a good time. She was also smart, sweet, and attractive. She had, I will say, many appeals: before becoming a lawyer she'd been a cheerleader for an NBA team; she was a lapsed Catholic; she was too polite to ever call me at home (though Hannah had grudgingly said it was fine—it seemed better, she said, than either of us sneaking off to the nearby Laundromat's pay phone). There was a bit of a lascivious element too, because in the early days of the affair, N. still lived at home. In a way, she was sneaking around more than I was because she was scandalously dating a married man. I think we identified with each other as outlaws.

Of course the little chemicals began to fire off again in my head—the emissaries of exhilaration that herald a new closeness with someone. But now I understood that this just went with the territory. Probably in a different situation we'd be dating, and maybe those chemical signals would lead to a traditional kind of relationship, at least for a while. But instead N. and I would see each other about once a week, have dinner or go to a movie, head to a hotel, and then each go back home afterward. In a real way it became an old-fashioned affair, regular in its intervals, except that it was allowed within my primary relationship. So it remained limited from inception but retained a romantic quality that certainly exceeded mere friendship. (Mere friends don't typically spend long evenings at the Snooz-Inn, though maybe they more often should.) And the fact that it was condoned never dissipated our natural attraction for each other.

For Hannah, on the other hand, my long-term affair created some difficulties. Sometimes the regularity of my meetings with N. led to some tension between us, as she saw the musician, G., more occasionally. And though we had minimized the jealousy problem, we hadn't solved the problem of how to feel close to each other in the immediate wake of our trysts. What regularly occurred—and this happened to me when our roles were reversed—is that upon my return she generally felt distant from me for a few hours or even a day. In contrast, I arrived back home from seeing N. feeling closer to Hannah because of the special quality and benevolence of our relationship. But from the other side, as I also knew, it's hard not to feel a little displaced by the homecoming. The other person returns with a kind of satisfied glow, the body lit up in a way that really has nothing to do with you. In other words, maybe once a week was a little too frequent, as it created some downtime in our relationship. Because, as everyone knows, it's impossible to hide that just-fucked glow. I think that's why so many partners intuitively know when someone is "cheating."

However, Hannah vaguely knew who N. was—just as I knew G.—and therefore we never obsessed about the other person's friend, the "unknown lover." We never fantasized about what unknowable threat or power this mystery person must hold. They were both just real people, and I think our knowing them as real helped with the inevitable insecurity that creeps into the situation.

And yet there was no escape from the sexual insecurity that is really just part of the deal, and which I sometimes felt I actually experienced more than Hannah. In fact, I think the sexual insecurity is perhaps just part of any long-term relationship—you know, ebb and flow. As I see it, we had a specific opportunity to figure it out, in amplified fashion. As it turns out, we both just needed a good amount of reassurance—a little compliment here, a flirtatious gesture there—that showed our continued interest in the other person. You might choose to call it seduction. Actually no more than what people need to do in a monogamous relationship, but with truly diligent application. And possibly our constancy in this matter never let us enter into the sexual drift that plagues many monogamous relationships. Which is not to say that you need to be in an open relationship to sustain intimacy with a long-term partner, just that an open relationship can't be sustained without that closeness.

·　　　·　　　·

But, unfortunately, I could *really* tell how much Hannah liked sleeping with G. Maybe she just didn't hide her pleasure quite as well as I did upon reentering the domicile, but I could always tell when she'd just had her brains fucked out. (Excuse my diction, but that's the only phrase that actually seems to fit the bewildered grin that always stretched across her face.) And so I had to work through my insecurity from the beginning, I had to talk about how I felt "diminished," so to speak. And maybe I had a more difficult time because of my own assumptions about sexuality—that men were naturally (or at least socially constructed to be) more promiscuous. But that smile on Hannah's face showed me one thing, that even if men were arguably more pleasure-seeking with regard to quantity, women were arguably more pleasure-seeking with regard to quality. It seemed all she needed was a few good men.

Apart from the insecurity that caused me in the beginning, it also gave me a sort of newfound respect for my wife. Because the bottom line is that new or occasional partners can be pretty damn fun. Yes, our culture admits this freely, but it condemns the actual act. My wife, apparently, did not.

So we did much better when we just accepted those events as a different sexual category, which was not competing with sex in the long, committed relationship. The former has newness while the latter has love, with its continuing potential for intimacy. As a surprising benefit of the mixing of the two, the feeling of another's body only heightened my awareness of Hannah's body, possibly because the language of the body, like all language, operates by relation. And I think having another lover also elevated my awareness of my own body, allowing me to feel more alive in my bones.

.   .   .

Eventually my affair with N. drew to a close, having had its day, and N. actually has a real boyfriend now. I once ran into them, and she and I met for coffee afterward, and it felt nostalgic. Since that long affair my experiences have been fairly random and fairly rare. On the other hand, Hannah's relationship with G. never really did fade away, possibly a function of the lesser frequency of their meetings (and possibly that grin on Hannah's face). In any event, we're still together and still very happy. Often we feel we're happier than anyone has a right to be. We're going to start a family soon, and we'll see, I suppose, if our open relationship continues after that or takes on a new form. But this week, G. is visiting us at our new house in the New England countryside—he is on break from touring with his band and is coming for rest. Of course Hannah says they're not going to sleep together here. ("That would be wrong!" she pronounced with false modesty over fried clams last night.) But really? I wouldn't mind—at least I don't think so. I'm lucky and I'm in love.

.   .   .

In the end, to be clear, I am not proselytizing for open relationships, nor am I promoting any kind of "lifestyle" choice. I admit I'd be happy if I opened a few minds, but I understand that different people have different needs in different situations. Still, is there anything I've described that is really so dangerous? Is my relationship inherently flawed and something to pathologize? Are other people's affairs for me to judge?

I think that we've been pretty good explorers. We've tried to put into play some honest ideas about sex and relationships, about desire and the body, ideas that most couples are afraid to confront. And for this I don't want any credit, or even an anonymous credit. I'd just like to be able to tell you my name.

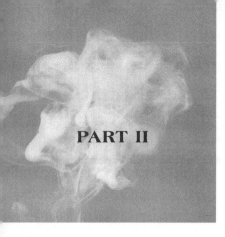

PART II

Can't Be Trusted with Simple Tasks

If the wife comes through as being too strong and too intelligent, it makes the husband look like a wimp.

—Richard Nixon

I Am Man, Hear Me Bleat

FRED LEEBRON

hen I first started dating my now-wife, Kathryn Rhett, my friends were horrified to discover that I'd been transformed into a new kind of man, a particular species they referred to as "Mr. Rhett." This was because I chauffeured my sweetheart from appointment to appointment, and on the rare nights that I did not stay over at her place, I picked her up promptly in the morning to take her to her job. After all, she didn't drive, and it was cold that first winter in Baltimore, and the neighborhood that surrounded her saw more than its share of crime. I was being chivalrous, of course, but my friends pronounced me "whipped." To them I was an inferior male, forever on call, willing to dance to the whims of my domineering woman.

They were wrong.

First of all, Kathryn was hardly a domineering woman. The domineering woman in my life back then was my previous girlfriend—the woman I was still seeing, in fact, when Kathryn and I met. A gun-toting Texan offspring of a retired CIA agent, this previous girlfriend had been christened Linda but was determined to change her name to Lee because she wanted a name whose gender was possible to escape. I, on the other hand, wanted a woman who would always be a woman. When Linda found out about Kathryn and me, she returned my kitchenware in a blowtorched condition, melted and bent into fractions, with an occasional bullet hole. (For a few days I displayed Linda's work in the kitchen Kathryn and I shared. I named it *Domestic Violence. Baltimore. 1986.*)

Besides, even if my friends did see Kathryn as domineering, I was hardly dancing to her whims. On the contrary, it was my car and my choice to offer her rides, which she could accept or decline as she wished. I've always had a macho, breast-beating streak in me, and the way I saw it, my behavior was rooted in a proud, masculine tradition going all the way back to the caveman days. I was protecting and wooing the woman who would be the mother of my children. And I did a good job of it. She became my woman who would always be a woman, and I became her man who would always be a man.

Or so I thought.

Flash-forward seventeen years to 2003.

Over this time, various things happened, most of them good. A bunch of years after Kathryn and I got married we had our first cute kid, and shortly thereafter we had another (and now we've just learned that a third is on the way—thanks, yes, we're very excited). We moved from San Francisco to Provincetown and then to Charlotte (all nice places) before finally settling here in Gettysburg, Pennsylvania (another nice place). We've followed our dreams and have pursued careers that have meaning to us.

So life should be great, right? And in many ways it is. Except there's one problem. During these years of raising kids and earning a living and putting down roots, something unsettling has crept into our marriage, or at least into my side of it. I'm not sure exactly how this troubling situation has come to pass, but the crux of it is this: I no longer feel like I know who I am or how I should be. Instead, there has been a gradual but undeniable shift in my relationship with Kathryn as these children have arrived and made their presence felt. My former chivalry has eroded into a sort of strained niceness and forced patience that drains me of energy, and my once proud, naturally animal personality has devolved into a short fuse I didn't recognize that I had.

Let's see—what to blame for this?

In some ways, I suppose, this is the saga of many contemporary husbands and fathers. For better or worse, we're expected to embrace our feminine side and domesticity, to express our feelings, to take care of our children when our wives are working, to do the housework, to cook, to be endlessly patient while our kids scribble on our upholstery and puke over our shoulders. And so we try to do these things, but what husband hasn't stood in the doorway of the typical scene of domestic tranquility (kids and wife sitting shoulder to shoulder on the carpet, playing "tea" or building with Legos) and wondered—just how the hell do I fit into all this?

When our first child was born, a nurse took me aside. "Don't try to copy your wife when you handle your child," she advised. "It will only confuse the baby. Be yourself."

But I thought this was the era of gender neutrality. I thought we were supposed to paint the girl's room avocado and the boy's room mango and give girls trucks and boys dolls. Now, after all that, I'm supposed to figure out how to appropriately manifest my masculinity yet again?

Actually, as I've lamented, I should know how to play that particular role. I'm a born and bred fighter, a guy who doesn't know when enough is enough, as my father used to tell me when I'd wrestle with him when I was seven and eight and nine and ten and sixteen and seventeen. I'm like a dog with a bone, and I can't let it go, and if the bone is more truly metaphoric—if the bone is something as intangible as one side of an argument—then I really cannot let it drop.

But as an adult husband and father you are no longer supposed to act this way. Perhaps the short temper I have now is the result of so many years of repressing this part of myself in the pursuit of being calm and domesticated. I don't know.

What I *do* know is that I'm not nearly as naturally patient with the kids as my wife is, hard as I might try. Nor can I ever hope to match her endlessly joyful tone. And as far as her ability to make games out of all the small but critical tasks the kids loathe—getting into pajamas, taking a bath, eating vegetables—well, she's in a different league.

Which is why I love it so much when Kathryn's temper reaches its limit and she rants and screams just like I do. But these moments are all too infrequent compared with my own propensity for outbursts. "Dad," my daughter said to me once, "your temper is so predictable it's practically boring."

And it's true. I exercise my temper too frequently and in socially unacceptable ways. I exercise it as soon as the insurance claims come back glibly denied; I exercise it when the drugstore misplaces the photographs of our daughter's birthday party; I exercise it whenever the kids resist bedtime or homework time or piano practice time for longer than five or six exchanges of dialogue. And in a way I relish those moments, lame as they are, because having my fuse ignited allows my own warped sense of myself full expression, and it gives me some semblance of the power and sense of control that I used to feel naturally. "This is reprehensible!" I shrieked at the drugstore clerk about the misplaced pictures, and when the prints finally came in and I went to pick them up, the note on the bill said, "Do NOT charge client. Client is VERY upset." I love getting upset. It's effective, and even the mere insinuation of my distemper can will the children into better behavior. "I have no problem with dragging you out of here kicking and screaming," I hotly told my six-year-old son as his whimpering began to crescendo when he couldn't decide on a toy at Wal-Mart. He gathered himself for a moment. "Okay, okay," he muttered, and he chose something for less than seven bucks.

But there's more to the temper—namely, a part of me believes this kind of retro fathering is actually *good* for kids. They need clear limits, right? They need a stern no every once in a while, without all kinds of explanations and negotiation. They need the law to be laid down in Father-knows-best fashion. They need discipline and rigor and maybe even a little jolt of fear in their tender hearts. A big part of me believes this. After all, growing up in my household, I learned that breakfast was at seven, lunch bags were provided without choice of menu, dinner was at five-thirty, chores took up most of any weekend, and we were shouted at and swatted at whenever we stepped out of line. Sometimes my mother would race up the stairs to see if she could catch us doing something as wrong as watching television on a school night, and if the damn thing was off, she'd feel the back of it to see if it was warm. While my dad was off making a living for the seven of us, my mom's child-rearing tactics began to cohere into an ultimately successful effort. We went to good colleges, we got good jobs. *Vive* my mom! But my wife thinks I'm a crackpot, an envious one too. She thinks I want to make sure my children don't get what I didn't get, that I'm an inverted cliché. And, buried not terribly far below the surface of her argument (if it isn't flat-out on the surface) is the age-old and yet sharpened supposition: *I know what's better for our kids.*

Three weeks ago I awoke in the middle of the night to find myself on the downstairs couch, covered in a pale-blue-and-pink mohair blanket with scratchy fringes. I sneered to myself. I was going to make it until morning. Kathryn and I had had a knock-down, drag-out forty-second scream fest at 9 P.M., and I'd shut myself into the study and thrown myself on the couch, determined to sleep through the night. What happened was this: my son had flown into one of his practically inexplicable and indefensible howling jags, which he had launched on account of being denied a second helping of chocolate ice cream. For him to throw a tantrum over such a thing further convinced me that we were ruining him with our lax parenting. My wife was convinced the rest of the family was ganging up on him. It came to a head when my daughter finally said, "He's a brat." And then I concurred. "Yes, he is. He's a brat."

In every family there are names that you aren't allowed to call one another, and in our family this name is brat. "Don't you dare say that!" Kathryn screamed at us. "Don't you dare, don't you dare, don't you dare!"

"He's a brat!" I screamed back, a six-year-old myself now. "We've made him into a brat."

She slammed the cabinets and I slammed myself into the study and Cade ran giggling upstairs and Jacob just howled and howled. Now I was going to spend the whole night on this couch. I'd never done anything like this before. I turned into the couch, and my underwear itched right along with the annoying fringe of the expensive blanket. I missed my pajamas. I turned on my side out from the couch and pulled the blanket more tightly around me. I could do this. I could spend the whole night on the couch. Men everywhere have been doing this for years. Decades. Centuries. I was fairly certain that this was the whole reason that couches were invented. After a while I couldn't even remember the exact reason for our fight. I just kept seeing myself as yet another guy spending a night on the couch, when there was an entire half of a big bed upstairs with his name on it.

At one-thirty, I climbed the stairs.

In the morning we did not bother to discuss it because we both knew I was wrong. I was wrong because I was older and he was younger, I was wrong because acting like a brat wasn't such a big deal unless you were forty-one and you were the one acting like a brat. I was wrong because I'd lost my patience, and these days, a parent without patience is not a parent at all but just another kid—and we had no room in the house for one more of them.

So all along this path of parenthood I have tried to be a grown-up, but sometimes even being a real adult—when you're a man—doesn't quite measure up in this world of screwy expectations and screwier biases. Case in point: one day, when my kids were five and one, when they seemed to be tearing us apart with their conflicting and arbitrary demands, when there wasn't a single night in seven when they were in their beds on time, my wife went on a four-day business trip, three thousand miles away. I had to work while the kids were at school and day care, and then I picked them up and ferried them around. No sweat. I took them out to dinner at one of those gaudy kid-type restaurants with sippy cups and gloppy entrées and paper placemats on which to scrawl with an infinite procession of crayons. That night they each had baths and were tucked into bed and definitively asleep at the proper times, and I slouched on the couch, full wineglass in hand, complimenting myself and idly speculating whether the whole drill just wouldn't be a whole hell of a lot easier if I were a single dad.

The next morning was Saturday. The wife wasn't getting back until Monday. No sweat. I made them simple breakfasts, wisely conserving my energy, and afterward I took them to a colleague's house, where they both played with his four-year-old, until, happily, it was the late afternoon and time to go home. I carried Jacob across the street and ferried Cade with my free hand. My buddy Mark followed with his son, Gavin, to see us off. I put Jacob into his car seat in the front seat (no air bag, thank you), but Cade was sassy, sassing me about why did she have to wait to get in the car while Jacob was getting such first-class attention, so as I was opening the back door and urging her to climb in, she was already climbing in, and somehow her thumb got clipped in the process of the door opening (to this day I cannot determine how this happened, and I have tried everything including reenactment), and she began to scream but of course I didn't see the thumb get clipped, so annoyed I turned to the backseat and said, "Cade, what *is* it?" And only then did I see that blood was everywhere, so much blood it looked like I'd stuck a knife into the belly of her thumb. And Mark's face went whiter than a Q-Tip, and he grabbed Cade and I grabbed Jacob and we raced back inside his house and together we bandaged Cade's thumb and then I called the pediatrician and took Cade and Jacob to the clinic, and the clinic sent us right back to the suture room and damn if the nurse, coming in and taking a look, didn't say, right off the fucking bat, "Dad's day out, huh?"

Sometimes I just want to give up trying to be a coparent. Sometime I think I am simply not cut out for it. I can't compete with my wife in this arena. She can compete with me in the career arena, sure, but I can't compete with her in the parenting arena. My kids sense the hunter in me, that I am always packing some kind of weapon, and I will never be my wife's equal in sweetness, kindness, patience, and warmth. So there it is. To cut my losses and gracefully bow out of this competition, I am hereby willing to consider a full surrender followed by an orderly transfer of power.

But this is what I don't get. I always wanted to marry my equal or my better—anyone less never occurred to me. This is what our generation of men does; we marry our equals. We seek out and partner up with women who will have careers at approximately the same level as ours. But you know what men give up when they venture into this kind of so-called equality? They give up equality. Why? Because there is no such thing as equality. Because men have long recognized that women are their domestic superiors, and perhaps that's why we've so staunchly and unjustly guarded our castles of work. Because women haven't had the so-called privileges we men have had for the entire history of the world, and now they are knocking on the door of the patriarchal fortress, and as that patriarchal door comes crashing down in my particular house, who is there to be squashed underneath it but me?

An example: a few years ago, when my wife got her first prestigious full-time job as a professor, she insisted on putting all the insurance in her name on the pretext of "I've never had a full-benefit job before. You have." Which was of course correct. And who cares, right? So she wants the insurance in her name like a goddamn badge of honor. Let her. But here's the catch. Who calls up when the claims get denied? Whose testosterone do we summon when it's time to do the dirty work of arguing with the company? Who's the one who gets on the phone and says "THIS IS REPREHENSIBLE"? Who lathers himself into a foam and reaches into his manly reservoir of anger to demand restitution, retribution, reimbursement, while railing against the system, against screwing the little guy, the middle guy, the unknowing, the uninformed, the goddamn-I-am-educated-and-I-have-a-voice kind of guy?

I do, that's who. And what do they say to me once I'm done?

"Uh, excuse me . . . uh, could you please calm down, Mr. Rhett?"

Chivalry on Ice

DANIEL JONES

One night about thirteen years ago—eight months after Cathi and I started seeing each other but two years before we got married—she called me around 11 P.M. to say there was a huge bug on the wall of her bedroom and would I please come over and get rid of it. She seemed embarrassed to ask this of me but was not embarrassed enough, apparently, to handle the situation herself or to ease up on me when I expressed a lack of desire at that time of night (I was already in bed) to get dressed and drive the mile or so over to her house to remove this bug from her wall.

This was in Tucson, Arizona, where, in all fairness, bugs tend to be large, swift, and armored, like miniature throwbacks to the Jurassic Age. Disposing of them was not a job I cherished, though I was a little braver about it than Cathi. Still, those times when I reached into the silverware drawer and felt something skitter across my hand I'd do the exact same freaked-out dance around the kitchen that she'd do. In short, I didn't see why the responsibility for getting rid of them shouldn't be considered an equal-opportunity nightmare.

Cathi and I were both twenty-eight then, in graduate school together and seeing each other exclusively, but we had no plans to live together. Partly this was because housing in Tucson was cheap—I paid $260 a month for my small two-story house, and Cathi's rent was comparable. But the main reason for living apart was that Cathi valued space and independence above all else. She was (and still is) strong-willed, competitive, and professionally successful, and for her simply being in a relationship was claustrophobic enough without having to live together. (In fact, we didn't live together until six months after we got married, when a move to New York City forced us, through financial necessity, to share a small sublet—a cohabitation Cathi entered into reluctantly and that turned out to be every bit as difficult for her as she'd feared.)

Anyway, I felt bad that Cathi was upset about the bug, and if I'd been in the other room or next-door or maybe even down the street I'd have made more of an effort to help her with it. But in my mind some additional threshold was crossed when the act involved getting out of bed and *driving* there, sirens wailing, to wage war on a single insect, as if I were some one-man pest-control SWAT team.

So I told Cathi she was welcome to come over to my place—in fact I would love it if she did—but I would not come and dispense with the bug.

Cathi grew increasingly baffled as she realized I wasn't going race to her rescue, and I grew increasingly baffled as she continued to insist that I come when I'd repeatedly said I didn't want to.

"Every other man I've ever dated would have come over in a second," she finally said with a huff. "Every other one."

Ouch. Nothing like dredging up the old boyfriends for comparison.

In the end, Cathi reluctantly agreed to come over to my house, where we slept together in bug-free safety. But she was not, to put it mildly, happy about it. And she's still not happy about it, thirteen years later. She gets flush-faced and tense at the mere mention of the issue.

I know, I know. I can already hear the jeers and boos from the studio audience, the finger-pointing demands that Cathi leave me rather than put up with such shabby treatment, and the gleeful shouts of "You go girl!" when the love of my life—sufficiently rallied by the mob—suggests that maybe she will.

But Cathi has not left me, and in fact we've been more or less happily married for eleven years, so presumably I have other attributes that make up for my failure to respond on that fateful night. According to her, these attributes are that I am decent and hardworking; I'm a "good father" (always the default quality of the otherwise lackluster husband); I make her laugh; I am her "soul mate" (another mealymouthed term that suggests a deficit in some other category); I am "handy" and maintain our house and yard in manly ways; I do all the driving on long trips so Cathi can sleep, read, and manhandle the children (and so I don't have to reign in her propensity for road rage); I am "laid-back"; I eat pretty much anything; I'm compliant and clean; I give her space when she needs it, and I've been well trained to handle my share of the kids and laundry and kitchen. Oh, I also have job skills and earn an income.

What I haven't done very well, I confess, is act like Cathi's knight in shining armor. I regularly fail to recognize the "damsel in distress" in her, or even, for that matter, the damsel in her that could really use a break. What I see instead is strength and strength alone, and on those rare occasions when she shows weakness, I find that I am more caught off-guard than spurred into protective action; I tend to step back and think, as if I'm some retro football coach from the School of Hard Knocks, *What? You, weak? C'mon. Dust yourself off and get back in the game!*

As you might guess, this attitude of mine—unspoken but implied—sometimes gets me into trouble. A generous judge of character might think, *How great that you have such confidence in your wife!* But Cathi doesn't quite see it this way. So on and off for the past decade (mostly off), we have been trying to hash out the reasons for my behavior—not only why I failed to act on that night but also why I continue to have ongoing lapses in the chivalry department, including but not limited to

1. Not offering to get her a cup of tea very often or ever;
2. Acting afraid for myself rather than concerned about her when she announces she's coming down with a cold;
3. Not leaping up to help her when she's staggering by with a basketful of laundry; and
4. Smiling like I "deserve an award" when I offer to give her a break by taking the kids out to eat some slop at Friendly's.

What's weird is that before I started going out with Cathi I was something of a paragon of chivalry. Actually, that's not true—I wasn't chivalrous with my previous two girlfriends either, who were both strong feminists just as Cathi is. But before *that*, back in college and especially in high school, I was a poster child for chivalrous behavior. During my senior year I was even favored to win the award for "Mother's Choice" (for the boy who's so clean-cut and gentlemanly mothers want him for a son-in-law). It's an embarrassing award— the equivalent of being thought of as "nice" by all the girls you want to sleep with—and I'm glad I didn't win it, ultimately losing to some Wally Cleaver geek who was even more straightlaced than I was. But the fact that I was a contender speaks to the sort of polite, traditional upbringing I'd had and my unquestioned allegiance to it.

During the postfeminist confusion that swirled through my college years, young women and men in progressive hot spots nationwide were challenging the assumptions of chivalry and exposing it for the antiquated deal it was. But where I went to school, a conservative state university in the South, posing a question like "Why should men open doors for women?" was unheard-of. Of course men opened doors for women. Of course men acted "protective" of the women they were dating. In fact, most of the men I knew could not have been more respectful of women in public; they were good old boys who'd been raised to treat women like delicate flowers, at least during the light of day. It was only at night and behind closed doors that the sewage of their disrespect flowed freely, in the back rooms of dormitories and fraternity houses where women were, at best, talked about in the most degrading language known to humanity and at worst spirited away into the darkness to be stripped down, felt up, drugged, date-raped, passed around. This was my four-year education in the hypocrisy of chivalry, and I began to want nothing to do with it.

Even so, I continued to march in step with chivalry's drumbeat—opening doors and paying for meals and forever being the manly driver who escorted my dates to the passenger side of my car, dutifully if awkwardly catering to women who were as able as I was in nearly every respect—who were, indeed, my competition for class standing and jobs and slots in graduate school—yet who still seemed to want to cling to the benefits of the old regime (if you consider being treated as weak, helpless, and penniless a benefit). And what further confused matters was that some of the women I went out with were progressive enough to no longer require the full chivalry package, which perhaps felt a bit patronizing. What they seemed to want instead was chivalry *lite*, or, better yet, chivalry à la carte, where they could choose from a menu of princely behavior and select which sexist behaviors they wished their boyfriends to retain and which to jettison. Some found the door opening and passenger-side escorting too old-fashioned but were happy to have their meals paid for. Others came armed with their own mysterious blend of preferences that you were supposed to divine during the course of the evening. Dating during this murky era was like an impromptu ballet where you tossed your partner into the air and sometimes you caught her and other times you sent her sprawling across the floor because neither of you knew the choreography. So if you fell out of step, say, by expecting to split the meal tab with a woman who, unbeknownst to you, had actually selected (in her mind) the "full-payment-by-man" option from the chivalry à la carte menu, you were shit out of luck.

For years I stumbled through this unchoreographed ballet until finally I went to graduate school and "evolved" (as those bumper stickers are always urging men to do)—that is, I stopped worrying about what I was supposed to do according to various courtship rituals dating back to the Middle Ages and allowed my membership in the chivalry knighthood to expire. I stopped dating dainty women who expected the princess treatment in favor of strong women who, within reason, could (and were willing to) do just about everything I could do. In these new relationships I let women open the door for me if they got to it first; I let them pick me up for dates in their own cars if that's how the transportation plan worked best; I even let them carry their own heavy bags unless they showed obvious signs of strain (in which case I'd ask once if they needed help but took them at their word if they said no—after all, no means no, right?).

And just like that, I felt comfortable. I finally realized the extent to which all of my earlier training and relationship experience had felt like a stiff tuxedo I'd been forced to wear, and now that I could "dress" however I pleased, jeans and T-shirts began to rule the day. Talk about liberation. My feeling about the death of chivalry in my own life was an unambiguous "Good riddance."

And nobody seemed better suited to match my feelings in this regard than Cathi, who exuded self-sufficiency more than any woman I've ever known. She may have been smaller and physically weaker than I (a foot shorter and petite enough to buy clothes at Gap Kids), but she was more determined, more gutsy, more ambitious, and less afraid (of most things).

After growing up as a smart, flirty, tough girl in New Jersey, she shot to career success in the New York magazine world by her mid-twenties, negotiating, financially and otherwise, life in that difficult and expensive city. She had even fought off a would-be sexual assault one night on a dark New Jersey street. When we first met, she pursued me just as I pursued her. She didn't tease, lie, or put on airs. She split all costs down the middle and never played the weakling. When she decided to leave New York and move to Tucson for graduate school, she bought a used Jeep with a standard transmission she didn't know how to drive, but she didn't want me to drive her anywhere—she expected that if millions of other people could learn to do something, she could too, and so she did.

On one of our early nights out in Tucson, at a rowdy dance bar, she decided I was talking to an old girlfriend in too flirtatious a manner and responded by heading to the bar and striking up a conversation with a man she didn't know, and she remained with this man for the rest of the evening, until, when I told her I was going, she bade him a fond farewell and accompanied me unapologetically back to the car. Her entire being screamed out, *I can take care of myself.* And I admit I loved this about her.

Here was a woman, I thought, who didn't need me, who didn't even want to live with me, who had no expectations or desire to be supported or catered to by a man. She was, in my mind, a feminist in the best sense—not a man hater or a bra burner but someone who wanted equality across the board, equal power and opportunities and treatment and expectations.

But she was also, as I learned on that fateful night, a feminist who expected her man to race through the night to protect her from a bug on the wall.

"The thing is," Cathi said to me the other day (newly fixated, as she has been, on our bug incident), "I *never* ask you to do stuff like that for me. I *hate* being dependent on anyone. And then the one time I asked you for it, you didn't come through."

Which is, I'm sorry to say, exactly the point. Cathi never asked that sort of thing of me and hated being dependent on me in any way, for anything (except, perhaps, in those rare instances when she asked me to lift something too heavy for her). But in general I didn't get off on protecting her and she didn't get off on being protected, and such was the foundation of our relationship. She'd built her private castle and dug her moat around it, and she liked being able to raise and lower her drawbridge as she pleased. And I was fine with this arrangement even when she used it to shut me out—I realized this was her need and prerogative and she was entitled to it.

It's just that when you define yourself by your independence to the extent that Cathi does, you allow your man to shove what's left of his already diminished "inner knight" even deeper into cold storage. And you've got to expect that he's going to be a little rusty with the sword if you suddenly try to draft him into action. Or worse, you might discover he doesn't even feel like he's obliged to get out of bed.

·　　　·　　　·

Cathi and I have good friends in New York, a "power" couple—I'll call them Mark and Cynthia—where Mark is a big deal in his company and makes good money but Cynthia is an even bigger deal in her company and makes even more money. Like Cathi, Cynthia is strong-willed, demanding, and fiercely independent. Like me, Mark has put a good-sized portion of his inner knight in cold storage. He is generally more knightly than I am (which, granted, isn't saying much), but he makes his own share of bad assumptions and is often chewed out by Cynthia for his lack of chivalry in a way that makes him my brother in this struggle for understanding. While our wives bond by complaining about us, Mark and I bond by being complained about (an interaction that includes a lot of sheepish grinning). And yes, we find comfort in the knowledge that we are not alone in our inadequacies, just as our wives find comfort in knowing they're not alone in their feelings of exasperation and moral superiority.

The last time we visited Mark and Cynthia in their New York apartment, they had spent the previous day out and about in the city with their two small children (one an infant), an exhausting marathon of shuttling the kids around, feeding them, and changing them in a city that can be rather inhospitable to these activities. And when they finally arrived home, stumbling into their apartment with their diaper bags, double stroller, empty sippy cups, and Cheerios containers, Mark promptly slipped into the kitchen and made himself a big Dagwood sandwich, leaving Cynthia and the kids to fend for themselves.

Of course, no sooner had he sat down at the dining room table than Cynthia came upon him in harried disbelief and snapped, "When you're with anyone who's smaller, sicker, or weaker than you are, *they eat first.*"

Now, it's possible that Mark was simply employing the well-known (among men) "oxygen-mask principle"—that counterintuitive in-flight instruction we've all heard a thousand times that tells parents in the event of a loss of cabin pressure they should affix the oxygen mask over their own faces before tending to the oxygen mask needs of their children. I'm guessing you could make an argument that this would apply to hunger too, though I wouldn't want to have to be in the position of making such an argument myself. It's more likely, however, that this was a moment when Mark's inner knight (as a result of the trying day) had been completely exiled to some remote arctic ice shelf—he was tired and hungry, and he really wanted to eat, and he knew Cynthia could make something for herself and the kids, as she does the majority of the time anyway. Okay, so maybe she'd have to nurse the baby first, but still. In the meantime, might as well eat.

Sound familiar? Know any men like this?

No doubt you do. Because it's not only *our* inner knights—mine and Mark's—that have been shoved deeper into cold storage. No, that collective freezer is jam-packed. All across the land there are men whose chivalrous tendencies have been put on ice—a whole subspecies of husbands and boyfriends who have been set loose from tradition to wander the dark forests of their relationships in search of new ways of being necessary and useful. And what have they found?

Here is a clue. Go to the supermarket and check out the men you see pushing carts. In the diminutive sheaths that now hang from their belts are not swords but cell phones, which are used by their wives to direct them through the dizzying mazes of Food King and Rite Aid, and on missions not of gallantry but of drudgery—"The chicken nuggets in the *blue* box. Can't you see it? Blue?" "No, the Tampax slender. The *slender!*" "You have to *smell* a cantaloupe to see if it's ripe—you can't just squeeze it."

Needless to say, it is hard for the men in this position to feel like they are following in the proud tradition of the Knights of the Round Table. In fact, I'd venture to say that if our identification lies anywhere in the old feudal system at moments like this, it is far down below the castle walls, in the fields and swamps and little thatched huts where the serfs gaze up from their menial duties in awe and wonderment (and possibly even remembrance) of what life must be like at the top of the hill.

·   ·   ·

And so the knights fell, and with their fall came the death of chivalry as men had to face the fact that they were no longer positioned to grant protection unto the "weak" from their perches of power, and women had to concede that they could no longer accept the benefits of chivalry without acknowledging the truth of its sexist and invalidated premise. Years ago I welcomed this news as liberation for both men and women, and maybe it was, for a time. Equality was supreme; self-sufficiency reigned.

The only problem with this sea change, I've since realized, is that chivalry—in my own life, anyway—didn't die alone. Unbeknownst to me, its roots had penetrated deep into the foundation of my personality, and when that tree went down, felled by an axe I'd swung myself, it also ripped out a few chunks of kindness and generosity. The gestures of chivalry may have been inherently patronizing and obsolete, but my liberation from having to perform them had the side effect of dulling my caretaking instincts, of turning me into someone who would cheer my wife on in one breath ("You can do it yourself!") only to brush her off in the next ("You can do it yourself").

And Cathi too—she's the first to admit it—suffered from a creeping loss of kindness and generosity in our oh-so-modern marriage. After all, when preparing a meal for your husband, washing the dishes, or folding the laundry starts to feel like just another step backward into domestic servitude, you tend to shelve the frying pan, order in your own preferred takeout, and leave your husband's clothes in the laundry basket. And before long neither of you is doing much of anything for the other, because every favor, every potentially nice act, starts to reek of the very kind of stereotypical behavior you've been so determined to avoid.

Not exactly a breeding ground for random acts of kindness, is it? As Rodney King might say if he were to observe our marriage or countless others like ours, "Can't we all just fold the laundry for each other?"

I don't know what Cathi's latest plan is to boost her generosity a notch, but as they say, admitting you have a problem is 90 percent of the battle, and she admitted this long ago. I'm just getting around to it now.

For my salvation, maybe I'll check myself into rehab to try and recover those lost scraps of my more gentlemanly self. I'll drag Mark along with me (he's always game for a few days away from the wife and kids). I can already see us sitting in a circle of the similarly afflicted, hunched in chairs with our plastic cups of meds and our hooded expressions, gripping the armrests to control our delirium tremens as the counselor asks us to repeat after him the mantra of the soon-to-be reborn—"When I'm with anyone who's smaller, sicker, or weaker than I am, THEY EAT FIRST."

Quality Time Keeps Love Fresh

Lewis Nordan

I was already fairly drunk and it was about 2 A.M. and the Library was closing—this was a redneck bar down in Arkansas, the Library, not a place where you checked out books. Somebody said there was a party over at the Skull Creek apartments and did I want to go. So I said, Yeah, okay, sounds good, I'll see if my wife wants to go too. I was devoted to that woman, Elizabeth, she's the love of my life, or was then. This was in the early eighties. I'm married to a different woman now, and so she's the love of my life. I had to shout to make Elizabeth hear me in the Library. There was this bluegrass band named Cornbread playing; they were exceedingly popular in the Ozarks at the time and had a washboard player with one glass eye and the other eye wouldn't focus either, so it would make you dizzy to watch that guy play. He had these metal things on his fingers, and they were going clickety-clack. He could make that scandal speak, as we used to say back then when we meant to say *scoundrel*. His eyes were spinning. There was a banjo too, and I don't know what-all.

This was back when I didn't think twice about driving while drunk, you know. We had a Dodge truck with a bad throw-out bearing that sounded like you were running over a bale of wire most of the time. I was MADD's worst nightmare, I'm not proud to admit it.

I had already run up on the sidewalk one time that night. The kids were staying over at their grandma's house, so we could have stayed out all night if we wanted to. You might say me and Elizabeth had treated ourselves to a romantic evening out. It was my idea. I was trying to make the marriage work. I would have done anything, but this was all I could think of. Elizabeth had already started to fall out of love with me, so I felt like I had to convince her.

I said, You've got to spend a little quality time together to keep love fresh. Anybody will tell you that.

She said, Oh all right.

But when I asked her did she want to go to the party at Skull Creek, and told her they might have some dope, she said, Naw, she didn't want to go to Skull Creek, she said she was too drunk and anyway somebody was always pulling a gun. This was a complete exaggeration, by the way. She said she had her reputation to think about, she was an elementary school teacher. It was one excuse after another. We left the Library and got in the truck, and I slammed the door so hard a hunk of rust the size of a dinner plate fell off the front fender.

When we got home the house was cold because I forgot to call the guy with the propane truck.

Elizabeth said, Damn it's cold in here.

I said, I wish you wouldn't be so critical all the time. It's because you're so critical that I'm always having to go to Skull Creek by myself. She said, I don't know why they had to name that apartment complex Skull Creek in the first place, it's morbid.

So I said in my charming way, Aw, shit, honey, don't be a party pooper, let's just go over and get fucked up, eat some pretzels, drink some Fresca, then we'll come on home, watch a little TV.

She said, At three o'clock in the morning?

I said, There you go again.

She said, No, really, I got to go to sleep.

I said, Why can't we ever just do what I want to do once in a while, why do we always have to do it your way?

She said, Go on ahead, be my guest. You can go to any low-life party you want to, feel up some big-haired college girl, get yourself shot too if you feel like it, but I'm going to stay home and puke, okay? Somebody's got to have some sense around here.

I said, What kind of marriage is this, you call this a marriage, this is no kind of damn marriage.

She looked at me with what you might call disgust. She said, What kind of marriage is this, what kind of marriage is this, is that what you are asking me? Do you know who asks their wives that question? Do you want me to tell you? Men whose wives won't give them a blow job are always asking what kind of marriage is this. Is that what you're trying to tell me, is that the ridiculous accusation I'm supposed to be taking seriously?

I said, Stay on the subject.

She said, I'm rubber and you're glue.

I said, Kiss my ass.

She said, Like the poet said, make it bare.

I said, I'll make it bare all right, I'll make my ass so bare you'll be singing "Moon River" in double harmony.

That stopped her. Eventually she said, That doesn't even make any sense.

I knew she was falling out of love with me. I was an idiot, I was a leech, I was living off her salary and trying to be a writer. It was a joke. I broke down crying. I hated to fight with Elizabeth. I couldn't stand the thought of losing her. If I'd been able to think one step ahead, I would have been crying about losing my boys, about not being around to see my older boy, Robin, graduate from high school or being there to sing my little one, Erik, to sleep at night. But no. I was only thinking about romance, and country-western songs and the blues, my baby left me, I'm taking the next train to Memphis and done lost my mojo and drinking wine in an alley and looking at her picture. Like I said, I was an idiot. I blubbered and cried. I said, Oh shit, oh God, oh boo fucking hoo.

She went on in the bathroom and puked, true to her word. I heard her gargling with mint-flavored generic mouthwash, which was all we could afford at the time.

Right that minute I knew how much I loved her. I said to myself, Now there's a classy lady. I had a good marriage. It might be sort of over, but it was good anyway.

I went on and cranked up that ragged truck and weaved on over to Skull Creek, with some cold rain coming down, going about five miles an hour the whole way just to be on the safe side. It was dark and the driver's-side windshield wiper wasn't working, so I had to drive while leaning way over to look out the passenger-side windshield. It's unsafe, I know. That bale-of-wire sound was still coming from the throw-out bearing, so I realized even then that I didn't cut much of a dashing figure. I did take one of the pistols, to make myself feel a little better, a little more secure. I took it out of the top of one of the closets. Elizabeth had dismantled it so it was in about seven or eight pieces. I was too drunk to put it back together. Putting that revolver back together when I'd been drinking was like failing an IQ test. You could hear the parts clanking around in my jacket pocket.

Nobody got hurt at Skull Creek. Some big drunk did tell me he was going to squash me like a bug, about something his hag witch of a wife said I had supposedly said to her, and so I told him I would be the last bug he squashed, I had a pistol in my pocket, I said. I put my hand in there and rattled the parts around some to show him I meant business. He went straight to the phone and called the police, who any other time wouldn't have given gun talk and Skull Creek another thought and would have gone right back to their donuts, but this time here they came, sirens, blue lights, everything, two cars, and one had a big dog caged up in the back going woof-woof.

I was out in the parking lot waiting for them. Everybody else was huddled up on the balcony of Skull Creek, already making a story out of what happened, what a dangerous character I was, how I had brandished a certain type of gun—"brandished," honest to God— that I had killed before, all kinds of embarrassing stuff that got back to me later. The police told me get on in the backseat, and we drove out of Skull Creek. They got a pretty good laugh out of my gun, how many pieces it was in. We drove around town for a while. They were nice guys, these two cops. They didn't want to put me in jail. One was a little guy name Bayles with red hair that stuck up when he took off his cap. I said, My stepdad's name was Bayles.

He said, Is that right.

The cop driving was a black man with a shaved head.

I said, Why do all black people shave their head?

He said, They just do.

We drove out to the Wal-Mart Super Store and then to the mall. We turned back then and went to the drive-in theater and then out to the racetrack. We shined the spotlight around but didn't see anything suspicious. The guy named Bayles said he thought I might have a drinking problem. He told me about some meetings I could go to. He looked back and said, You don't know who you might meet up with there, and winked. I think he was implying that he was a member.

The black cop said, They make you shave your head for the initiation.

I said, I'm trying to be a writer. I said, I stay home and look after my two boys while my wife works. I said, I cook supper every night.

The black cop said, I might marry your ass my own self.

I said, I'm the one sitting in the doctor's office when the younger boy is running a high fever. I said, I'm not much of a writer, but I wouldn't take anything for the feel of his hot parched cheek against my own.

The black cop said, You're a regular Elizabeth Barrett Browning.

I said, I was the one there when the braces went on the older boy, Robin, and when they came off. I'm the one home when they get home from school. I give them their afternoon cookies and milk and make them their lunches. I feed and walk the dogs. I was there when Robin picked out his clarinet and when Erik caught the bus to his swim meets.

The cop named Bayles said, What are you doing at Skull Creek with a gun? Why ain't you home with your kids if you care about them so much?

So that was that. They drove me home and I got out and thanked them and waved good-bye and went on in the house and slipped in between the covers beside Elizabeth. Her body's heat had made the bed toasty and fragrant. She woke up, halfway, and said in a thick voice, Everything okay?

I said, Can you take me over to get the truck tomorrow?

She said, You left the truck?

·   ·   ·

Not long after this, when everything really went to hell, Elizabeth is the one who stayed in that house with the boys and I was the one who moved a long way away and got myself sober and got a job and even managed to get rid of some of my romantic self-pity.

In this new life I could only know my boys on the telephone and on holiday visits, so that's what we did, and I felt terrible about it, but there it is. At least in those days when Elizabeth was working and I was home taking care of my boys I got to know them better than most fathers with real jobs probably ever do. At least there's that.

My List of Chores

Christopher Russell

1. The List and Chief Moose

My friend Dean was in New York on a business trip and had spent the night with us in our apartment in the West Village. On weekday mornings our apartment has the hum of most get-up-and-go homes, with its particular patterns. In our case my wife, Gina, who is an executive in a large corporation, gets up first—bustling around, showering, ironing, making breakfast and lunch for our son, Jacob, who is eight years old. She eventually starts urging Jacob, who on most nights eventually drifts into our bed, to get up and eat his breakfast. And while I am still in bed and more or less asleep, Gina brings me in a cup of coffee.

I work as a ceramic artist, struggling to turn a profit, and getting out of bed in the morning is not my strong suit. On a typical day I hope to be awake and functioning by the time Gina and Jacob leave to walk to school at around eight-fifteen. Then I have my own breakfast, get dressed, and wander over to my studio, where I spend a few hours making tiles for the production line or working on one of my commissioned projects that needs attention.

On that morning, however, I got up at the same time as everyone else so that I might have coffee and chat with Dean before he left for his business meetings.

That day was also special in that the D.C. sniper was still on the loose. During that dramatic time, each day's news was filled with details of his movements and motives, with talking heads speculating about his next step. And, as always, there was the tantalizing prospect of another one of those surreal press conferences held by the fabulous Chief Moose, in which he would speak directly to the sniper in cryptic, personalized pleas. I was fascinated, and I was pleased to discover that Dean was too. We both agreed it was top-notch TV.

Gina, however, did not share our interest. She regarded the entire affair, and especially the delicious media orgy Dean and I so enjoyed and looked forward to, with not-unexpected scorn. So there was a tension in the house that morning as Dean and I both champed at the bit to check out the latest update on CNN. Had the sniper struck again? Had Chief Moose finally caught him? Had there been a new flurry of exchanged, coded messages? But with Gina preparing in such a focused manner for her productive workday, we both sensed that sitting down with our coffee on the couch with Paula Zahn—I was still in my bathrobe—was simply not the right thing to do. So instead we sat talking, biding our time until Gina and Jacob's departure, while the remote control burned a hole in my hand.

Ever directed toward leaving, Gina zeroed in on me at our kitchen's island and proceeded with a daily household ritual, a ritual that captivated Dean to almost the same degree as the events in D.C. He watched, spellbound, as Gina, in her officious way, presented me with my List of Chores. Every day Gina prepares this list for me, with all the household tasks and details that I am responsible for completing before she arrives home from work that evening.

"Okay, Chris," she began. "It's really important that you actually get the things on the list done this time. Okay?"

My answer to this is almost always "I really will do my best."

And then Gina commenced the next ritual of the daily list—going over each item, one by one, to reinforce the importance of the task or to clarify or simply to cheerlead me into doing it. "First you've got to call Sarah and set up a play date with Drew. Jacob hasn't seen him in two weeks, and you know they had us over last time. Then e-mail John and family with a thank-you theme . . . you know, the presents they gave Jacob at the brunch? Go to the post office—it's really important this one gets done today. Those packages have been sitting around forever. Then, let's see—call the exterminator. The place is absolutely crawling. Call the door guy to come and fix the lock. Jacob needs more vitamins, the chewy kind with the blue top—you can only get them at Integral Yoga . . . And we need printer paper, Cheer Free, and Bounty. Call Esther to say hello; call your parents about the plane tickets; and call Julie about lunch. That's been on the list for weeks. You've got to do your taxes. And Jacob needs a haircut. So, Chris—I can depend on you to get these things done today?"

"I really will do my best."

Gina gave me a kiss and hugged Dean good-bye, and then she and Jacob headed for the door. As she got close to her actual departure, Dean, who had grown increasingly anxious about turning on CNN for the sniper update, began to narrate a play-by-play of Gina and Jacob's exodus under his breath—"They've got their coats on . . . they're at the door . . . they open the door . . . they're out . . . the door closes. Okay! Where's the remote?"

And then it was just us—me, Dean, Paula Zahn, and the chief.

2. What Gina Expected When She Was Expecting

When Gina was pregnant, a huge number of objects came into our house from I don't know where. Receiving blankets, bottles, sippy cups, diapers, booties—they just flooded in. There was a whole new vocabulary for things I had not even known existed (onesies?). Somehow Gina, who had not been particularly interested in babies before her pregnancy, had learned about all these things that Jacob would need, and now she was in the process of gathering them. I, for

my part, had no idea about any of it. I imagine that some of the information had come out of the pile of books on Gina's night table
that she kept urging me to read, those books about babying that all
soon-to-be-parents suddenly find in their homes, like *What to Expect
When You're Expecting*—which really is the Mother of All Lists. I hate
this book, with its overzealousness, its exaggerated demand for per-
fection in the management of innumerable, incomprehensible details. It really is horrible. Its tone is that of the bossy, arrogant mother
to the naïve mother-to-be, and I'm sure this tone, and perhaps the
average new mother's deep-seated need for this sort of bossiness, is
why the book holds such dark attraction and remains on the best-
seller lists. The *What to Expect* diet is notoriously fascistic, with its
blanket condemnation of eating the exact kind of unhealthy, satisfying foods so many pregnant women desperately crave (a friend of
mine actually refers to the book as *Eating Disorders to Expect When
You're Expecting*). The beatific, calicoed, insipid woman in the rocking chair on the book's cover is the implied ideal. It's just hideous.

Maybe it was all those books, or maybe it was the long chats with
all of her new mothering friends, but somehow Gina had a whole vision of what had to be done to prepare for our baby's arrival. And I
simply had missed the whole thing. When a friend asked me what she
could give us as a baby present, I conferred with Gina, and she instantly produced a list of detailed notes and relayed that we could really use a large Thermos for holding the warm water one needs on
the baby's changing table. Chrome would be great.

I knew nothing about the changing table or its accessories. Nor
did I know about the plastic-covered foam tray that you fasten to the
changing table, to which you then strap the soiled baby when you do
the changing. This foam work surface, which I now recognize as an
essential component of the oncoming baby's environment, simply arrived in our apartment in one of the many bags that Gina brought
home from Schneider's Juvenile Furniture Store nearly every week-

end. I don't know how she became aware that we could not possibly have a child without that foam tray, or without the Thermos of hot water next to it, or without the drawer of one-yard-square blankets with which to swaddle the baby after the change, or without the many chemical and natural agents needed in the battle against cradle cap and diaper rash and infant acne, or without a cloth baby carrier, or without a car seat. It was as if Gina had been an open receiver to a broadcast that I now realize must have been blaring at both of us loud and clear. While she'd acted on this transmitted list of commands with her usual unfailing attention to detail, I'd been oblivious.

And that list continues to broadcast, and Gina is the one who continues to hear it. When Jacob was of an age where it was appropriate for him to begin eating whole vegetables, requests from Gina for cherry tomatoes and bags of tiny carrots appeared on the shopping list. Requests for juice boxes, 1 percent organic milk, kiwi fruit, and soy-based chicken nuggets magically appeared on the list too. Gina was all over the baby-sitter issue, the preschool problem, the elementary school selection conundrum; it had never occurred to me to even think about these concerns. I often think that Jacob would have starved to death—actually starved to death by now—if I had been taking care of him without Gina's instruction. From the beginning, I would grab him, strap him into the Baby Björn, and rush off to wherever we were going—a restaurant, my studio, a birthday party, wherever. And then during the outing I would gradually remember all of the things I'd forgotten in my rush—a bottle, diapers, wipes, baby food. I still have those sudden daily epiphanies—*Jacob should probably eat something!* Each time it hits me like a whole new idea.

So should it surprise anyone that Gina writes a list for me each day, and that she asks me at the end of each day how I did with the list? Or that she wakes up the next day to copy yesterday's list onto a new piece of paper, to present these unfinished tasks to me again?

3. But Sometimes She Doesn't Know How Easy She Has It

Last Halloween I went trick-or-treating with a friend and three children. We were in Greenwich Village, and though it was early, the sidewalk was already crazy with Halloweeners and partygoers. We'd been all over the neighborhood; the kids' eyes were glazing. My friend and I agreed it was time to get everybody home via cab. Cabs are not easy to find on Halloween, so when I spotted one I grabbed Jacob's hand and ran for it, darting between two double-parked cars—one of which, as it happened, was an idling police ambulance. But the space between the two cars was tighter than I had expected because we couldn't make it through. As I stood there trying to figure out what to do, the ambulance driver leaned his head out the window, looked at me with a kind of bored scowl, and told me that it wasn't a very good idea to have my child between two parked vehicles, particularly when one of them not only wasn't parked but was a police ambulance that could move at any moment.

Duly admonished, I backed out, dragging Jacob with me. By now the cab had come around the far side of the ambulance and was waiting at the light, still empty. So I ran for it again, and, after reaching it and knocking on the window to get the driver's attention, I yanked open the door and got Jacob in. As I looked for the others, I heard one of the girls let out a horrible moan. The bottom of her trick-or-treat bag had fallen through, and there she stood in a frozen state of heartbroken shock, her entire collection of candy at her feet. I didn't want to lose the cab, particularly with Jacob still in it, so I hesitated about going over to help. That was when I heard a loud animal yelp and a scream. My friend's son had stepped on a passing dog's foot, and while the dog yowled and the boy shrieked and the girl with the spilled candy sobbed and the cabbie bluntly demanded to know whether we were getting in or *not*, I believe I actually lost consciousness for a moment.

Somehow everybody ended up in the taxi. My friend, a successful lawyer now working as a stay-at-home mom, looked over at me and said, "We really deserve a drink. Our partners have no idea how easy they have it, do they?"

4. IF I'M A BIT LAX, GINA IS A BIT BOSSY

On a recent winter evening, searching for an address that didn't seem to exist, I led Gina and Jacob around the snow-packed sidewalks of Brooklyn Heights. We were late for dinner with friends, and though we had called them from our cell phone in an attempt to get better directions and to notify them of our lateness, we were only able to reach their answering machine. As is often the personnel arrangement in our family, I was striking out ahead—to read the name of the next street—while Gina and Jacob lagged behind, taking the messy sidewalks a little more tentatively. As I scooted along, very much wanting to arrive (we had stopped at a liquor store on the way, and the large bottle of vodka I was carrying was growing cold and heavy in my grip), I was vaguely aware of the other members of my family conversing behind me.

"Now Jacob," I heard Gina say. "When you and Daddy are out walking together, you make sure that he doesn't run ahead like this. You make sure he holds your hand so you're safe!"

I was taken aback. No, I was completely pissed off. Gina's suggestion that Jacob should concern himself with keeping an eye on me through the big mean streets conjured up an image in my mind of a Dickensian urchin walking his aged, blind, mentally ill grandfather through the streets of a smoky old London, looking for a free doorway where they could spend the night. I stopped in my tracks, turned around, and called out, "Jacob, next time when you're out with your mother, could you please make sure that she walks a little faster!"

I don't get angry very often, and even less often do I yell. But as they pulled up to me, I snapped at Gina, "What the hell was that about?"

Gina gave me one of those looks that means, *You know perfectly well what I am referring to, and if you weren't so defensive—*

But then my cell phone rang, and it was our friends calling with directions.

After I hung up, and as we made our way along the illogical route, I went on: "I walk with Jacob all the time. And we have managed to get home alive every time so far! You were back there, dawdling along, with him! Do you think that I hadn't taken that into account? Do you really think I would have just let him walk into the middle of the street if we had been alone?"

We rode up our friends' elevator in silence, I glowering while mentally preparing my defense, and Gina with that same defiant look on her face.

5. SPECIALNESS

Jacob attends a wonderful private elementary school several blocks from where we live. A few years ago, when we applied for Jacob— back when the stock market was sky-high and there were so many young families who believed they were rich enough to afford both a family-sized home in New York City and to send their kids to private schools—getting into this school was ridiculously competitive. The school has a studied casualness, though one that is, in fact, available almost exclusively to privileged families. It is very confident in its neighborhoody specialness. I love the place, but anyone can see its contradictions.

On the first day back from spring vacation, everyone has a tan and asks you, "Where did you go?"

The mothers all wear Ted Muehling jewelry. Ted Muehling is a very special SoHo jewelry designer who makes perfect little earrings. Ted Muehling jewelry is relaxed and casual yet quite expensive. When people ask me about Jacob's school, I tell them all the mothers wear Ted Muehling, and they—or those in the know, anyway— immediately understand.

One of my daily duties is to pick up Jacob after school. The mothers I see picking up their kids always look as relaxed as their Teds. They arrive breezily early to chat with one another and catch up on the gossip.

I, on the other hand, am in a frantic whirlwind, always on the way to getting something else done. I'm chronically late, rushing back from my short time at the studio. Three days a week I have to get Jacob to his tutor, and often I am rushing to get some design or office work done at home. And then there is always my List of Chores, with the daily trips to the grocery store, and the endless home fix-it projects, and the required thank-you correspondence and play-date planning.

When I look around at these women, I somehow doubt that any of them are carrying with them a list of chores from their husbands detailing the various tasks they must perform that day. I would think that any of these women would laugh at her husband if he tried to give her such a list. Every woman seems to have her clear agenda, confident that she knows how a household should be constructed and run, and the husband's opinion about this agenda, about how he would do things if he were in charge (even if he is the one at home most of the time), is secondary.

As a man in my position—not being the main wage earner in the household, not having a *real* job—I concede that I am vulnerable to being subjected to Gina's List. And this daily struggle that Gina and I have over the List, with her aggressively writing it and me passive-aggressively not completing it, is not just a skirmish of our personalities (although I can see that my lack of attention in the housekeeping arena could make anyone want to tell me what to do) but to some extent a microbattle in the war of the sexes.

Gina and I will make the most of it, and the war does have some honors. I may not be able to feel the same kind of pride as a woman who runs her own household and makes her own lists, but that doesn't mean I don't feel pride. When Gina comes around the corner and finds me at the top of a ladder changing a burnt-out lightbulb—a task that might have been on the list for days or weeks—she'll look up at me with a surprised, fetching smile and say, "Oh, great, you're changing the bulb. Look at you up there! So manly . . ."

And, sometimes, a comment like this is all I need.

Men in Houses

RON CARLSON

y career as a cartographer was an exciting career. In 1958 at Edison Elementary School, Brent Griffiths showed me how to trace maps out of the *World Book*, and I could take a plain, blank piece of paper, and, working close with my Dixon Ticonderoga pencil for twenty minutes, capture the contour, the major rivers, and the mountain ranges of Africa. I also did Australia, South America, and Antarctica. It was the year we learned cursive writing, but I printed the names of cities and rivers and mountain ranges onto these maps, and I used other pencils to shade various districts and divisions on each. Brent had a folder of his maps and I had a folder of my maps. These maps, linked to the independent research project we'd done the year before—writing the numbers from 1 to 120,000 in order in a notebook—made me feel pretty much that the sky was the limit in terms of what the future held for us. Under the rich influence of old Tarzan movies, a documentary we saw on piranhas, and a sense that the jungle was in fact deep and dark holding mysteries yet unplundered, Brent and I made a pact that year that when we grew up we would not get married, but we would take our maps and go partners in a Jeep and take it to Africa and let adventure take us. I was sure in my heart that this would happen. I could picture myself in that vehicle, an old army

Jeep I'd seen in a movie. We had provisions in it, stowed neatly in crates. As we bumped along, I wiped the road grime from my safari glasses with a big blue bandana. The roads were uneven and rough and unnamed. The streams were choked with carnivorous fish. Wild birds called from the leafy darkness. My plan was to drive to the end, where no roads went, and then right into the uncharted; taking my pith helmet and my pencils, I would go into the unknown.

And, of course, that is exactly what has happened.

I met a girl in high school and married her the week we graduated college.

I've been married a long time now. How long? So long, people don't even ask about it. My wife and I look like each other. Ten thousand nights, exactly. Eleven thousand. Something. So, what, should I come at you with some story of high adventure, misadventure, crime, exultation, honor? Let's be frank. I'm the man in this deal, and so my adventure involves modified bohemianism, abbreviated foreplay, a mortgage or two, questionable table manners, and lost car keys. It's an adventure. It is an adventure. You've got to be open to the word. It is true that my adventure has transpired indoors, on couches and under a roof, snacks at close range, the only growling from the garage door or the television.

I was against all this at the beginning. I was happy with marriage, but that was as settled as I was going to get. And I was okay with living inside a permanent structure as long as it wasn't mine, as long as I could still cut and run at a moment's notice. Then we started acquiring furniture, and I should have seen it coming, but I didn't.

We had been married six or seven years, and it seemed to me that things were going fine for the man in the marriage: I was a schoolteacher and we were in a school apartment living with secondhand furniture. Our first couch was a surplus couch courtesy of the admission office of the prep school where we'd taken work. It was a classic maroon leather wingback on which ten thousand nervous parents have lost their pocket change. Then for twenty bucks we bought a beige Naughahyde sofa bed used from the math teacher. A sofa bed! Now we could sleep in the living room! Talk about sexy. Like all men, I liked this notion of waking up in the wrong room, and I welcomed this new device into our household. But we still had no real roots, no permanent possessions; I was still basically footloose except for the job and the wife. Then my wife informed me that we were going into the world to purchase a brand-new couch. I declared the man's six-word credo: *What's wrong with the old one?* It's torn up and ruined, but what?

Really, we stood in the furniture store and my wife explained, in that endless jungle of easy chairs and divans, that I was looking at our new couch. Well, my feelings were not unique. It wasn't a surprise that when confronted by two hundred alcoves of seating arrangements, I wanted to sit down. I had that old feeling that Thoreau describes: I wondered if I would own the couch or the couch would own me.

I must here admit that my dear wife and I had words. We're in the furniture store and I'm being passive aggressive ten years before that phrase even appears in a book title. I'm so smug and so smart and so right. I'm affronted by the materialistic turn our relationship has taken. I pull out all my sixties cant frosted with sarcasm, and what I do is hurt my wife's feelings in a way that will be called in twenty-five years "big time." The whole conversation, my huffing and haughty capitulation, and the silent ride home reminded me of our first such moment, the fifth day of our marriage, when in a small grocery store my wife appeared at the checkout with a mop and a bucket. A mop! It was the very first tiny recognition of what was coming. I didn't want a mop! Yes, we were moving into a borrowed apartment for the summer, but a mop! We're not taking a mop on our adventure into the unknown! Yes, my wife patiently explained we are going to be the proud owners of a mop and bucket. It's what grown-ups do.

And so, a new couch found its way into the apartment. It was the color of oatmeal and looked like something rich people would own.

A few years later we let go of the apartment and bought a house. There goes nomadic wandering. There goes pack up everything and leave in the middle of the night. Men in houses! How is that going to work? A house is the antithesis of adventure. Houses glare menacingly at adventure from opposite sides in the big book of antonyms: domestic and foreign. Suddenly you have a mortgage, which is so obviously related to that other word, *mortuary*. You're essentially stuck. Thus runs the sorry litany of boy-think. You start out in your mother's house, maybe you even have your own room, and then there's a short season staying in the rooms of the world, maybe a dorm or an apartment, and then you're in your wife's house. (There's maybe going to be one more place, the geezer's repository, but as they say: Let's not go there.) It is amazing the percentage of our lives we live with a roof over our heads. I'm not asking you to look up right now, but if you did, even sitting here almost a year from you, I know what you'll see. We live lives where opening the window is seen as a gambit. Let me say right here: I don't get out much.

The first thing cavemen did, after the fire was going, was scratch a deer or a bison on the wall. Some folks think this was sympathetic magic for the hunt to come. In reality, they were simply bringing the outdoors inside, drawing a picture of *where they wanted to be*. Now it doesn't take a man long to see the true purpose of a house: to keep the television out of the weather. The purpose of the television: to bring the outdoors in for safe viewing. Suddenly a roof makes sense. In that light, furniture suddenly assumes a meaningful glow; a man can see that every stick of furniture in the house serves a supporting role for the television. Especially the couch. Even the proper living room with that overstuffed or leather or rattan furniture is just a place to sit and wait until you're permitted to watch television again.

Of course the other thing a house is good for is keeping your children out of the midday sun and the periodic rain. As the big book on the stages of matrimony has it: after the mop and the couch come the children. Children are the steel-coated, grade-A, four-star bona fide separator of men and women. All the other issues in a relationship—sex (every element of sex including frequency, variety, positions, inventions, discussions, unique bodily features, preambles, postscripts, et cetera), money (every aspect of finances including pocket money, beer money, retirement funds, luxury purchases, blistering debt, discussions, positions, et cetera), communication (every scrip-scrap of data exchanged, including written, oral, fax, e-mail, refrigerator notes, hand signals, et cetera) pale—these issues absolutely dry up and blow away—when they are placed against the one true test: children.

Now, men have a child-caring style. I certainly do. My sons arrived within a year of each other, and my style emerged immediately. My style is best characterized by surprise. When you layer that on the other surprises that my marriage had delivered unto me, you can begin to put together a more comprehensive picture of my total style, which is a state of chronic surprise. I was surprised (and pleased) to be married, and then I was surprised to have a job. My surprise doubled when we began to get furniture. I had thought furniture was for other people, and as I noted, I was surprised to have a house. All of these surprises are not lack of forethought; they are inherent in my wiring as a man. It is not a fault; it's a condition.

Women do not have a child-caring style. You can't label it a style, when it is part of their core fabric. I am not saying that caring for children is easier for women than it is for men but simply that they have a God-given, dyed-in-the-wool, deep-blood, native, atavistic, chromosomal understanding of how to care for children that men do not have. They know what to do if someone runs a temperature, swallows a penny, cries. I know what to do some of the time, but these are things I've learned. I had to learn them. Oh, look, the little person is crying—which of the five major reasons could it be? Let me go down the list, after I find the list. Where is the list? Meanwhile, my wife will have solved the problem. She doesn't have to consult the list; she is the list. As a man in my house with my wife and children, I have seen some things with my eyes, which I take as empirical proof of women's abilities in this regard. One comparison might be this: if you play infield, say third base, for ten years, you develop a fair understanding of what is going to happen next. You can tell by the batter's stance and the variables of the pitch as it goes in whether the batter is going to swing and, if he does, if the ball is going to be hit to your left or right (or straight at your nose), and almost imperceptibly you begin to move toward the play. I saw my wife move that same way in the first week of having kids; there'd be a blink or a shudder or a lifted chin or a start, and she would move up and make the play. Listen: I tried to imitate it and I could not.

Our boys were less than ten months apart, so there was a blim-blamming in the nursery. At one point in those dirty-diaper days, I thought I'd give Elaine a hand and change the boys before I went off to give an interview and reading at a radio station. Deftly, I got both boys on a towel on the bed. See, this is a man's approach: two at once. I peeled off the heavy diapers and immediately saw that this was a poor approach. How could I clean one guy up while the other guy was squirming around? Two hands were inadequate, and it was a poor idea to have already put on my tie. We got through it, I'll say, but half an hour later in the tiny radio studio, my host pushed her chair as far from mine as she could, her nose rearing like a horse in a barn fire.

Kids are the unknown. They are the uncharted territories that come into your own house. For me, they stilled the powerful pull of dark nights sleeping on the ground near the end of the road. They made me rethink the house. I planted trees, another set of things that are going to be hard to move in a hurry, built a redwood fence, fixed and painted all our doors, carpeted the nursery, assembled the cribs, and I loved how the little gates lifted like the last little fence between the world and our boys. Now look, you have a couple kids and you provide the shelter, as well as movie money, dental care, and clean socks. You follow your wife's example when you can, but mainly you try to be around. Your approach to the enterprise is a kind of good spirited trial and error. There are errors, but you can't bail.

The boys knew immediately what to do with the couch. They boarded it like pirates and fished from the bow with the sash of my robe. They informed me when I walked through the room that by touching the floor, my feet had been eaten completely by alligators. I could have slapped my forehead. I knew that all along. The couch keeps you out of danger. They stayed on the thing for hours, finally quitting the sport by walking across the coffee table and two chairs and leaping onto the kitchen tile and safety.

We bought other couches: a wicker deal that weighed about forty pounds total, a plush green L-shaped seating arrangement big as a train wreck, a ten-foot marshmallow that used to trap my parents when they came to dinner, a Mission-style sofa with wonderful wooden arms for your books and coffee. Well, you go through three or four couches, your kids are going to grow up. By the fourth couch, they'll be in high school. You recover one, they'll be packing for college.

When our boys got into high school, our little family started going in different directions. Everyone was trying to develop a private life but me. We ate together when we could. It was worrisome; we were prosperous, which in America means everyone goes to his room. It becomes less clear how everybody is doing in school and who their friends are and what they're doing until 1 A.M. Our house was just a dorm where people came and went on their way to greater adventure. It took about a year to see that we were losing touch.

So here is where it ends. When I was a kid I wanted to be out of the house, away, gone, and the quality of being away called to me like a tide. Now, as a father with my two boys, I just wanted to be home. And the fact is plain that I wanted them home with me. I wanted to talk to them, to know their friends, their pursuits. I wanted to look them in the eye when they came in, and I wanted to smell them, and let them know I was still around. I certainly hadn't used all my advice or bad jokes. I wasn't, regardless of their opinion, done.

I could remember the season when our boys took the living room couch apart and made a duplex out of the cushions. They had food in there and a flashlight and reading material. I think they had a television. No one over ten admitted. They even had a password, which turned out to be my wife's maiden name. And, if you thought about it right, they had a couch, most of one. It is my favorite architecture, those cushions—a house within a house. I haven't seen one of those forts for a few years now. That was the couch we had recovered last spring.

The most famous couch in America is in Springfield, of course, and belongs to Homer and Marge, and has brought their brood together in hundreds of combinations for years. It was probably this last couch that was my inspiration.

I did an astounding thing—something that, frankly, surprised me.

I told Elaine I wanted to buy a new couch. This is nonfiction. Last fall I took Elaine out to a big furniture warehouse north of town, and we bought a couch. Listen: I couldn't wait to get it home. We tore out the dining room—where we never ate—and I bought a cabinet and a big television. We installed this stuff in that room, right next to the kitchen, so close to the fridge. Suddenly our house had a new center. It became the station where everyone flopped out when they came home. We sat on it and watched all the effluvia of Western civilization. I saw men and women conquer Everest, challenge asteroids, float the Amazon. We've had the couch just over a year now, and it's shot the way the great couches are shot. If you sit in a certain place, good luck getting up. There's a strong chance that if you come in and sit down second, you're going to end up with someone's ankles on your lap. It's a posture that shows you're related.

So now maybe I get it. I think I have finally gotten the thing about men in houses. I'd like to thank my boys for coming along and teaching me the importance of houses and furniture, which I have used all these years to keep them nearby, and also for teaching me, just lately, that even with the TV and the couch you can only keep them with you for a limited amount of time. But I'll stay here and watch the guys on television drive their Jeeps through the jungle (MacGyver isn't even married). Maybe Elaine will join me every now and then. But my boys have seen the map and they want to go—they need to. This very year, this month in fact, they are headed off to college. It's a big world.

The Lock Box

SEAN ELDER

y wife and I were lying in bed after making love one morning—okay, I know that must sound very sophisticated and child-free, but this was an exceptional morning; our daughter had spent the night at a friend's house, and my teenage son was not yet out of bed. Anyway, there we were, as close to contentment as I could hope to get on this earth, when I made a bush-league error. I asked her what she was thinking about.

"The trim size of the magazine," she replied, "which we may have to reduce."

I should explain that for the last year my wife has been the editor in chief of a new women's magazine, and as anyone who has worked on such a launch can tell you, the work never really stops. Or at least you never stop thinking about it. Even during those moments when work talk was once banished.

I'd like to report that I ignored her and lit two Gauloises, but she doesn't smoke, and if memory serves, I simply fell into step and began discussing the fate of oversized magazines in this competitive newsstand environment. It's nice to share an interest—or in this case, a profession—with your mate. But there is a time and place for everything, no?

What's depressing is that it doesn't seem very long ago that I held my wife's bedroom attention for just a little longer. In our early days, like most couples, we tangoed 'til we were sore (to borrow a line from Tom Waits). But lately I have come to feel that, like Billy Idol, I'm mostly dancing with myself.

Not that I expected marriage, and the sex therein, to be a cake-walk. But like a lot of men I've always put sex high on the list of domestic prerequisites, somewhere between food and basic cable. I did not think it was something that would have to be constantly negotiated and appraised, and I admit I was sort of caught with my pants down (read: up) when the trajectory of our sex life spiraled from nightly to weekly to "What's wrong with you?" Is this common to marriage? I wondered. How could I tell? Most of my male friends are married and no doubt have similar tales to tell, but despite what some women may fear, grown men don't spend much time talking about sex (especially if they're not getting much). When you're young and not getting any you talk about it all the time, but as an adult it's not quite the same thing. In fact, it's the opposite thing.

Now, despite Dr. Phil's assertion that "sexless marriages are an undeniable epidemic," that's not what I'm talking about. A sexless marriage story would quickly devolve into a divorce story, and my wife and I have both invested too much love and energy into our marital vehicle to sit here and watch the wheels come off. No, my wife likes sex as much as I do. She really does. She may not like it as frequently as I do. Or as urgently. Or with as many possible variations . . .

But here's the thing: For many long, pulsating, undulating years there seemed to be no reason to talk about sex. Like the car in *The Phantom Tollbooth*, it went without saying. Then one day the car was stalling, the timing was off. I remember clearly the first time we came back from a night out and she didn't want to sleep with me—I was stunned. *Was it something I did?* No, she assured me. Nor did she plead tiredness, drunkenness, or any of the physical complaints that traditionally stop the show. "No, I'm just not in the mood," she said. Does any phrase strike greater fear in the hearts of married men?

But that's what happens. In so many couples, especially those with two careers and children, sex just falls off the list, like some dance craze from our youth that everyone's forgotten. And men who opt for divorce and trade their old wives in for a younger, more pneumatic model appear in public as graceless as Grandpa doing the Funky Chicken—and, soon enough, they find themselves back in the same boat anyway when the pneumatic version too starts yawning at eight o'clock and proclaiming she's not in the mood.

·   ·   ·

Our situation may be complicated by the nature of our jobs. I work at home, and as such, our house and its needs constitute half of my work. I've been a freelance writer and editor for the eleven years we've been married, a sometimes lucrative period of self-employment broken up by occasional staff jobs, while my wife has gone from one magazine to another, ascending the editorial masthead as she's moved. As her work has become more demanding as well as more remunerative, the tasks of cooking, cleaning, and keeping track of the children have fallen to me. Nothing wrong with that: I like to cook, and after my parents divorced I became accustomed to doing household chores. But it does put us in a rather different frame of mind at day's end. When she leaves work she's fleeing minions demanding her time: editors, art directors, publicists, and publishers—they all want something and they want it now. The last thing she wants to deal with when she gets home is somebody else's needs. And though I have been gnawed by my own ducks (a son who's lost his keys again, an editor who wants a new lead, a daughter who wants help with her homework), I, unlike her, am pretty much starved for adult conversation by the time she gets home.

Nothing in my wife's feminist life has prepared her for the Freaky Friday feeling of suddenly finding herself cast in the role of fifties dad. "The whiplash effect can be kind of intense," she tells me. And I can't blame her for not wanting to come home some nights—though of course I do.

One night my son wanders into the kitchen, guitar slung around his neck, to inquire when dinner might be ready. "As soon as Peggy deigns to make an appearance," I tell him. Then the phone rings, and it's my wife herself, who claims she's now leaving for real—she just got caught up in a meeting and then there was an e-mail she had to answer.

"Did you ever hear of the phone?" I snap before hanging up on her. Yes, it's come to this.

•   •   •

Helen Gurley Brown, no stranger to sexy cover-lines, once suggested that a wife greet her husband at the door wearing a negligée and carrying a martini. While my wife likes a stiff drink now and then, I don't think the sight of me in see-through pajamas would do much for her libido. No, what she wants after ten hours of meetings and display copy is more along the lines of fettuccine Alfredo, or a chicken roasted in olive oil and lemon, and this I duly provide for her. (Young women bitterly joke that the perfect girl for most men would be one who turned into pizza after sex. On work nights my wife would skip the sex and take the pizza—provided it was baked in a brick oven and topped with goat cheese and roasted peppers.)

After dinner comes the nightly ritual of putting our daughter to bed (something we share, or break up into shifts, with me doing the reading and Mom acting as the closer). Then maybe a little evening news and the promise of sleep, sweeter it seems—for her at least—than any sexual fantasy. ("Sleep is the new sex," Margaret Carlson proclaimed in a recent essay in *Time* magazine that considered the working wife's desire for rest and respite from day-job drudgery, clinging children, and that ogre of the modern marriage, the pawing, prying husband.)

But hope springs again on the weekends. Of course, there's the usual forest of responsibilities to coordinate: play dates, music classes, and an endless procession of birthday parties for the kids, various tasks related to our home and animals, and even more work (for both of us) that must be done by Monday. That's precisely why stealing moments of pleasure seems all the more imperative to me. Finding ourselves unexpectedly without children or chores one afternoon—someone had called to see if our daughter could stay at her house longer, my son was at a matinee—I raised the subject, and also an eyebrow. My wife looked at me as if I was speaking Urdu.

"That's the last thing you think of at times like that," I accused her later, "but it's always the first thing that occurs to me." She couldn't argue with my assessment. She hasn't equated free time with foreplay since the last time we were trying to conceive. But for me, what sweeter revenge against this world and its injuries could you imagine than lounging in bed with the one you love? Everything in my life seems better after sex. New York doesn't smell so bad, and the GOP isn't *really* the Nazi Party, after all. I think most men are like me in this regard. Given the choice between fucking and just about anything else, they'll go for the former.

Does that make us stupider than women? It certainly makes us simpler. My brother once sent me an e-mail with the subject line "The difference." Within the body of the message was an image of two identical boxes, roughly the shape of a stereo tuner. The one labeled WOMEN was covered with knobs and buttons, as complex as the cockpit of an airplane. The MEN box had but a single switch, labeled ON and OFF. (My wife is still trying to find a way to turn me off.)

•   •   •

Weekend evenings would seem to be a lock for some marital recreation, wouldn't you think? Barring illness, exhaustion, or dinner guests that just won't leave, there is little that comes between us—except, perhaps, a novel. The narrator of the *Arabian Nights*, you may recall, had to keep telling tales to her husband or he would kill her. In our variation of this Scheherazade routine, my wife seems to believe that she needs to keep reading tales of her own or I will ravish her.

A few Saturdays ago we had a real date: a movie, a baby-sitter (okay, my son, but he didn't let anything happen to his sister while we were out), the prospect of an early bed. I shaved and brushed my teeth, practically humming "I'm in the Mood for Love" as I came down the hall. My wife was about halfway through one of Alan Furst's sublime novels of espionage—a shared passion of ours of a different sort—and begged a moment more. "Just let me get to the end of this chapter."

What could I say? It's hard to start a romantic encounter with someone by denying her what she wants.

When she got up to use the bathroom, however, I stole a look at her book and discovered, to my considerable dismay, that the chapter had another seventy-five pages to go.

Upon her return I pointed this out to her and she assured me she didn't mean the end of the *whole* chapter—there would surely, she promised, be a natural break in the narrative . . . sometime. Then she picked up the book and resumed her reading.

Rather than sit there and sigh like Al Gore, I took the dog out for a late constitutional, cleaned up in the kitchen a bit, read some of the paper, and finally came back to our bedroom to get my cigarettes. She was still deep in the intrigues of the French Resistance and seemed surprised to see me.

"I don't know why you're avoiding me by hiding behind that book," I told her. "I'm not even sure *you* know. But when you do decide that you want me, I trust you'll remember how to let me know."

She put down the book, mole-eyed. "Don't be that way."

But the game was up. One of the first rules of this sex tango is that you don't speak its name. The second is: no complaints. You can make logical, unassailable observations, try and be good-humored and gracious, but once you express any hint of disappointment or frustration, you're dead. No éclairs for you, pal. (Is this what Al meant by "the Lock Box"?)

The next day was Mother's Day. After I brought my wife coffee in bed (something I do every single morning, for the record), she apologized. "This week has been such a burnout," she said. "Sometimes I just need to disappear inside my little snail shell." It's true; she is far more independent than I am, and this difference is probably one of the things that keeps our marriage together. Once, long before marriage, we separated, with me the one wielding the cleaver. "I'm like a dog, you're like a cat," I told her then, by way of explaining our different (and in my mind incompatible) personalities. "But dogs and cats can get along!" she told me then, and over the years she has proven right. When we finally got a cat last year, at my daughter's insistence and against my wishes, I rapidly adapted to the cat's temperament by treating her just the way I treat my wife: letting her go off on her own, not forcing my attentions on her, waiting for her to come to me. It's a working strategy for cat and woman alike, though in my wife's case I get a little lonely from waiting.

So after a long, slightly bumpy Mother's Day—marked by some petty bickering and an absence of shaving on my part—we make love and it's sweet and salty as escargots served in butter and garlic. It's getting past the shell that's the tricky part.

.   .   .

There have been many explanations offered for the man-woman disconnect on this matter. Biology gets a lot of grief, with the simplest explanation being that women have less need for sex once the husband-children thing is locked in, while men ride their heat-seeking missiles off into oblivion, like Slim Pickens at the end of *Dr. Strangelove.* (There is no OFF switch.) Society too gets its lumps as feminists find most men's expectations about sex and marriage based in patriarchy and an obsolete sense of entitlement. Wives used to put out for their husbands because they had to, this line of thinking goes. It was part of paying the rent, part of what women gave in exchange for food and lodging, to say nothing of the college fund for the children.

But as that sort of traditional marriage grows scarce, at least in many Western countries, the old answers don't work. For men such as myself—outearned by their wives, with their very work identities cast into doubt—the mantle of breadwinner, and the assumed benefits thereof, simply no longer apply.

A modern marriage is held together by a thousand tiny threads, of course, and there is no crude quid pro quo of the meat-for-sex variety that sustained early societies. But if my wife doesn't depend on me for her financial solvency (and a good thing, too), she does depend on me for myriad other things—cooking and child care, yes, but also for humor and companionship, for moral support and critical insight, for reality checks and trivial information. Farther down the list, almost falling off the page, is sexual gratification. I think women know it's something we're much keener on than they are and occasionally they try to indulge us without being completely condescending.

"It's a very romantic complaint," my wife says, reading an early draft of this essay. (You try writing about your sex life without letting your spouse vet the piece.) And she's right: I am yearning for something that seems long gone but is still within reach, not just sex but love in all its lost intensity, immediacy, and impulsiveness. Women roll their eyes as men are forever clinging to the scraps of former glory—that guitar pick Joe Strummer threw into the crowd, the ticket stubs to that playoff game you attended twenty years ago. And like all romantics, we believe that by hanging on to the vestiges of fulfillment past we might just bring it back to life. To give up on this, to me, feels like a kind of death.

•   •   •

If you took all the mostly useless literature out there concerning men and women and sex, you could probably boil it all down to one complaint. "I don't see why it has to be such a big deal!" we yell to each other across a chasm. Men meaning, What's the big deal, let's go to bed; women meaning, What's the big deal, can't you give it a rest? A fair question, but the answer seems to be no. Because, let's face it, if men weren't always hungry for it, nothing would ever happen. There would be no sex and our species would perish.

Okay, maybe that's a bit melodramatic. But married sex beyond procreation might well become a thing of the past. If women associate sex with new life and new relationships, men tend to associate it with life itself. I remember making love to my wife a few days after learning of my mother's death. We were headed west for the funeral, staying in a friend's cabin in the Rockies, and the sensation was as intense and urgent as any baby's wail. Each passionate kiss refuted death, every caress said to the earth, *You ain't got me yet.* I know my wife loves me, she shows it in a hundred ways. But without my resilient desire I sometimes wonder what our marriage would be. A book club?

•   •   •

Another evening at home. My wife is getting ready for an event her magazine is hosting the next day, printing out a speech she'll be giving, worrying about the dry cleaning that hasn't arrived. She has a million things on her mind, and I am not one of them. She pauses in flight to kiss me.

"And think of how much more relaxed you'll feel after I fuck you against the wall in the hallway," I say, grabbing her and holding on.

On instinct she tries to pull away, unprying my fingers from her arm—she doesn't have time for this. But then she returns with a surprise of her own. She kisses me again, more voluptuously this time. With a smile, she says, "That does bring back a happy memory."

And there it was. For a minute I made her remember—for an instant she wanted me. And that was enough—or at least enough to tide me over until I try again to get inside.

My Problem with Her Anger

Eric Bartels

y wife and kids were sleeping when I finished the dishes the other night, shook the water off my hands, and dried them on one of the grimy towels hanging on the oven door. I gave the kitchen floor a quick sweep, clearing it of all but the gossamer tufts of cat hair that always jet away from the broom as if under their own power, then turned to shut the lights, happy to have finally finished my nightly chores. That's when I noticed the two metal grills I had left to soak in the basin. They're the detachable, cast iron type that we occasionally use atop the stove to affect an outdoor, open-flame cooking experience. Submerging them in water for a while makes it easier to remove the carbonized juices and bits of flesh that get welded on during use. It's a good, sensible way to save labor.

The problem was that they'd been in the sink for several days now. I really wanted to go to bed, but I knew if I left them, my wife would surely think something less than kind about it. And then it occurred to me: what I was facing, in my decision over whether or not to return to the sink and clean them, was the dark heart of the divide between men and women.

It's unlikely I was any less harried or tired the previous few nights as I went about my kitchen cleanup, a responsibility that has fallen to me more or less exclusively of late while she takes the kids up to bathe. No, my energy level is fairly constant—that is to say, depleted—at that particular point of any day. I could, and probably should, have finished the grill-cleaning project sooner. Just as I should make the bed every morning instead of occasionally. Just as I should always throw my underwear into the hamper before showering rather than leaving it on top of it or on the floor next to it. But I don't, just as I hadn't quickly scrubbed clean the grill on, at very latest, the day after it had soaked overnight.

And these—we'll call them domestic lapses, for lack of a better term—are the things a husband does that quietly annoy the living shit out of his wife. That is, until his wife becomes a mother, at which point they inspire fury. And that fury won't be kept secret. No, it will be unleashed on her husband, and, of course to a lesser extent, on the children. On the receiving end, the husband will be left to wonder why the punishment is so wildly out of line with the crime. This is the kind of vitriol, he thinks, that should be reserved for lying politicians, corporate greed-mongers, and hitters who won't take a pitch when their team trails in the late innings. Not a dedicated marriage partner with garden-variety human foibles.

Yet here we are, my wife and I. We're both good people. We have a lot of friends. We make a decent living at relatively satisfying professional jobs—she as a half-time account executive at a small advertising firm, I as a full-time newspaper journalist. And we're dedicated, attentive parents to a six-year-old daughter and a two-year-old son. We wanted these kids and had a vague idea that it would involve some work. We knew, or should have known, what we were getting into. We signed the contract. Shook on it. Kissed, actually. But I think we missed some of the small print.

Still, we try. We never use profanity in front of our children, unless we're arguing angrily. We never talk to each other disrespectfully, except when arguing angrily. And we never ever say bad things about each other to our kids—unless, of course, we've just finished arguing angrily.

My wife is a talented and lovely woman. She has a quick mind, both analytical and imaginative. She hates convention and looks easily through hypocrisy of all kinds. She also has big-time type-A tendencies, character traits that make her the choice for many of the organizational and administrative duties in our shared life, such as paying bills and scheduling the kids' activities.

But these proclivities also work against her. The chaotic, unpredictable reality of having two small children threatens and at times overwhelms her compulsion for order. Traveling, with the on-the-fly time management it requires, makes her crazy. I watched her walk face-first into a glass door at the airport. Another time, near the baggage carousel, she distractedly pushed our son's stroller into another child. A pointless quarrel over a trip to the Home Depot led to her backing out of the driveway and into a parked mail truck one morning. My point is, she isn't perfect—though her cleaning skills may be—and I like to think there are things that my less compulsive tendencies bring to our marriage too.

I know my wife's life is hard. Motherhood asks the modern woman, who has grown up seeing professional success as hers for the taking, to add the loss of a linear career path to an already considerable burden: child rearing, body issues, a shifting self-image, and a husband who fell off his white horse long, long ago. My wife spends more time with the kids than I do and is almost completely responsible for running them around to day care and school. I contribute regularly and earnestly to the shopping, cooking, and cleaning, but a significant amount of it still falls to her, just as some two thirds of the income production now falls to me. And her job, although part-time for the last six years, still presents her with hell's own revolving door of guilt over neglecting her work for her kids and vice versa—a kind of guilt that men don't and probably never will feel to the degree women do. Men whose work keeps them from their wives and children may sincerely regret the loss, but they won't necessarily feel that regret as guilt. They are breadwinners. They are doing what their conditioning prepared them to do.

But I too have had my life take a turn for the more challenging since our first child was born. And I've given up plenty of freedoms: time with friends, regular pickup basketball games, beer. And I honestly don't mind living without these things. I understand the trade. I'm not saying I deserve an award for my commonplace efforts and sacrifices. But I don't deserve a war either.

At times I suspect my wife's thinking moves back and forth in an ugly zigzag pattern. If, in her mind, my shortcomings provide the justification for her anger, then the perception of me as someone with only shortcomings must be groomed like the playing field of a game I can't seem to win. The helpful things I do that might contradict her preferred image of my ineffectuality don't even show up on the scoreboard. Until, finally, nothing I do is right.

My efforts to organize the contents of the armoire one day—a project she'd suggested—led to a screaming fight when she complained that the clutter I was planning to move to the basement would just create more junk down there. The other night she came into the kitchen as I was cleaning up after a dinner that I had both cooked and served, and announced, with barely veiled resentment, that it would be nice if I helped her get the kids to bed every once in a while—as if she had just found me drinking beer and playing video games. And a few nights later, after bathing the kids in succession, getting them in pajamas, and feeding them their vitamins, I was rocking our son to sleep when I heard my wife's telltale annoyed stomp coming up the stairs from where she'd been folding laundry. She walked into the bathroom and scornfully announced, with me down the hall as the implied audience, "Why is there still water in the bathtub?" At times like this, I don't really know what she wants from me. It seems I can't win.

I'll make a nice dinner after a long day at work—broiled curry pork chops with steamed zucchini, perhaps—and she asks, politely but not so politely that I don't take it as criticism—why I made rice instead of pasta. At the grocery store, I try to buy food that's somewhere between not entirely toxic and prohibitively expensive, but my choices often meet with disapproval. I wash clothes the wrong way, failing to properly separate them by shades of color I seem permanently blind to. I even, according to her, spend too much time rinsing off dishes before loading them into the dishwasher; after all, why waste water and time when the dishwasher would do the work?

I know—I realize it doesn't mean much for me to go on like this. I realize, in the end, my trail of tears probably all sounds like so much "He said, She said" (or, actually, "He said, He said"). All I'm saying is this: If my home is my castle, it is under siege. From within.

And my head is not the only one on the chopping block of all this liberated anger. As I said, the kids get their share of it too. Sure, children need to learn the meaning of *no,* and my wife is the one who will do a lot of the teaching. But I'm certain there's got to be a kinder, gentler way of explaining the concept than she chooses in many instances.

I try to make this point calmly at such times, and when that doesn't work, I make it more forcefully. Then, of course, we fight— she says I'm too critical, and where do I get off anyway, as in, "Where have *you* been all day?" I tell her I think her general rage toward everything is unfair to all of us, me *and* the children—and she gets angrier and I get angrier until the futility of this fighting leaves me feeling deflated and distant, in a place where passion of any kind has slipped into a coma. I tell her, in the quietest, most reasonable tone I can manage, to please relax. She responds by telling me one more time, through gritted teeth, what she is angry about. But I didn't ask her what she was angry about; I asked her to stay calm. Aren't those different things?

Anyone who's ever watched a young child's face crumple in fear and bewilderment as parents unleash their anger, in any direction, knows instantly what the stakes are. Parents do not need the toxic stew of anger coursing through them while in charge of small, impressionable children. And partners who are struggling to remember what particular disease of the brain led to their union won't be helped back to the right path by the rotating wheel of frustration, resentment, and blame.

My greatest fear is that when my wife's anger is totally liberated, as it too often is in our little house—at times I watch her mercury rise steadily and predictably to that point where she lashes out, and I almost feel as if she *wants* to get there—it becomes less and less necessary for her to question its origins. No need to examine it, no need to work backward in the hope of identifying and defusing the triggers to the fast-replicating chain of events. And what is the hope of altering a behavior if you don't know where it came from and never see it coming?

.   .   .

Which leads me to the past—mine and hers. My wife grew up in a place populated by people who, despite their individual charms and professional achievements, struggled to escape a deeply embedded set of old habits—the intolerance, blame, and recrimination that often deranges the family dynamic.

My own family of origin is far from perfect. My mother kicked my father out of the house when I was nine years old. Their divorce was sudden and shocking. But my father was never the bad guy and my parents quickly forged a decorous relationship that exists to this day. Anger was never a regular feature in our household.

That's not to say I'm unfamiliar with anger. I was a boy. Boys are the ones whose favorite childhood entertainments run to breaking windows, starting fires, and playing sports that allow you to beat the crap out of yourself and others. The ones who instantly want to know if their first car will do a hundred miles per hour. The ones who attend beery high school parties with the goal of getting laid, but who'll settle for a good fistfight. I'm no Boy Scout. Unchecked anger has made me treat coworkers unkindly, throw elbows on the basketball court, and destroy many a small appliance. When I was a bartender, which is how I made my living for many years, I would often lose my cool, kicking a refrigerator door closed or whipping an empty bottle into a bin with an ear-splitting explosion. I imagined I was just blowing off a little steam.

Then, one night, as a patron at someone else's bar, I watched a bartender momentarily capture everyone's attention with a loud fit of pique. He was slamming the cash register, cursing it out, and then he turned away from the bar and kicked over a garbage can. And I realized something: that the many witnesses to his antics, including myself, saw the whole thing as somewhere between laughable and pathetic. We didn't care what was bothering him. We were having drinks and a good time. Too bad he wasn't enjoying the evening himself, we thought before turning away. Too bad he was such a *child*.

It was a revelation for me. Anger, justified or not—if acted mostly as a release without the clear-cut agenda of provoking change—is selfish and juvenile, obnoxious and unattractive, and it got you nowhere. No matter how determinedly this guy sought the empathy of others for the bullshit he was enduring, he wasn't going to get it— at least not this way. For the first time, I understood that the kind of behavior he was exhibiting was nothing more than an indulgent plea for attention that people weren't interested in hearing.

Was the guy under a lot of pressure? Yes. Was he being frustrated by all manner of impediments to his ability to do his job? Almost certainly. Did anybody care? No.

I did a lot less kicking doors and throwing things after that. Which is not to say I never lose my temper. But it becomes clearer to me every day that our reactions to circumstances are exactly what we permit or deny ourselves. It's dangerous to embrace the notion that anger is something we've earned a right to express and that it takes expressions of anger to earn respect. Lashing out angrily is less an expression of emotion than enslavement by emotion. And to believe otherwise is damaging to ourselves and especially damaging to those we love.

.   .   .

I think it's been fairly well established by now that parenthood is a challenge and that marriage is a creaky, old institution that may not have fully adapted itself to modern life, one that now, in fact, fails in this country more often than not. Put children in the picture, and you have a degree of difficulty exponentially higher. And, as I said, things may be even more complicated for women; after all, they now contribute substantially and necessarily to most household income, while also, of course, biologically carrying, birthing, and in many cases nursing the children for anywhere from several weeks to several years. Not surprising that many of them are exhausted and frustrated, particularly in the kids' early years. And the power of their premarriage years of autonomy and careers—possibly even bossing underlings around—has made them consider expressions of anger to be their right and privilege.

For women of my generation, anger appears to have replaced the quiet desperation of the past, which seems to me—and I'm sure to them—like a healthy stage in the development process. But the key word here is *stage*. There's got to be a next evolutionary step, don't you think? Sure, men have made some strides and accommodations, but if I were a woman, I wouldn't want my future happiness and peace of mind to depend on a man's continuing ability to improve his clairvoyance for what must be done around the house.

No, any woman struggling with the potentially toxic trio of career, marriage, and motherhood should now focus only secondarily on what the world and, more specifically, her partner can do for her during the challenging early years of child rearing. To truly empower herself, she will need to find a way to get beyond—on her own, with help, or however—the destructive impulses that the frustrations of modern motherhood can bring out in her.

In other words, buck up.

I know—this is fine advice coming from a man, right? And so typical, yes, I concede, for a man to propose some pat solution like that. But if men are expected to learn from women as we become more domesticated, then why shouldn't women also learn from men? And if men are good at anything, it's pat solutions. Absent the degree of intuition and empathy that seem an integral part of a woman's nurturing instinct, men grow up in a simpler milieu in which challenges are to be quickly surmounted without a great deal of fanfare. Something breaks? You fix it and move on.

This may not be a mindset that lends itself to a great deal of introspection and deep thought. But you know what? That may be a good thing. In fact, I would go so far as to say that it *is* a good thing. Men don't worry about things before they happen, and this imbues them with a confidence that, however vexing a problem might seem, it can and will be resolved.

A friend of mine says that everything in a woman's world starts with fear. Everything becomes tied in some way to fears of disapproval and abandonment and loss of control and God knows what else. Men, generally, don't go there. We don't, for better or worse, traffic in low self-esteem. Ours is the world of the hierarchy, not the group hug. If you falter, you have two choices: get back up and do better, or live with it.

•   •   •

My wife and I need to fix this anger thing together. I know it looms as large as it does, in part, because of my fervor to confront and defeat it. Maybe I've been too much like a man in this. Our home has been a battlefield at times. My wife and I have been mean and fought dirty, and we've hurt each other.

But with little steps, my wife and I are breaking free. We've started to stand back and see where frustration starts. We no longer yell to each other from different rooms of the house. We've turned down the volume on the stereo and the TV. We insist that our daughter wait her turn to talk and even take turns ourselves.

Maybe we're past the worst. Our children, whom we love so dearly, are growing up. They're getting bigger and easier. Every day we can count on the reassuring rhythms of life: the sun rises in the morning, a weather system drifts in from the Cascades to blot it out, our cats barf up hairballs. I'm optimistic. I don't think we've done any permanent damage. I don't think it's anything we can't fix. But that's just the guy I am.

PART III

Bicycles for Fish

It's lovely to be a feminist and all. Have gotten in *plenty* a tizzy over the inequity of the female role in this bizarre universe. Have even tried out the independent, "A woman needs a man like a fish needs a bicycle" track and been quite good at it. Eventually, however, I settled upon this conclusion:

This fish needs a bicycle.

If not for comfort, at least for entertainment's sake.

—*Opening statement from Heather L. Hunter's*
"This Fish Needs a Bicycle" web log at www.thisfish.com

My Life as a Housewife

ROB JACKSON

 doubt that many, if any, boys dream of a career as a stay-at-home dad. I certainly didn't. NFL quarterback or business mastermind, sure, but not as a man whose main job is to take care of the children and keep the house. Then again, I never believed I'd actually meet a woman like Shelley, and that we'd marry and her four little children would become mine too, and that when we split up the parental roles I'd be the one at home doing the cooking, cleaning, and parenting for fifteen years while my wife worked full-time. But, as the saying goes, life is what happens while you're planning to do something else. And in my case, I guess you could say life happened—my life—because I couldn't figure out what my plan was.

It all started back at my college graduation, which may forever stand as my life's premier nonevent. At Denison University, in Ohio, I'd spent four years studying women, and there were no gold ropes or tassels for that. I'd received no awards, set no records, left no legacy at the school newspaper or radio station. I'd come in as a soft suburban boy, raised on the naïve expectation that the step-by-step process of schooling my parents had set into motion eventually would lead to the expected reward of a high-paying business job, whether I applied myself or not.

Anticipating this, I bought my first suit and a pair of wingtips in the fall of my senior year and commenced to interview for internships in advertising. I must have looked the part, because I quickly landed a January internship at an agency in Pittsburgh, my hometown. As jobs go, shooting miniature hoops in a cool office while brainstorming funny ad campaigns appealed to me, but the reality was bottom-rung monotony.

That suit and shoes got me through a few on-campus job interviews before graduation, but they couldn't make up for the fact that my file was the narrative of a C student who'd left no mark. It wasn't a big surprise when I wasn't called back after any of them.

With graduation only weeks away, a friend asked me if I'd join him in Colorado in the fall and be a ski bum for the winter. Having no other prospects, I agreed. That just left a summer to fill. I wish I could say I immediately began researching summer employment, but I didn't. With my fall plan in place, I sat back and waited for a summer plan to present itself. And then it did.

While sitting in the Student Union watching girls walk by, I noticed a discarded career-resource newsletter on the floor and picked it up. As I lazily flipped through it, an ad caught my eye.

"Mother's Helper Needed," it read. "Local family with four small children needs mother's helper for summer on the coast of Maine."

Now, I realize the position of "mother's helper" hardly sounds like the most attractive job for your average red-blooded American college man. But for me it made a strange kind of sense. First of all, I wanted something flexible enough to give me some time to write (which, like skiing, was another unprofitable activity I wanted to pursue—I pictured myself on the rugged coast writing a screenplay about an average girl-chasing dork in college). And second, how hard could it be to hang out with a family on summer vacation for twelve weeks?

I called the number on the flyer, and the nice-sounding woman who answered told me straight out that she'd always hired women for this job. But as we talked she seemed to become intrigued with the idea of hiring a man. She wondered aloud about the fact that she had three boys (aged seven, five, and one) and only one girl (who was three), and maybe it would be a good idea for the boys to have a man to roughhouse with and teach them things? She also seized on the fact that I'd been a lifeguard—with four little kids scrambling around the surf, she admitted this experience would give her great peace of mind. She scheduled the interview.

What about the father? I thought, hanging up. But it turned out he was largely absent in the summer months; he had ambitions of joining the PGA tour, and his summer was full of qualifying tournaments. I learned this at the interview, an hourlong process during which I spent the first half hour trying to stay focused in the presence of this young mother, who turned out to be only eight years older than I and stunningly beautiful.

Shelley and I hit it off during the interview, and I was hired. Being a mother's helper was fine with me, but I didn't think that job title would play too well with my friends and family, so instead I told them I was going to be the family handyman for the summer. Nobody questioned me, and off I went.

On vacation in Maine with these kids I barely knew, I was surprised by my capacity for play. Pushing over rotten trees in the woods, making a bear outline with masking tape on the hedgerow and throwing a boomerang at it, rowing to small islands we then named, constructing little boats and creating storm conditions to test them—these were my days, and I reveled in them.

Shelley loved how I got along with her kids, but soon it became evident that there was more to her appreciation of me than that. I hadn't realized in signing up for this job that I was walking into a marriage on the rocks, but after a while I got the picture. There were a few difficult weekend visits from her husband when I kept my distance, but otherwise Shelley and I were fast becoming a team in more ways than one—in fact, I was beginning to feel like a hired husband. I confess that during this period my job responsibilities began to dwindle rapidly. Shelley and I stayed up late talking night after night, and then I often slept in while she got up (early) with the kids and did, presumably, exactly what I'd been hired to do. When I emerged (well rested) each day, I'd happily join in. After a few weeks of this, what was supposed to be merely filling in my summer gap was starting to feel like a lifetime gig. I had fallen for all five of them.

Bit by bit Shelley told me about the troubles in her marriage and her longing to escape it. At the end of the summer, she called her husband to say she wasn't coming back to Ohio and she wanted a divorce.

This was a gutsy move on her part, particularly since she was completely dependent on him financially; she had nothing without him, and needless to say, I wasn't promising much. But she didn't feel like she had any choice. As she filed for divorce and got a lawyer, I helped her and the children move out of the beautiful vacation cottage and into the modest employee quarters of an old inn, where she'd gotten an offer of a house-sitting job. I rented a small place for myself nearby and got a menial job in a woodworking shop, and we continued to see each other.

Over the next year, Shelley worked through her divorce and I worked my way through three more menial jobs (ad sales for the newspaper, production assistant on a movie being shot locally, and Sheetrocking houses). Shelley also scrabbled from job to job and moved herself and the kids from place to place. This was in a little town called Brooklin, Maine, where most people were laborers of one kind or another (boatbuilders, commercial fishermen, construction workers) and opportunities other than that were scarce. Luckily Shelley had some teaching experience from earlier in her life, and that fall she secured a job teaching English at the local junior high school—a position with low pay but all-important benefits.

Although I still had my own place, we were always together. There wasn't talk of marriage, but we could feel it coming, and, sure enough, a year later we started planning for our wedding.

We sat down then and talked about what to do with the children—who would take care of them with both of us working? Day care, where they'd been, was expensive, and my pay as a Sheetrocker hardly justified paying someone else to take care of them while I worked. Plus, I'd just had a depressing meeting with my foreman in which he told me, flat out, that I wasn't a very good Sheetrocker. I hated it anyway, but still, it was pretty bleak being told I sucked at my eight-dollar-an-hour job. By contrast, I thought, I was good at taking care of Shelley's kids, and I liked it infinitely better than Sheetrocking.

So it was decided. I would take care of the kids and house, and Shelley would work. It was 1988 and I was twenty-four years old. I had no idea what I was signing up for.

Although I'd helped with the kids for almost two years, my time with them had always been sporadic and unstructured. Now, however, their lives were my structure, and their needs dictated my every waking move. The first day of school that fall, with the three older kids gone and Shelley teaching, was technically my first real day on the job. That morning I took a picture out at the bus stop of our new fourth-, second-, and first-graders before heading back inside with little John, who was now four. Suddenly time seemed to be on a new continuum—it slowed to half its normal speed. John's existence was simple. He giggled or cried, was happy or angry, bored or thoroughly entertained. I'd be lying if I said it wasn't boring much of the time, but still, John was my coworker, and we were a half-decent team. I had a college degree, and he needed help wiping after a trip to the bathroom. Okay, I could do that.

Eventually our routine improved, or I just got more used to it. Every morning we had "quiet news time" while I watched the *Today* show and John played on the floor nearby. Cable was not available, and satellite TV was a decade away, so children's programming or cartoon channels were not an option, and despite my lobbying, John didn't like *Sesame Street*. The *Today* show was relatively tame, but from time to time there was graphic footage or promotional movie clips with explosions or shouted conversations that inevitably got John's attention. Seeing a small boy idly fumbling with a tiny plastic motorcycle while his eyes were locked on disturbing images from the grown-up, real world gave me pause. I began to understand that passing the time, cleaning, and cooking were only going to be the most obvious demands of the job.

The less obvious element was that I would be presenting the world to four newcomers. I would be the filter, the promoter, the advisor, the dissenter. In short, I was in a position to shape them. The stakes were even higher than I'd expected. And the ego boosts I needed to give me the energy to get through it were few and far between.

Furthermore, I quickly learned (if I didn't know it already) that a man who doesn't earn money is not held in high regard. Even before I married Shelley and became a "housewife" I was aware of this undeniable truth. When I'd return to my suburban hometown for holidays, the Comparison Game was always being played at a fevered pitch. The model of your car, the size of your house, the Regional Vice President of Special Systems Consultation and Analysis job titles—these were the elements that comprised one's worth. During one visit back home for a wedding before Shelley and I were married, I found myself at a brunch trying to pass off my job at the woodworking shop (a tiny operation where we made things like Adirondack chairs and towel racks) as the first step toward buying the shop and developing a "must have" product. But my story was thin gruel, and my parents' friends saw right through it. The father of an old girlfriend finally asked me outright if I was making *any* money. As I squirmed for an answer, I could sense his relief at knowing I was already in his daughter's *case closed* file.

I wish I could say that my old friends saw things my way—that they respected me as a guy who chooses to live in a cabin on the ridge, the rugged individualist. But they regarded me with the same polite smiles as their parents. I sensed I was a big loser in their eyes. At least the woodworking shop was a manly job—working with tools and building things. How was I supposed to compete after I became a housewife? How could they possibly conceive of any job that had no paycheck at all? And it's true. In my fifteen years as a housewife I haven't seen a paycheck that would impress anyone but an eighth-grader with a summer job. Two hundred dollars was a windfall when I was a teenager, and it stayed that way right through my thirties.

At times I've thought, *Maybe I do need a paycheck. Maybe I do need to be admired and envied a bit.* Because the fact is, the housework I've done has been of consequence to exactly one person—Shelley. Not even the kids have cared about it. I knew that I'd gone down a radically different path. In the mid-eighties I was a rare species indeed. *Mr. Mom,* a popular movie at the time starring Michael Keaton, was considered "high-concept." The storyline—Dad stays home with the kids while Mom goes to work—must have struck the producers as just crazy enough to be entertaining.

But the fact that my life was high-concept and that I was an innovator, defying convention, didn't give me much solace when I was cleaning up wet messes of all consistencies and aromas. Such moments, and there are hundreds of them, are simply not fulfilling. The work my mother did—work that I very much took for granted when I was growing up—was now my daily routine, and it could be mind-numbing. Over the years I have returned every conceivable type of object that could be picked up by miniature hands to its proper place, stood before piles of laundry that could be classified as small hills, and scoured acres of porcelain. I've put thousands of home-cooked meals on the table and broken up just as many arguments.

In any family the breadwinner has an extra measure of influence, and ours was no different. I quickly came to understand that I was the man of the house but not the power. The kids knew they had food in their bellies and sneakers on their feet because of their mother, even if I was the one who cooked the food and shopped for the sneakers. Shelley knew it too, but she was careful to protect me.

"The paychecks are both of ours," she assured me many times. "I couldn't do what I do without you."

Unfortunately, Shelley's notion of "our" income was not acceptable to credit-card companies. I've been notified countless times in mailers from Visa and American Express of my "pre-approved" status, but in following up on these offers I have never actually been approved. This, to me, is a metaphor for my standing as a housewife. For all outward appearances we were a progressive family, but being thought of as "progressive" doesn't really do as much for a father's ego as having an income and a career. I knew the kids loved me, but on a gut level they just couldn't appreciate what I did for them. They seemed to judge me only by my moods, and having an even temperament, which I did, at times felt like a liability. I tried not to get angry at their little mistakes (or big ones) because once you head down that road, you run the risk of being angry all the time. But staying below that threshold also took its toll—I'd be either emotionally flat or irritable to the point where the kids would start wondering, *What's wrong with Dad?*

"Maybe I should scream at everyone periodically," I once barked at Shelley. "I can't pass through the room dancing a jig all the time. Cleaning toilets doesn't always make my spirit soar that way."

Deep down I felt that a slow process of appreciation by them all was under way, one that would eventually make me a legend among my grandchildren. But when the parents of those future grandchildren were in my face arguing instead of apologizing for things bent, broken, and shattered, the slow process of appreciation was far from my mind. When it came to support I had to rely solely on Shelley, but she, of course, had her own low moments and workplace stresses.

And like any working parent who returns in the evening to the chaos of home life with kids, she'd sometimes bring her stress home and take it out on me.

Generations of fathers have behaved this way, acting like tyrants around their wives and kids. And now I'm convinced that this behavior is not gender-related but instead stems from a sense of entitlement that develops when one person is supporting the other financially. Shelley had already done what I was doing, having been the full-time parent and housewife in her first marriage, so perhaps she was more inclined than your average husband to be sensitive to my situation. But this wasn't always enough to override a tendency for her to slide into the role of the temperamental husband. She would stride in the front door and complain that lights were on all over the house, or that dinner was not yet under way, or that the kids were watching TV before they'd done their homework. If she was returning from one of her many night meetings (she was now the school principal), I could usually expect some criticism about showers and baths not being taken or homework not checked. I was asked to make sure that the house was especially clean on Fridays so that she could immediately unwind instead of succumbing to her own cleaning impulses. I needed to remember that she didn't like tossed salads in cold weather and never with iceberg lettuce. She's a vegetarian but has no particular fondness for fruit and doesn't like pies. If I didn't have a vegetable option for dinner, she'd look annoyed. Once I threw out catalogues before she had a chance to look them over, and I was quickly set straight. If the clothes hadn't been folded immediately after drying, she'd snap, "Well, they may as well not have been washed at all, because now you've got to start all over." "Filthy," "out-of-control," and "tenementlike" were some of the words Shelley liked to use to describe the state of the house.

Needless to say, these moments didn't inspire much affection from me. As the days and years mounted, our mutual respect and admiration increased, but those times—most frequently when she re-turned from work—invariably put the process on hold. She was transformed into another person altogether. Running a school is highly demanding, and Shelley never let down on any front. In deal-ing with students, parents, faculty, and staff she'd spend all of her diplomacy and patience, and by the time she came home in the eve-ning there was little of these qualities left for me. I knew where Shel-ley was coming from, though. There was reasonable justification in what she expected to find when she came home—in what would re-lax her. And though it didn't exactly feel great to be chewed out by her, I have to say that for the most part it was effective.

Housekeeping and providing that relaxing atmosphere for her were, after all, my end of the bargain. If doubt and self-pity slowed me down, well then, I needed a kick in the ass. That it came from my wife instead of a boss or a supervisor was all right with me as long as she didn't enjoy it too much. Don't get me wrong; I never reacted to her queen-hell-bitch persona in ways that would encourage the be-havior. In truth, I was in a struggle to eliminate it completely. I've been quick to defend my housework in general, and I haven't been above isolating her complaints in order to make them sound trivial. I'd explain how it insults my intelligence when she rehangs (by the hems) something on the summer clothesline.

"Call the house filthy, but the kids are healthy and smart," I'd counter, trying to make her feel like she was being hysterical. "How bad can it be?"

Underneath it all was my sustaining belief in the kind of superior housewife I considered myself to be. This was one element of my de-fense that went unspoken. I wasn't naturally tidy as a boy or a teenager or a young man, and I suppose housewives who keep the home sparkling were instinctive cleaners from early on. But if they could make the bathroom tiles shine, could they also replace the tiles and regrout them? How about gutting the bathroom? Sure, they can scour the toilet (a dirty job), but can they remove it and install a new one (considerably dirtier)? Can they spend a month and a half redigging a leach field, by hand? Can they unearth a concrete sewage junction box and stem the resulting geyser of shit, a job that is both illegal and disgusting, all to save a few thousand dollars in contractor fees? Well, I can, and I did. Let me clarify. I kept the *entire* house, from shingles on the roof to frozen pipes in the darkest, most cobweb-draped recesses of the basement. And at this, unlike the past "real world" jobs I'd had, I was damned good. In fact, I was incomparable—I've never seen anyone in the field with my range. I could handle Shelley's criticism on the particulars and be patient with her idiosyncrasies, but if I smelled any doubt about my commitment, my reaction was sharp.

If there was a milestone argument in the first five years of our marriage that "explored" my commitment, it was the one about my announced desire to stay behind while the rest of the family went to Florida for our annual—and totally exhausting—spring-break vacation. My reason for trying to pass on the trip that year was that as a full-time parent I questioned what kind of vacation it was for me. In my mind it was the toughest parenting challenge of the entire year. Instead of me being in charge of my own domain, as I was normally, parental authority was spread out among me, Shelley, and my in-laws, and that fact along with all the choices any vacation presents invariably led to fights and chaos. No matter how Shelley and I handled the decisions about what to do and where to go, there were always tearful losers and smug victors carrying grudges right through to the next toss-up between Jungle Golf and TGI Friday's on one side, or a manatee-watch boat ride, dinner back at the condo, and a treat at DQ on the other.

No, I felt I needed and deserved a reprieve that year, and I tried to explain to Shelley that her failure to understand my need for a break indicated to me that she didn't recognize what I did as work. The matter was far simpler in her eyes—abandonment. And at high volume she questioned my commitment to the arrangement we'd agreed to years before.

I can't remember the words that squeaked out of my constricted throat, but my intent was to let her know that my commitment was self-evident. I was in my late twenties and spending my afternoons trying to determine who pulled the head off of Malibu Barbie instead of climbing the first rungs of the six-figure ladder. In a decade that made wealth a virtue and status a character trait, I stood alone as a male Brownie-troop leader in his prime. "Oh, I'm committed all right," I told her. "You're saying I'm not committed?"

But the only way to prove it, I realized, was to suck it up and go along on the vacation. After all, how many female housewives would be able to opt out of the family vacation to get a break for themselves? None. In fact, they'd never even dare ask.

So there I was once again, driving us through the cold March rain, unloading four half-asleep children and herding them across gray slush into the airport and onto the plane. Flying scares Shelley a bit, and she squeezed my hand on takeoff—a reassuring sign that I was still the man of the house in some respect.

With the argument as a prelude to the trip, Shelley was especially sensitive to my needs and moods. For example, I was determined to keep from getting sunburned, but I can't stand slathering lotion on my face, so while Shelley's parents watched the kids one afternoon she helped me shop for a hat. As we went from store to store, she was patient with my particulars and unconcerned with the cost or the time we spent looking. This led to the perfect hat. White canvas with a wide and stiff brim, it was a like cross between a pith helmet and a cowboy hat.

Later that day, as I strode around the hotel pool catching glimpses of myself wearing that hat in windows and mirrors, I felt like I was the successful business executive I'd always expected to be when I was growing up. After all, who but a big shot taking a break from his high-powered job would wear a macho hat like that on vacation? And the funny thing was, it really cheered me up to feel that way. It made my whole vacation. I'm not proud that something so superficial had an effect on me, but there it is. Something powerful in me must have still needed to believe in that vision of myself. What's more, something powerful in me must have really wanted other people—total strangers, in fact—to see me that way too, even if it was just a mirage.

The hat is gone now, and the kids are gone too—all of them either off in college or already out. For the first time in our lives together, it's just me and Shelley. Four years ago, Shelley got a job running a prestigious boarding school in Deerfield, Massachusetts, and we live in the 250-year-old house that comes with the job. There are more rooms to vacuum, but I have help now—namely, the school's buildings-and-groundskeeping staff, who are only a phone call away. Even if there is no more kids' stuff to pick up, I walk from room to room and think about when there was.

Recently our oldest son, Frederick, turned twenty-four—the exact age I was when I got married and became an instant father. It begs the question: how would I feel if Fred were to call up tomorrow and announce he was marrying a divorcée with four children and that he intended to forego a career to raise the kids while his wife worked? Would I be proud of his decision? Would I think he was making the best choice for himself? Would you?

A Brief History of the (Over)involved Father

ANTHONY GIARDINA

ometimes it's possible to locate the exact moment when your life changed. In my case, though, it's not so much the moment of change that remains vivid for me; it is the moment of coalescence, when changes that had already taken place began, finally, to make sense. Given how important the movies have always been to me, it seems appropriate that this epiphany hit me while I was watching a movie.

The movie in question was *Kramer vs. Kramer*. It had opened in December 1979, roughly coincidental with the birth of my first daughter. But I didn't see it at that time; I was too busy. I was living then the life I had always wanted to live: in a too-small apartment on the Upper West Side of Manhattan, writing plays that were getting produced off-off-Broadway, halfway through a first novel. Oh, did I mention that I had a wife? Mentioning her this late in the game is in-dicative, I suppose, of how I thought of my life then: achievement was important, with everything else taking a distant second place. Relationships, the birth of children, these were items in the bil-dungsroman but in no way central. If I could be said to contour my life in those days around any image, I think it would be one I grew up with in the fifties and sixties. It was the image affixed to all those pa-perback covers I studied in drugstores and supermarket racks, the one featuring a guy with a raincoat slung over his shoulder, a guy on the verge of needing a haircut, with a quizzical, slightly weary, but (don't be fooled) absolutely thrilled look about him. Surrounding this central image were the disembodied heads of women; they were all to somehow feed into this man's story, but the message of the image, and the arrangement of the image, was that he was not to lose any vital part of himself to them. At the end, he was to walk off alone.

In the first two or three years after my daughter was born, I went on trying to live that life, with the raincoat thrown over my shoulder and the weary, sexy, thrilled expression. I went on writing plays and seeing them produced and writing that first novel and seeing it published, and on weekends joining the other parents in Riverside Park, pushing my daughter on the swings and enduring the jostling, competitive chatter of the other Upper West Side parents, until one day I realized I had come to the end of things, or at least to the end of a chapter. It announced itself in nothing very dramatic. One afternoon, after hoisting our daughter's stroller up the stairs of our walkup and entering the dim light of our cramped quarters, I just turned to my wife and said, without knowing I was going to say it, "Let's move."

I didn't mean to another apartment or to a suburb. I meant, *let's move*. To western Massachusetts, in our case, and given the nature of our marriage then, my wife didn't resist. She was looking to break out of her job as the dessert chef at an insane SoHo restaurant, and the notion of searching for a new career in a more relaxed atmosphere appealed to her. The truth is that I had always been the one to call the shots, the one who cared more about his career, and she was willing to go where I wanted to go. But almost immediately, it seemed, life began to change in ways I'd been unprepared for. My wife took on an interim baking job that required her to work more, not less, than she had in New York, and me . . . well, all those big thoughts about "career" seemed to get subsumed into a different life, one I hadn't been fully conscious that I was choosing. All I knew was that in place of meetings in theaters and editors' offices, I found myself spending a lot of time in the park, reading to my daughter about a man named Mr. Pumblechoke, and from a book about a mysterious cranberry recipe, a salty sea captain, and a foiled robbery.

Our daughter was in day care then, but hell, I was a writer, I could take afternoons off (and it would save us money as well), so I picked her up midway through the day. I gained a new conception of time in that first year: how *long* afternoons with a child can be. Life seemed to have gone from a tightly shaped thing to something amorphous: sleep, day care, children's books, doctors' visits, puppet shows, library hours. And, oh yes, writing. But writing—the whole way I thought about it, at least—began to take on a different weight than it had in the city. In Manhattan I had thought of children as delightful appendages to the serious business of life: strap them on your back and take them where you need to go. That was where my daughter was— on my back—the day I delivered the revised manuscript of my novel to my editor, and one of my all-time favorite moments was standing outside the old Manhattan Theatre Club on East Seventy-third Street while a play of mine was going on inside. It was May, but one of the play's effects had the actors entering the theater from out of a snowstorm. We stood on the street and watched the techie working the snow machine, to my little two-year-old's delight. But now such moments were gone. When a play of mine was done (increasingly rarely), it was done long-distance. Mostly, I was in the park, strapped on the back of my daughter's life; she was taking me where *she* wanted to go.

It's tempting to say that childhood itself changed when we moved out of the city. But it wouldn't be true. I was the one who had changed. I was undergoing what I imagine a lot of men undergo in their mid-thirties, particularly those with young kids: that slight dampening of energy, that awareness that the testosterone-fueled will to dominance has given way to a new set of questions: does my life really have to go the way I believed it must in my twenties? The vexing part was, though I can phrase these questions now, I couldn't then. Or maybe I just didn't want to admit to what was happening to me. When my daughter turned five and started kindergarten, there was a particular lunch box she insisted on having, and I remember now the intensity of the search for that lunch box, which was, of course, out of stock everywhere. We drove far afield, in the beautiful late-summer dusk, to Ames and Caldor's and Kmart, each of them a tall, beckoning, neon-lit tree on the branches of which the Holy Grail of that phantom lunch box might be found hanging. Though I felt it intensely, it was still not possible for me to admit consciously that this quest had become more important to me than the quest to complete my troublesome second novel.

At the time, the mid-eighties, there was a kind of cultural surround helping me along (one might even say *pushing* me along) in this direction. Every Sunday I looked forward to reading the now-defunct "About Men" column in *The New York Times Magazine*, in which, week after week, like reciters at an AA meeting, one sensitive-guy writer after another would stand up and profess to having lopped off whatever offending organ had stood in the way of his ascension to Better Fatherhood, Better Husbandhood, Better Manhood. (Full disclosure: I wrote one of those columns myself.) The one I remember best was Carey Winfrey's "Taming Ambition," about losing the old fire in the belly after the birth of twins. Everywhere I turned then, it seemed someone was telling me that my less ambitious, more lunch-box-conscious life was the new male life of my times.

But it really wasn't until I saw *Kramer vs. Kramer* that it all came together for me. I saw the movie on video, or maybe on network TV, years after its first release. But life—at least *my* life—had caught up with *Kramer vs. Kramer*. I remember being struck by one scene in particular. It is the one in which Dustin Hoffman, playing Ted

Kramer, the hustling ad executive turned full-time dad, is sitting in Central Park, distractedly talking to another child's mother while his son plays on the jungle gym nearby. Suddenly, there's one of those eerie silences in which you know something has gone wrong, followed by a child's wail. Dustin turns to look. His little boy has fallen, his little boy is wounded. He picks the child up and begins running. No empty cabs are to be found on the Upper East Side. He doesn't think to call for an ambulance. He simply runs, presumably toward a hospital, embracing the hurt child, a look on his face of total absorption-in-the-role. Whatever he has been before, he has whittled himself down now to one pure thing: a father.

For Ted Kramer, it pretty much ends there: work will never again have the same meaning for him. He will do it, but only for the money, only so that he can provide for his son. The world of hustle, of power lunches, of office flirtations, all those lubricants of his previously exciting, superficial existence has been seen through. So has ambition itself. He has ascended to a kind of saintliness, and that is where he will stay.

It ought to have settled things for me as well. The "About Men" column, *Kramer vs. Kramer*, and all those sons and daughters of it that filled my Saturday afternoons at the movies in the years to come—*Mr. Mom, Mrs. Doubtfire, Baby Boom, Parenthood, Hook*. They all cohered around a central premise: we (men) were better off when we let go of hustle and allowed our inner nurturer out. I ought to have relaxed and just accepted this. My daughter, after all, was apparently thriving. My wife had gone back to school to become a labor-and-delivery nurse, and I had landed a nice, soft job teaching at a college. But a part of me couldn't accept this familycentric drift as the inevitable direction life had to take. I didn't know how to name this other part of me, but it bothered me the way grit bothers you when it gathers in the crotch of your bathing suit: only mildly annoying, perhaps removable, but still something to make you twitch. That was what I did for a couple of years after seeing *Kramer vs. Kramer,* those years when I was supposedly lapsing into acceptance of this new role: I twitched, without knowing why.

It's doubly appropriate that the answer (if that was what it was) came to me through another movie. This one I didn't really have to watch, but only to glimpse briefly, on the TV screen of a beach house in Ocean City, Maryland. We were there with friends, and my daughter, then about six or seven, had turned on the TV midday. We discovered her watching, rapt, an old movie I recognized immediately. It was *40 Pounds of Trouble,* a largely forgettable early-sixties concoction in which Tony Curtis plays a Las Vegas casino owner, a man-about-town who is suddenly handed responsibility for a little girl. There is no point in glossing the plot of *40 Pounds of Trouble* except to say that Tony Curtis does not accept this responsibility as Ted Kramer does, by jettisoning everything about his life that made it exciting and fun. Instead, he takes the little girl along. There he was, on that screen, Tony Curtis in all his glory—sharkskin suit, porkpie hat, shiny sports car—living the vivid life of an American bachelor, circa 1963. And the little girl beside him in the red sports car—did she look deprived because Tony hadn't cast all his selfish pursuits aside in order to settle down and read to her about Mr. Pumblechoke? Did she look as though what she wanted above all was to be clasped to his bosom while he ran through the streets of the Upper East Side, a Saint of Fatherly Protection? Hell no. The little girl was having a ball.

Two things happened to me, simultaneously, as I focused for five or ten minutes on that movie. The first was that I recognized how much inadmissible pain I carried around at the thought of the life I had abandoned: the life of fun and excitement, the life that I once thought had been my natural inheritance as a man. (Whether he is represented by Tony Curtis or the man in the raincoat, he is the same man: call him—though, admittedly, it doesn't sound quite right—*homo fifties*). As much as the culture had gone to work debunking that man's life, as much as the ascension of women as full partners had utterly changed the way most people would regard *homo fifties,* I found I couldn't dismiss him, not all the way. His power was still there to haunt me, in the movies, even the *silly* movies, that stood as testaments to a way men had once believed it was right to live.

The other part of my response had to do with my daughter's reaction, or with what I read into my daughter's reaction. She looked— well, is *envious* the proper word? Had she too been deprived of something in having a father who'd signed on to the eighties notion of fatherhood? There was no way I could know these things, of course, but it began, at the very least, a line of questioning. Hadn't I grown up under the sway of movies like *40 Pounds of Trouble,* and hadn't they created in me a fierce desire to become an adult?

What were the images of *Hook* and *Mrs. Doubtfire*—those adulthood-hating stories we were now telling our children—doing to my daughter's sense of what was to come? In those movies, whether the parental figure is Robin Williams as the hustling businessman of *Hook* or Michelle Pfeiffer as his female counterpart in *One Fine Day,* the main narrative thrust has to do with getting this worker drone to face the boss, jettison work, and sacrifice the career so that he or she can make it to the place where we all truly belong— *on the sidelines of the soccer game!*

It may seem silly, or at least wildly eccentric, to have been this affected by watching ten minutes of an old movie. Nonetheless, it began something for me. I started watching more carefully the movies of the fifties and sixties, comparing the culture of those years to the one in which my daughter and I were living. And as a result, I found myself asking more and more questions about the new cult of Presence.

Where did it come from, exactly, this insistence that parents be always present at their children's sporting events, and even at the most minor of school events? Fifties children like me had seemed to do fine spending their childhoods in roles largely subservient to their parents', unwatched much of the time at our baseball games and school activities, at least not watched with the anxiety with which today's parents watch. As always, the movies offered helpful clues as to what might be going on: at a certain point in the movie *Multiplicity,* the chronically overworked Michael Keaton comes home, late at night, to watch a video of his child's grammar school play, one that work has forced him to miss. So dreadful does the play seem that you find yourself thinking he must be secretly glad he missed it, until you look at the screen and see Michael Keaton *weeping uncontrollably.* It's a deeply unbelievable moment, but it says a great deal about the ways in which, between 1979, when *Kramer vs. Kramer* opened, and 1996, when *Multiplicity* made its bow, a generation of parents enshrined the notion of itself as childhood-worshippers, *unforgivable unless we're there,* a notion profoundly at odds with the experience many of us had as children. No one had bought into this notion more than I had. But I became determined, once I'd seen through it, to sneak away from my identification with Ted Kramer and to move ever more consciously back toward an earlier version of myself.

Seven years after our first daughter was born, my wife and I found ourselves pregnant with a second. Just as she was about to be born, I was invited to premiere my new play at a prestigious venue that would require me to be away from home for a month. *Perish the thought!* the more enlightened of our friends all shouted. (The women, mostly; the men tended to keep silent, while looking at me out of the corners of their eyes with a certain envy.) Of course I went. I committed the cardinal sin of missing my new daughter's sixth through tenth weeks on this earth. Further, I did it pretty much without guilt.

It has been, in fact, a different experience with this second child, one who came into existence just as I had determined to take a fresh look at my old, banked ambition. I vowed from the beginning that I would bring her up less guiltily, less voraciously, that I would deliberately *miss* some of her events, that I would try consciously (at least some of the time) to put Career ahead of Presence. In the past several years, there have indeed been moments when I catch sight of myself in the mirror and can almost see, like the covered page of a palimpsest, the old image—the man in the raincoat—looking back at me.

Almost. Mostly what I see in the mirror is a man on whom fatherhood and domestic life have exerted undeniable claims. Yes, I drove this new baby back and forth to rehearsals of a play of mine in New Haven, clutching her in the famous crotch-hold while delivering direction to the actors. And yes, ten years later, at another of my plays, I got the tech crew to give her rides on the moving sets, and as I watched her, I could *almost* convince myself that I was as footloose a careerist as Tony Curtis in *40 Pounds of Trouble.* But mostly, what I have to admit is that, having once given myself over to fatherhood as I did, it requires an extreme effort to boost career up to something like an equal footing. In spite of all my "seeing through" what the culture of the eighties and nineties tried to do to us as parents, I have to own up to the fact that those movies were onto something. Give yourself over to a child, and you are more or less spoiled for overweening ambition.

The remarkable thing about all this is how little it has manifested itself in a struggle between me and my wife. There have been fights, to be sure, but she's also been remarkably generous, and largely unburdened by the conflicts between career and home life that drive me. (It might also help that when I am home, which is most of the time, I am so overbearingly overinvolved with domestic detail that she could well be relieved when I divert a little energy to career.) The battle has come to seem not a marital one but a struggle between competing ideologies I hold within myself: the image of men I grew up with, and could not quite let go of, and the emotional discoveries

I made on those long afternoons with my first daughter in the park, which pointed to another way of being. Perhaps the best you can ever expect from a battle between internal contradictions is a truce. As my younger daughter turns fifteen, and wriggles out of my grasp, the pain I feel at this loss makes it clear that I have used my identification with *homo fifties* not as a clear directive but as a kind of guardianship against excess, a handhold to keep me from slipping entirely into the much-desired embrace.

The Dog in Me

KEVIN CANTY

uilty, guilty, guilty as charged. I'm the one, Officer; I've got a box of cigars in the glove compartment of my truck and a condom rattling around in the bottom of my toiletries kit. That was me who skipped my daughter's grade-school Christmas show and then went out and got hog-drunk with the graduate students later that night. I was the one who told my wife we didn't have the money to buy a new couch and then bought a new fishing reel that same week. In fact, don't get me started on fishing junk: I've got enough of that lying around to convict two or three of us.

Deep into middle age I still have a band, and we play Muddy Waters into the small hours of the morning in smoky bars full of disreputable people. If somebody hands me a joint at a party, I will smoke it. If someone hands me a bottle of tequila, I will drink from it. And it's true, my idea of a fine evening at home involves drinking beer and watching *Monday Night Football* while playing electric guitar loudly enough to keep the children awake.

I am, in short, that well-known figure of fun, that feckless boy/man so many married and ex-married women are so permanently pissed off at. They should be pissed. It's all true: I do things sometimes for selfish reasons and not for the good of the family. I can spend hours on solitary work (writing) that makes me spaced-out and irritable and then spend further hours in solitary recreation (fishing), which puts me in a fine mood, most of the time, but well away from the house and its travails. I would rather eat broken glass and drink iodine than do the dishes.

It's the dog in me. And you know what? I kind of like the dog in me. I kind of trust him.

The dog in me has got a pretty good nose, for one thing—he notices things that we're normally too polite to notice. Like, for instance, it's *a lot* easier to get forgiveness than it is to get permission. It's way easier to just buy that electric guitar and let the Loved One find out later, if she ever does. (The trick is to leave the house with an empty case that will hold the new acquisition.) The idea that the Loved One and I would be able to sit down and negotiate the purchase in a reasonable and rational fashion is a total fiction. If you want the guitar (fly rod/golf clubs/exhaust manifold), you had best go out and just buy it, because you will never, ever get permission.

And even if you do, it won't matter. A few years ago I came into a decent pile of unexpected money, not life-changingly large but a pile nevertheless. Out of that pot of money I built a fence around the backyard, put up a deck, had the old asbestos-covered furnace removed and a new one installed, and bought the biggest, flashiest electric guitar known to mankind, a Gibson ES-295 in Les Paul gold with an engraved floral pick guard and a Bigsby vibrato unit.

And how did that work out? You can guess. Three years later the virtue I hoped to accumulate with the deck, fence, and furnace has evaporated entirely (if ever it existed in the first place). And yet the solid-gold ES-295 is still around to cause offense. Every day I am guilty of continuing to own such an expensive and frivolous object.

Now, it may very well be that this kind of sin-first-and-ask-questions-later approach contributes to a certain amount of tension around the house, may even promote seething and sulking. It may be that a more straightforward approach would not.

But this purchase *was* negotiated in advance; it was contextualized with the good of the family in mind, it was talked about, given a seal of approval. Three years later, none of that makes any difference. Just wanting such a thing in the first place is wrong, and having such a thing is doubly wrong. No slack. No possibility of slack. The point here being—as the dog in me would like to suggest—that there is no way to win in this situation. There's no way for me to legitimately want what I want. And at that point, in choosing between what I want and what, according to the Loved One, I *ought to want,* it's really not that difficult.

Now, obviously the way to avoid all this friction is for men to act more like women: less impulsive, more cooperative, more rational and group-oriented and family-centered. The dog in me wonders, though, whether this is the way women *are*—or the way women *imagine themselves to be.* Just curious.

It's a fine line, though, isn't it? Something's come loose, something's come unglued in the last couple of decades. We no longer feel quite comfortable in our roles, no longer quite fit the people we imagine ourselves to be. It seems a lot clearer when I look back at my parents' lives: Dad made the money, Mom took care of the house and the kids. Sure there were limitations—Mom never really took her rightful place in the world until all of us were grown and gone, and we never saw a lot of Dad—but overall, they knew where they stood. They knew what they were supposed to do. They did what they were supposed to do, and everything worked out fine. The nice thing about these roles was that they were inherited; they didn't have to make anything up, didn't have to improvise. They were grounded in tradition and, at least in part, in economic reality.

In the aftermath of the feminist revolution, though, we all find ourselves scrambling to adapt to new ideas of equality and democracy, to find new roles that seem to make sense. Everything's suddenly up for grabs—and haunting the whole process is the knowledge that we are actually making all of this up, that none of these new roles are blessed by anything other than our own convictions. We are supposed to be open and equal and democratic and straightforward. All those old, unspoken compacts—all those chains that bound our parents to outdated roles—are to be brought out into the daylight of reason. In reason and equality we will proceed together into a new, bright future.

Well, maybe. But the dog in me can't help noticing that I'm still paying for everything. The dog in me wonders if this isn't just a way to make me take care of half of your business while I'm still taking care of all of mine.

Now before you come after me with the tar and feathers and the rail, let me point out that we started in the same place everybody else did. In the years before marriage and children, the Loved One and I practiced the new doctrine of independence and equality: our financial and professional lives (she a photographer; I a writer and teacher) were as separate as separate gets, the housework split unevenly but nearly equally. I did the cars and the cooking, the Loved One did the dusting and organized the bills. We lived in blissful independence for more than a decade, and in fact we still have separate friendships and separate checking accounts, and we like it that way.

Throw a couple of kids into the mix, though, and everything goes to hell. When I count around the circle of my acquaintance, I find exactly one couple with children who split fifty/fifty, a few (a *very* few) in which the woman is the primary breadwinner, and a slew of marriages in which the responsibility is centrally on the man. He's the one with the retirement plan and the health plan, he's the one making the mortgage payments, he's doing the car insurance.

Now, wait a minute, I hear you say. *Somebody's* got to take care of the children.

Well, yeah. And somebody's got to make a living. Somebody's got to put a floor under the family to make sure that when your fulfilling, interesting, entirely worthwhile job hits a dry spell, you won't have to auction off the children. Don't get me wrong—I like my job. I teach creative writing in a good master of fine arts program; it's engaging work and there's not too much of it, with summers off and all. There are times when I think I have the best job on earth.

But even the best job on earth is hell some days: the student from hell, the faculty meeting from hell, the class from hell, the crucial chapter broken off midsentence so I can attend a meeting of the faculty evaluation subcommittee. I know you don't feel sorry for me. I don't expect you to. My point is that even a good job can feel on some days like eating a peck of shit. And in a ten- or twenty- or thirty-year career, there are going to be plenty of days that feel like that; days when all you can do is soldier on and hope that things get better. And that most of the time, still, it's the man in the house that's doing the soldiering. We don't have the luxury of a return to school, a career crisis, a nervous breakdown.

Okay, I know: you work, I work, everybody works. Everybody struggles through.

And sometimes, it's true, it's the woman carrying the weight and the man—in my experience, writers and artists, mainly—who has the luxury of pursuing his ambitions regardless of his ability to make any money with those ambitions. But not often; not as often as you would think, given the revolutions of the last thirty years. And even more rare, in my experience, is the couple that shares the roles equally.

What happened? Where did this idea of equality go off the rails? It's those damn kids, is my opinion. Somebody's got to take care of the kids, it's true—and I don't think anybody who doesn't have kids can appreciate what vicious little time-suckers and energy-suckers and emotion-suckers they are. It's like being Miss America, or being blind: you can *imagine* the experience beforehand, but your imagination has nothing to do with the actual experience, which you will not understand until you have it.

When my first child was born, my son, Turner, he came into the world not breathing. A kind of purposeful hush fell over the room, then began a rush of activity that was quick and grim and terror-inspiring. And in that moment my life changed—I felt myself turned inside out, I saw that everything I had held as important up until that moment was trivial, and that what mattered, the only thing that mattered, was that child's life. I prayed, I bargained, I held my breath. And when he started to breathe again, no more than a minute later—though it felt like an hour—I was no longer the same person as a minute before. I am still not. Every day, every minute he breathes—he's fourteen now, taller than his mother, taking kick-boxing classes and preparing to kick my ass—feels like a gift, and I am grateful for it. Turner and Nora, my son and my daughter, go first. On the way out of the burning building, they go first. When we're trying to figure out where to live, how to spend the summer, when we're making the thousand large and small decisions about our lives together, their interests go first. If you have not had children, you will think I am dramatizing. If you have had children, though, you will understand that I am merely reporting.

Somebody's got to take care of the kids. It's nice and primal, isn't it? The dog in me has no trouble understanding this thing. There is no substitute for time and care.

I don't at all mean that the woman in the partnership has to do it; like you, I know households in which it is the man who is in the house, changing the diapers, holding hands, whispering nursery rhymes. And these days it's nearly unimaginable that this work is not shared in part. But still: somebody has got to sign up to be the primary homemaker and make sure that the child is taken care of. And somebody needs to be the breadwinner, to make sure there's food on the table and a roof over everybody's head. And there are not enough hours in the day or enough days in the week for this to be the same person.

Can't we share? Sure we can share. In fact I even know one couple that seem to be sharing everything equally: money, planning, child care. (Although, come to think of it, he's a couple of rungs up the career ladder already, and she's a little behind . . .) But nearly all the couples-with-children I know relapse into some version of the old roles, breadwinner and homemaker. Sometimes it's the man wearing the skirt—and the dog in me would like to talk to him about this—mostly it's the woman, but some version of this home-at-home versus home-in-the-world seems to resurface.

With one change: the primary parent, whether it's Mom or Dad, isn't staying home very much anymore.

Go to the day care. Watch the parents dropping their children off. Watch their faces. Mostly just busy, harried, preoccupied, late—always late—but sometimes you see the regret as well. Does anybody think this is entirely a good idea? Dropping little Alexandria into a nurturing place for a few hours while Mom goes to work or Dad hammers away on his novel, sure—no problem. Stashing the kids in day care for forty hours a week so both parents can have their careers? This is not just stressful, this is not just anxiety-producing; this is wrong.

So what are we supposed to do? you say. We need the money.

Well, exactly. The roles of homemaker and breadwinner—the roles we inherited from our parents, not to mention the Brady Bunch—evolved at a time when the average household could be supported on a single income. But those days are over.

We have been approaching this idea of who does what and where we all fit in terms of ideology and emotion, in terms of feminism and equality and injury and lovingness. I wonder, though, if it would not be better approached in terms of political economy. What I'm getting at is, how did we get priced out of the market for our own lives? My mother would say—has said, in fact—that she didn't have a fancy kitchen or a fancy second car; she didn't spend thirty dollars a week on coffee or two hundred dollars a month on telephones, Internet access, and cable TV. She's right, of course. On the other hand, even if we were making our own coffee, bringing our lunch to work, driving secondhand Volvos, and dialing (gasp) an actual telephone connected to the wall by an actual cord, we still couldn't afford little Susie's ballet classes and Timmy's tennis lessons—not to mention a decent house in a decent neighborhood.

Also: we grew up in affluent times. Many of us had cars and trips and nice clothes and spending money in high school and college. Not only do we want the same things for our children, but the prospect of living worse in midlife than we did in high school seems completely strange and unacceptable.

Maybe it's as simple as that: maybe it's not our lives we can't afford but our aspirations, the things we were brought up to believe we could get from life. The dog in me is balled up over in the corner, muttering something about yuppie perfectionism, about materialist greed and advertising culture, about how we think we can buy our way into happiness—and isn't this the desire behind all this "living simple" hoo-ha? The notion that we can somehow dematerialize our lives and return to that mythical homespun yesteryear, where love is truly all you need. Of course, what this turns into is a glossy *Living Simple* magazine and a range of simple, tasteful products for your easy, low-key lifestyle, all elegantly designed and yet, somehow, quite expensive . . .

Where did that money go, anyway? I'm not going to touch that one, except to say that the richest 5 percent of our population has seen their share of the wealth skyrocket while the middle class has seen their share fall. And our country, alone in the Western world, has decided to allocate almost no resources to support working families. Spend a minute and imagine how much easier all of this would be—work, children, marriage—if there was a real family-leave policy, or if there was a system of child care run by professionals, trained caregivers who were paid more than the help at McDonald's . . .

But here in the real world it's impossible to take the time off to care for small children without trashing your career. Here in the real world it's every family for itself to improvise child care.

Here in the real world the "breadwinner" role continues to make sense, though. I can work hard—get through whatever I have to get through—show some discipline and persistence and grit, and I can make the money to take care of my family. Maybe not entirely, but I can put money in the retirement account, pay for the health insurance, keep the cars in shape and relatively new. And you know what? I find this completely satisfying. When things go to hell at work, I can remember why I'm sticking it through; it gives me a sense of purpose, a place in the world. I know what I'm supposed to be doing. I do it. It makes me feel purposeful and whole, a feeling even the dog in me can understand.

I like having kids. I like taking care of them. It's not crazy complicated.

Where it gets crazy complicated is when you get to the "home-maker" role. Lately one person is supposed to assume primary responsibility for the day-to-day care of the children, plus maintain a fulfilling and profitable career, plus keep the household going? Even with whatever degree of help the breadwinner is willing to come up with (wildly variable, in my experience), it still seems impossible.

What it turns into in our house is a big Mexican standoff, with the Loved One saying, I'm making more money than my mother ever did! and the Jerk saying, I'm doing way more housework than my father ever did! and the Loved One saying, You don't even pick up your socks! and the Jerk saying, You wouldn't know an electric bill if it bit you in the ass! and the Loved One saying, It was supposed to be different.

Maybe.

This is the place where the dog in me checks out, takes himself for a nice little walk, sniffs around to see what's happening. Because, you know, I can't force it all to make sense. I can't take care of you that way. I can only do what I do: get up in the morning, punch the clock, keep the credit cards in line and change the oil and cook dinner a few times a week and go to a Christmas pageant when forced to. I can keep my own head above water, and I can make sure that, whatever else happens, you and the children are not going to go homeless or hungry or without modern-dance lessons.

Here's a confession: a couple of years ago the Loved One had a huge photographic project down on the Navaho Nation in Arizona and New Mexico. She spent the first half of the summer on and off shooting pictures in the Southwest and the second half in a frenzy of developing, sorting, and printing the resulting pictures, leaving me with the kids. And you know what? I really liked it. We went to the river. We went camping. We talked about why Turner's tennis instructor was cool and why Nora's dance teacher was a freak, and we sat around eating pizza and watching terrible movies, and for a few weeks, I felt like I understood what the world looked like to them. It turns out that they are actually interesting people, and good company. When the university cranked up again and the Loved One came home, I was even, for a moment, jealous of the life she led with the children.

But this was a summer more or less off—no deadlines, nothing looming. I nickel-and-dimed my way through a little magazine work and a couple of short stories, but really, I didn't get a lot done. I don't see how you could, to tell you the truth. I don't see how that script works, not with small children.

Here's another confession: that condom in my toiletries bag came from a campus safe-sex drive about five years ago, and it's still sitting there. Those cigars in my glove compartment have sat there untouched since I quit smoking on my daughter's birthday two years ago, on the grounds that if I wanted to see her married, I was going to have to live for another twenty years or so. The band, the parties, the occasional late nights with the grad students—all these are, it pains me to admit, entirely harmless ways of blowing off steam, of getting through the week. I do what I do, as best I can. I take care of the people I was put here to take care of. I take the dog in me out for a walk, every once in a while, just so he won't get too restless. But I don't let him off the leash, not anymore.

And the guitars? Womankind will rejoice to know that I finally sold the solid-gold ES-295 last week—just wasn't playing it enough. I did, though, keep the money in the guitar account, and right now I'm eyeing a National Reso-Phonic style 1 tricone resonator guitar in chrome-plated bell brass, with a little engraved band around the edge—the biggest, flashiest, loudest acoustic guitar in existence. The Loved One still thinks we need a new couch, but the dog in me wants this thing. We'll see.

Why My Kids Like Me

STEVEN RINEHART

I correspond online with a senior citizen who likes to say that parents today are going about things completely the wrong way. "They just want to be friends to their kids, not parents." Somehow she blames hippies and the seventies for allowing this behavior to get a toehold in our society.

"You know, the hippies were raised by World War II vets," I type back to her. "Those guys may have done a great job over there, but then they came home and raised some serious whack jobs, you have to admit. I wouldn't be surprised if Squeaky Fromme's old man spent the winter of '44 in the Ardennes."

But you don't mess with the Greatest Generation, I found out, at least not out loud. They sacrificed. Nobody after them knows from sacrifice.

Now, I don't know if my kids consider me their friend, but I have to say that if they don't, it's not for lack of trying on my part. Most adults will have very little to do with me. My own kids are much less discriminating (but not completely; my younger daughter recently took me in hand for some "private time," just the two of us, swinging gently in the hammock in the backyard. "You yell too much," she said seriously. "Use your inside voice more"). She's four.

I use my kids as sounding boards a lot, which is probably one reason why we're so close.

"At the status meeting today the operations director moaned during my PowerPoint presentation," I told my son, also four. "What do you think?"

"*Ohhhhhhhhhh,*" he said.

"Yes. Exactly like that. What do you think that was all about?"

He immediately flopped to the floor and writhed in imitation of an electrocuted executive. "It's Big Train Day," he gasped. "We're supposed to play with the *big trains* today."

We played with the big trains, and before long I realized that the immaturity of the operations director was something for his kids to work out in therapy, not me.

My older daughter and my wife are also my close friends, and that pretty much rounds out the picture. My wife has tackled the project of Grown-up Friends for Steve on and off again over our nine years together, but none of her candidates took except for the kids, who, when it's all said and done, have very little choice in the matter.

"You're the best boy," I whisper to my son when he's tired and I've got him pinned to the bed after we were both chortling wildly at some book about talking mice with no pants. "You're my hero," my wife says to me when I've somehow managed to match her exertions keeping the family afloat. You see the connection?

At my older daughter's school there are a lot of dads who remind me of the operations director. A couple of them have mistaken me, dropping off my daughter in the classroom, for the teaching assistant. I'm forty-three, for Christ's sake. Maybe it's my size thirteen Converse All-Stars, which for some of us never needed to come back into vogue. At the parents' mixers, invariably hosted in the richest parents' duplex, I stick close to my wife, joking that it's our only time to talk. Around us, operations directors, male and female, trade wisdom, debate the ouster of problem teachers (*fire a* *teacher?* I could just as easily sue my grandmother), the annual fund, curriculum shortcomings. My wife is eager to join them, and in the end she finds another sad-sack man-child to fob me off on. He and I hang out by the food, quickly discovering how little we have in common after all, curricula and teacher sacking notwithstanding. At the end of the evening I manage to pay for the cab home, even remembering to request a receipt, which ends up being washed in my jeans.

·   ·   ·

Several years ago I got a chance to meet the photographer Sally Mann and, oddly, help her name some of her photographs of her naked children. She was very polite about rejecting my ideas.

"That one looks like, you know, nymphs and stuff," I said. *Asshole*, I thought. They were naked middle-schoolers; of course they looked like nymphs.

I was hanging out at Sally's gallery with her, my wife, and another photographer-mother. For the most part, all three of these women were successful artists, mothers, and professionals. All three were comfortable at art openings, private-school fund-raising events, and Filofaxing, which meant their husbands didn't have to be, which is the way we like it. I kept my mouth shut, mostly.

A little later Sally told us that her son had told her recently that, from that point forward, he wanted to have his clothes on in any photographs she took of him, and she'd of course agreed to this. She'd made a lot of great art around those kids' asses, probably put them all through school and paid the light bill too, but she said no problem, no more bare-ass for her son.

Now, I'd read a lot of affronted bitching about those pictures when that book came out. Everyone had an opinion, even Republicans who were just then hearing about this Internet thing that in a few years would enable them to build child-porn libraries that would make her book *Immediate Family* look like "The Family Circus." Sally

Mann took naked pictures of her kids, and God only knows how that will affect their development as citizens and voters. But in the gallery that day I suspected that there was someone else in the picture, that gallery-absent, non-Filofaxing dad, someone just like me back in Virginia or wherever, shooting the shit with the boy and his nymph sisters while Mom did her shows. And with great results all around, apparently, because at the end of the day, any kid who had the stones to tell his mother not to take naked pictures of him and put them in a book would, unlike me, be able to tell his folks later on that he didn't really want to go after that Air Force ROTC scholarship after all. He'd be able to tell his wife that dragging a seven-year-old and two toddlers to the Million Mom March to see Raffi on a liquid-vision display from a quarter-mile away was solid insanity and he'd rather be kneecapped. He'd be able to tell the operations director to please save all the moans for the moaning-and-answer period at the end of the presentation.

That kid would save a lot of people a lot of time, and that's not a bad thing.

Our kids are wise to all of this anyway, so we might as well square with them. It's not about innocence anymore. This country has already decided that where the kids are is also where the big money is. I picked up an Archie comic book the other night and was instantly transported back to my early teens, desperate again to have the cartooning talent to be able to depict Betty and Veronica naked. But it's different for kids now. Today Veronica poses for *Playboy*'s "Women of Enron"; Betty's on tap for "Women of Wal-Mart." They're no longer inaccessible, insufferable cockteases, their cleavage a knee-weakeningly simple black line. Now they're moms, their kids are all on the college track; their husbands read *Men's Health* and want to be Bono when they grow up.

I imagine Veronica's husband, Mr. Lodge-Whatever, one night when Veronica's working late and he's doing the Outback Steakhouse thing with the kids. "That's a pretty lady there," he says, nodding at a woman in the salad line. "Look at that total horse's ass she came in with, though. Jeez."

"I'm telling Mom," his kids announce.

"Guys," he says. "Mom says I'm allowed to look if I don't touch."

"You're *ogling*," his daughter says. "Mom says you've got midlife issues."

"Mom said that?" Veronica's husband trembles a little now. He's made the mistake of putting himself in a position of weakness with his children. Never do that. East German schoolchildren turned their parents into the Stasi, remember. Imagine trying to take away those kids' Napster. If you're going to befriend them, be consistent. You're the older kid; you'll suffer their advice, and even the occasional soft reprimand, but don't get so blabby that you end up giving them information they could use against you. Trust me.

Many fathers my age, at least those in New York City, have mastered the public face of this buddy-dad role. On the bus, hanging out in line at the planetarium, or even just riding the subway, we practice the rap with our little chums, and it's easy to get a whole subway car listening.

"Daddy, why do they close the doors on people?"

"Because the conductor lacks simple human decency," I answer. "He probably needs a lot more time-outs." Chuckles from around us, even from the tattooed gangsta rappers, or the Juilliard students pretending to be tattooed gangsta rappers.

"Is the conductor a bad man, like the president?"

"Yes. That's why you can never understand a word any of them are saying."

Unfortunately, this art is lost on those who wear our rings.

"No more television, ever," says my wife one day out of the clear blue. "And no more videos." Because, it turns out, our son had a meltdown with her in Blockbuster, a meltdown that apparently made the Big Train flap look like a Japanese tea ceremony.

"Next time," I say, "just threaten to throw him out the window."

But my wife won't tell him that. She never takes my advice, which is too bad, because not only do I miss the TV, but also, threatening to throw your toddler out a window is a surefire meltdown-stopper, as it's something irresistible for them to chew on. ("Does he mean it? Does he even know we're on the ground floor? *Dad!!*") It's like when your best friend says he's going to kill you. Idle threats carelessly tossed build intimacy. When my four-year-old says she's never going to speak to me again, *ever*, I can easily counter with, "If 'ever' ever comes, then I won't even *care!*" The only real trick is to remember to say it with my inside voice.

It's sad that this kind of sophisticated dialectic isn't really available to women. Sally Mann can take naked pictures of her kids, but if she threatened to throw them out of a window even her dealer would testify against her at the custody hearing. And that's a shame, because women ought to be able to exercise their "inner Roseanne" more, or maybe even revert to Diet Coke–swilling, backpack-toting best girl-friends around their kids. After all the practice they have handling their husbands' whore-Madonna complexes, it would be a great relief for them to kick back and release their goofy, giggly inner nymph. But for some reason women can't perform this devolution (my pet theory is that the behavior of adolescent girls is so venal and base that most women are only too eager to put those days far behind them), and when they catch us doing it, you can count, at the very least, on that sharp intake of breath that signifies "I don't like what you're doing. It's not in any of the books, but the books do say not to debate parenting in front of the kids so all I'm going to do about it is suck this lungful of air between my teeth."

Because of this, I mostly practice my parenting out of my wife's earshot, similar to the way I practiced the trombone in junior high. Does this mean my wife has taken the place of my father? Probably, but in all honesty my most genuine reaction to that realization is relief. My father was an athlete, a disciplined ex-Marine who could work fifty hours a week and build an addition to the house in his spare time. I live in an environment where I can drop three hundred dollars at Home Depot on power tools, use them primarily to sever their own electrical cords, and my wife still tells her friends that I'm "handy." She's my dad minus *his* dad. If I ever let her watch *This Old House* she'd instantly wise up and leave me.

·   ·   ·

In the end, it's true, this new breakdown of roles is not fair to women. Their new roles are the result of additional pressure, added responsibilities. Just about every one of them could use a personal assistant to help them run their lives, and you can't really say that about the men, even the ones who, like me, bust their asses with a forty-plus-hour workweek, do most of the cooking, and have forsaken the Dagwood Sunday-morning nap on the couch as a quaint custom in the same league as whittling. We don't need assistants; when push comes to shove, we just become the weak link. Our wives can fume and fret about the details; we buy the kids junk food and take them to Adam Sandler movies. Someone has to stop and smell the rose-scented Hello Kitty lip gloss and ogle the ninety-five-dollar Yu-Gi-Oh cards behind the glass of the display case, and we're just the guys to do it.

But women are still living longer than we are, so the basic unfairness doesn't trouble me too much. I suppose I do wonder, sometimes very late at night, about the kids, though. You're really not supposed to be your kids' friend because they need to feel safe to develop a rich inner life. They need someone in charge so they don't have to bear that burden themselves. Will my son one day grab me by the shirt, like James Dean did to Mr. Howell in *Rebel Without a Cause,* and toss me around the living room for not being enough of a man? Will my daughters drop out, tattoo themselves from coccyx to elbow, and abandon their unwanted newborns in a Dumpster because I hindered their childhood development?

I have no idea. When the time comes, I'll probably just ask them.

Ward and June R Us

ROB SPILLMAN

Lately, when I'm whipped into a domestic frenzy, I feel like Ray Liotta in the movie *GoodFellas*—the scene near the end where he is trying to make the perfect spaghetti and take care of his scrambling kids while FBI helicopters hover overhead, his cocaine business about to explode in his face, his arms flailing around like an octopus as he attempts to cover multiple boiling-over pots. This exact sort of frenzy seems to take place nearly every day in my house from three to five in the afternoon, those brutal postschool hours, when I have to figure out how to get a four- and a seven-year-old to play dates, gymnastics, art or guitar classes, and then, oh shit, what are they going to eat for dinner? And in this horrible daily crisis I'm all alone, completely without help, as my able-bodied wife, Elissa, lounges nearby at the computer, where I sense she's not *really* working on her novel but instead forwarding joke e-mails and eating the proverbial bonbons.

Why isn't she helping me? Because this is my week to be June Cleaver, and she gets to be Ward. Next week we'll switch, and *she'll* be the one caught in the domestic vortex while I rest my feet on the ottoman and entertain the kids like the quintessential fifties dad just home from work. This is how we have come to manage our lives: by completely giving in to gender stereotypes, but on an alternating basis.

After years of frustration, of bickering, of seething resentment, my wife and I finally gave up on trying to have the perfect egalitarian, postfeminist marriage and embraced our inner Ward and June, because when we were doing it our *old* way—which is actually the "modern" way—we simply couldn't figure out how to share everything (work, kids, domesticity) without driving each other crazy.

A bit of background: both of us are writers/editors, and we work mostly at home. We have constructed our lives to have flexible work schedules because we wanted to be able to spend as much time with our kids as possible: even *this* time—the postschool, predinner, hunger-fatigued, whiny-wasteland hour or two.

Before our Ward and June arrangement, Elissa and I attempted to be as equitable as possible in the distribution of family responsibilities, sharing everything in our marriage from financial duties to domestic chores. We operated on the assumption that our time was equally valuable and that we should share all of the parenting burdens. The two of us met when we were twenty-one and married at twenty-three (we've now been married fifteen years), and we came of age in the postfeminist era where equality, in our circles, was a foregone conclusion. When we met, we were in complete agreement about splitting everything down the middle and rejecting any kind of gender stereotypes.

And we did. We started our careers at the same time, working entry-level jobs at magazines, and decided together to leap into the literary world with all its uncertainties. Instead of growing apart, as do many couples who marry young, we grew together. Maybe it helped that we had almost no money. In our first apartment—a ninety-dollar-a-month share in a run-down part of Staten Island— we had one bowl and two spoons. We pooled our meager resources into a joint banking account; we shared a bicycle and even clothes. We lived in monastic simplicity, and—except for our monthly scramble to pay the rent—the stress level was relatively low.

Buttressing our relationship was a strong belief in each other's ability to become fully actualized creative people. Since "creative" and "poor" generally go hand in hand, we settled into a mutually supportive financial system. One of us would try to hold down a decent-paying job for up to two years so the other wouldn't have to worry as much about making money and could concentrate on creative work. When my wife decided she wanted to attend graduate school for an M.A. in creative writing, I had no problem punching a clock for two years as a fact checker so that she could. After she received her degree, she found a steady job as an editor at a literary magazine and I was able to concentrate on my writing. In each "down" period, there was an understanding that the other would still contribute financially, but with lower-paying creative gigs, and that the person not at the office would handle more than the normal share of the domestic responsibilities, which, in prechildren hindsight seems like a joke—"Honey, did you make sure to stock up on Top ramen and Pernod?"

When both of us were freelancing, the financial strain increased, but since we were both in the same boat, the self-inflicted burdens were easy to bear. When we decided to have children, we figured we would both continue to work at home, assuming that our children's care and feeding would fit seamlessly into our current arrangement. We had this utopian vision of being able to work at home *and* somehow spend all of our time with the kids. *We'll work when they're napping,* I remember thinking. Ha.

Early on we discovered that there was a fundamental problem with our flexible, subsistence-level approach to life: children are inflexible. They need to eat regularly and sleep regularly. They like routine and certainty. And where it used to be charming and artsy for us to be financially crunched—eating canned soup or PB&J while we waited for an overdue paycheck—our children weren't as amused or sustained by the interesting fare one can create with twenty-nine cents' worth of dry noodles. Reality set in one late night when our overdraft was tapped out and our credit card was denied when we tried to buy diapers at Rite Aid. At this low moment, we wondered aloud if it wasn't time for one of us to get a Real Job. Just under the surface was the assumption that I should be the one, since I, as the male, should be "the provider." And also just under the surface was our embarrassment at thinking along these sexist lines.

So instead of one of us punching a clock, we decided to redouble our creative efforts and take on as much freelance work as we could handle. And sometimes it worked. Some months were better than others, and we made nearly equal amounts of money, depending on whom the freelance gods were smiling upon that week or month. Yet, admittedly, each of us couldn't help but think of the other, "You could be making more money if you weren't spending so much time on low-paying creative gigs." And when times were lean this feeling was heightened, which would lead us to dwell on one inevitable but unspoken truth: each of us believed our work was more important than the other's.

Part of the problem was that we had no role models for what we were trying to accomplish. Elissa comes from a traditional, stable family where her father worked and her mother took care of the kids—each one's role clear and defined and each supportive of the other. As for me, my parents divorced when I was three, after which I lived with my father, who is openly gay, until I was ten. This was in Berlin, in the mostly gay opera world, and there weren't a whole lot of parental role models around, functional or dysfunctional. We were rarely at home, and I ate and slept in and around the opera house and in concert halls. After the age of ten I lived with my mother, who had remarried, in Baltimore, and there I was treated as a domestic partner, with assigned nights for cooking and cleaning. None of these options seemed particularly appealing to us.

But with our chosen alternative of working and living together, the freedom from domestic duties we each needed in order to advance ourselves professionally came at a direct cost, in time, to our spouse. Since we couldn't afford to hire out all of our domestic and child-care needs (assuming we'd even want to), one of us had to pick up the slack around the house while the other was on deadline. And needless to say, the person stuck picking up the slack around the house was not advancing his or her career, which created the Catch-22 of "How am I supposed to get out of the 'picking up the slack' role when I don't have the time to get the assignments and the deadlines I need to put myself in the position to ask *you* to pick up the slack?"

Elissa and I felt like we were constantly groping in the dark about who was supposed to do what and when, and the problem was that everything was in play and open to negotiation—every responsibility, every meal, every errand. We were both available for all of it, and yet we both had to do our work if we were to keep a roof over our heads and food on the table. So at the end of the day, after the kids had been wrestled into bed and read to and the house was finally quiet, who was supposed to attack the sink full of dishes and who was supposed to slink off to the computer? Adding to the complexity of the situation is the fact that we both love to cook and to take care of each other. What's more, we both enjoy spending as much time as possible with our children. But in the real world, you can't spend all of your time cooking and taking care of each other and spending time with your children. At least not without a trust fund and a total lack of ambition.

We tried dividing up tasks on the fly—one person cooks, the other sets the table; one does laundry, the other folds. Yet with this system there was a constant weighing of tasks—does one easily prepared dinner really equal a load of laundry? Didn't I shop the last time? Can't you for once change the damn lightbulbs?

In a recent article in *The Atlantic*, about the epidemic of sexlessness in modern-day marriages, Caitlin Flanagan says, "Once children come along, it's easy for parents to regard each other as co-presidents of an industrious little corporation."

Okay, I can see that. Except I felt we were more like co–middle managers, struggling to figure out who would deal with all the higher forces: the school functions, the alpha-organizing parents, the social events requiring baby-sitters, doctors, and trips to visit family, not to mention work deadlines.

Elissa and I were up to our necks in the details of our lives—we were close to drowning. I kept thinking of Raymond Carver, who characterized parenting as "unrelieved responsibility and permanent distraction." I can't say that we weren't happy at least some of the time. Yet with multiple forces pulling at us from every direction, we both felt close to flying apart.

Luckily, Elissa and I loved each other, and our shared history, not to mention our shared offspring, kept us from snapping most of the time. But still, we both knew something had to change. And so it did.

I think what precipitated our change was the fact that my wife and I began to travel for our work, occasionally leaving home for a week at a time, and during these trips the parent left at home was naturally forced to take full responsibility for the house and kids. I dreaded this the first time it neared. After all, we could barely manage with two parents—how could it possibly be handled by just one of us? But strangely enough, we discovered that the household actually functioned much better when only one of us was home, mainly because the parent who was "on" had to fully dedicate himself to the tasks at hand with no one to resent for not helping enough. School lunches had to be made the night before, and dinners had to be planned in advance. Shopping had to be done for those meals, and who else was going to do it? The house suddenly became a smooth-running machine and the kids were strangely relaxed and compliant. In fact, when Elissa was away that first time, on her book tour, I found myself actually enjoying the shopping, the cooking, and the making of the kids' lunches. I felt pride in a job well done instead of resentment in a job I had to do by default because I'd somehow wound up on the losing end of that moment's competition over career versus chores.

And this, of course, was precisely the advantage of the traditional marriage—the *Father Knows Best* and *Leave It to Beaver* marriages of the fifties and before. Ward Cleaver was off at work all day—he couldn't possibly help—and so, with only one captain (June) running the ship at home, everything sailed along smoothly. As many of the previous generation (and even the current one) would argue, there is a lot to be said for this: roles are fixed and certain, and everyone's expectations are met. The problem, as we all know, was that a lot of women were suicidal from being at home with the kids all the time and a lot of men were having heart attacks from having to be at work all the time.

So here was my solution: I proposed that we become Ward and June Cleaver—that we scrap our broken, resentment-laced egalitarian marriage and embrace the arrangement of that beloved retro couple of TV Land, where June does all of the domestic duties—shopping, cooking, cleaning, and laundry—and Ward works full-time and comes home in the evening to entertain the kids, guilt-free and harangue-free. The catch? We'd alternate, on a weekly basis, who is Ward and who is June. Each week, whoever is June gets fully burdened with the domestic duties from Monday through Friday, and whoever is Ward disappears to his "office" all day. There would be no negotiating and no trading chores. It's just the way it would be.

Elissa was initially hesitant—after all, hadn't we both embraced the liberation that feminism had promised? Wasn't there a way for two supposedly educated, progressive people like us to share these responsibilities on a daily basis without resorting to retro stereotypes?

No, she finally conceded, there wasn't.

A year later we're still Ward and June, and I think it's fair to say that the system has worked amazingly well for us. In this arrangement there are no nagging worries that things aren't getting done, no guilt over hasty, crappy, last-minute dinners. Each day, time is budgeted for a series of tasks that one person is responsible for. There is comfort in knowing that it will all get done, even when I am the one doing it all. With responsibility comes control, and control equals power. June rules the house—all of the house. Obey her or feel her wrath. But don't get too carried away, because next week you'll be at the other end of the whip.

We've both learned that while having the power and control over the house is satisfying, it is equally enjoyable to relinquish power. Our generation has been groomed to superachieve in every aspect of our lives. We have to do everything fully—be the best at our jobs while still being able to make a Taj Mahal model out of sugar cubes with our kids after school while cooking a well-balanced organic meal and never, God forbid, letting the TV do the baby-sitting. But with June in control, Ward can focus on work. And when he's done, he can pick up the kids from school and start gluing sugar cubes with abandon. Even June winds up working more freely, because although she still needs to budget time for shopping, cleaning, and cooking each day, resentment has been taken out of the equation. It's part of her day, every day, for a week, and because June is responsible, June gets efficient with her domestic duties and thus can budget time for her own work. With the parental roles thusly defined, the collateral effect on the kids has been stunning. With reduced levels of hazardous resentment in our marriage, our kids (who, like frogs in the Amazon, are the first to notice environmental pollution) are also much more relaxed.

Of course, there's still the murky swamp of weekends, which we haven't figured out how to divide up along Ward/June lines, and the occasional business trip or unplanned-for deadline can instantly

plunge our "perfect" solution into a morass of reassigned responsibilities and promises of makeup favors. And then there's the week, I
confess, when I just can't get it up to make anything for dinner better
than hot dogs/chicken nuggets/mac-and-cheese/frozen pizza, or the
week Elissa's idea of cleaning the bathroom is wiping the faucet with
a tissue. And, as I described at the start, resentment can still creep in
now and then—for June, mostly, when Ward is reading *Artforum*
while the kids are melting down and the spaghetti is boiling over, or
when June gets a little too uppity about her puttanesca sauce being
preferable to last week's June take-out pizza. (Needless to say, neither
Elissa nor I would have cut it as a fifties housewife.)

And yes, there are still days when our evening conversation de-
volves into grunts about tasks done and tasks left undone. (Often
when the kids go to bed, out come the computers and it's back to
work for both of us. Just before bedtime is reserved for the review of
finances and "Can we afford summer camp?" discussions. Very sexy,
right?) In fact, money is still tricky, even with both of us working as
hard as we can (at least during our Ward weeks). Elissa and I sometimes joke that what we really need is a *Palm Beach Story* solution to
our financial problems: one of us goes down to Palm Beach, marries
a gazillionaire, and we live happily ever after. But overall, our
Ward/June arrangement is still a vast improvement over what we had
before.

Is our arrangement for everyone? No. First of all, you've got to be
able to schedule your career into alternating weeks and compact it
into the evenings after the kids have gone to bed. But second, and perhaps more important, most men I know loathe the prospect and
would never willingly agree to it. In fact, when I've mentioned our
arrangement to my married friends, their standard reaction has been,
"Don't tell my wife!" The notion of total abandonment to domesticity, even on a week-on, week-off basis, seems to strike fear in the
hearts of even my most liberated friends. They would rather trade

and barter tasks as they have been, the power balance an essential element of the frisson of their relationships and the illusion of hanging on to to their permanent Wardness—no matter the actuality—simply too difficult to jettison.

But for us, the totally egalitarian marriage was a mirage, an illusion that we were knocking ourselves out futilely chasing. This way—by giving up power and then taking control, week after week—we do manage to have it all. Just not all at the same time.

She Didn't Want a S.N.A.G.; She Wanted Me

ELWOOD REID

I met my wife, Nina, in a dingy rock/punk club called the Blind Pig/8Ball Saloon. There were no gold chains, buttery nipples, or sex on the beach involved, nor did I pepper her with cheesy pickup lines. I followed orders and used my fists, sprinkled in some head butts, and she was mine—but more on that later.

We both worked at the Pig. She was the sexy, tip-sucking waitress—a Sarah Lawrence grad who directed improvisational plays at the local theater. Rumor had it she was in retreat from a bad breakup somewhere back east. I was the silent ex-jock—a former Michigan defensive lineman—who'd found a numbing niche as a bouncer, dispensing law and order to the bar's unruly patrons: drunks, crack heads, street brawlers, and the occasional beer-brave frat boy who thought tangling with a bouncer and losing would somehow confer cool.

This was in Ann Arbor, Michigan—a so-called enlightened college town full of food co-ops, contra dancing, "Take Back the Night" marches, and sandal-wearing faux hippies who were quick to pull out Daddy's gold card to gas up their Limited Edition Eddie Bauer Jeeps en route to a Dead show. Political correctness had swept through the campus, lingering like patchouli oil. After years of locker rooms and football stadiums where I participated in the exact sort of caveman behavior regularly denounced by the enlightened, I was struggling to fit into this new, postcollege, nonsports world and figure out the rules. The John Wayne bullshit was out, and I didn't know what was in or how I was supposed to behave, so I kept quiet, grew my hair long, and read a lot. I wanted to be somebody else, but I had this body built for hunkering down and hitting. The problem was that I could no longer do that; despite what the coaches said, life was not like football. My ability to lay someone out with a forearm shiver impressed no one except perhaps the manager, who frequently had me bounce guys he owed money or dealers he'd screwed over. And although I was smothering the post–glory days of college sports with booze and whatever else I could get my hands on, I wanted better, but I didn't know how to get it. Fortunately, the bar was a sort of halfway house where, among the slumming grad students, late-stage alkies, and townies, I hoped to remake myself—no easy task for a six-foot-six jamoke who tipped the scales north of two and a half bills. When I walked into a room, ducking under some low-hung fixture, certain expectations were raised, and most of them involved lifting heavy objects.

More than once I'd overheard women at the bar describe the perfect man as a S.N.A.G., or Sensitive New Age Guy. Having grown up in blue-collar Cleveland, I had no fucking idea what they were talking about, except that a lot of the guys these women identified as S.N.A.G.s were to me just pussy hounds spouting sensitive rhetoric they had no intention of living up to. They'd say things like "My favorite book is *The Color Purple*," or "You want to go to the Del Rio and have a seitan burger with me?" These were the same guys who'd sported pooka-shell necklaces, cream Docksiders, and Members Only jackets during the *St. Elmo's Fire* eighties, when getting chicks meant channeling Rob Lowe and David Hasselhoff. If S.N.A.G.s were what the women I desired (troubled, arty, a little bitchy, and whip smart) wanted, then I was pretty much out of luck, because my "I am what I am" midwestern philosophy prevented me from striking a pose or donning a costume to impress the girls. The women I liked thought football players were stupid, base, and violent, and with my size there was no hiding the fact that I'd played. And so I took to my post at the door, happy to have found a job where my size and willingness to take both punch and insult were assets. And although I was routinely called a fascist or pea-brained Nazi for refusing service or showing a belligerent minor the door with his face, I was the one folks looked to when a fight erupted or some homeless dude off his meds shat his pants and started screaming about the CIA and the Easter Bunny. In other words, even in this oh-so-correct college town people like me were acceptable when our thumping skills were needed. So sometimes life was like football. And as much as I wished I could trade my body or become someone else, I admit it still felt good to have people depend upon me for this duty, even if it meant digging myself deeper into the hole I was trying to get myself out of.

I'd already deemed Nina way out of my league, and so I played the obedient Lurch who, after closing time, would help her put up the stools and bus empty bottles. In return I got a few dollars in tip-out, a smile, and the un-*Cheers*-like impression that she did not know my name. Par for the course, because Nina, like all the other waitresses, regarded the bouncers as unglamorous grunts who basically sat on stools all night staring at IDs—dumb lugs who for a smile and flirt would pitch in and help with the waitress work, wiping down tables and emptying ashtrays. After a month of secret pining and cataloguing of Nina's apparent likes and dislikes, I allowed my crush to fade into just another dull ache and added her to the long list of unattainable women who paraded around the bar with unworthy S.N.A.G.s or the always dependable rebel-in-leather-jacket dude who—once you got past his problems—was really sweet.

But every once in a while Nina would slip through the sweaty crowd to point out potential trouble. The blaring amps forced her to lean close and scream a few words like "There's a guy passed out by the stage," or "Somebody broke a bottle." For a few brief moments I had her attention. My services were needed.

I began making sure we worked the same nights, and as I sat on my stool under the WE RESERVE THE RIGHT TO REFUSE SERVICE TO ANYONE sign, stamping hands and taking cover charges, I secretly hoped for trouble—anything that might send Nina my way to huddle close to me and shout into my ear over the yowl of guitars and jabbering drunks.

Then one night it happened—not a fight but something better. A guy had not only grabbed Nina's ass, he'd also tossed a tip in her face after she'd refused to let him slip it down her blouse.

"I want him gone," she told me. I looked over at the bartender for confirmation. He drew his finger across his throat and pointed at the door—translation, cut off and eight-six the bastard.

Usually I approached these situations with a detached cool: I would explain the rules and ask the guy to leave, and if he chose violence, I was only too happy to oblige. It was nothing personal, I'd tell him; I'm just doing my job (even if that meant head-butting him until his nose split or wrapping my arms around his chest and squeezing until things began to crack). It was his choice. After dozens of fights and near-tangles, I'd learned to master the prefight jitters. The odds were in my favor, and most guys, even the vicious drunks and crack heads, could see the endgame and find a graceful way to exit the bar without injury. However, there were always a few who, despite all sober and rational evidence to the contrary, thought it a good idea to swing first. Once that happened I had the green light to mangle in the name of the Blind Pig/8Ball, because in the words of our lawyer, I feared for my life and was only trying to protect myself. In other words, any guy who made the mistake of throwing the first punch got his dose of pain and public humiliation.

I pushed through the crowd as Nina led me to a dark corner. There were a few locals drinking Bud and yammering about sports, some college kids pooled around the jukebox, and the usual collection of diehards hunched over their drinks trying to maintain the illusion that they were killing another Friday night for some social reason and not because they were full-time drunks.

Nina pointed at a blocky, red-faced guy wearing a cheap leather jacket over a stained T-shirt, his hands thick from work or cigarettes, I didn't know, and a home-job haircut. She peeled off and went back to her rounds, leaving me to size up the situation. He was drunk and loud and didn't seem to have many friends who might jump in and try to park a beer mug upside my head. And so I approached him with the nice I'm-just-doing-my-job act and gave him the bottom line. "We're asking you to leave," I said.

Embarrassed, he turned to the nearest fellow drunk and began a loud one-sided conversation. "Can you believe this shit, man?"

I reminded him not only that he'd touched a waitress, but also that he'd had too much to drink and it was time to go home while he was still ahead.

He called her a crazy bitch and worse. I smiled and again told him he had to leave even though I wanted to split his head open and tell him he was wrong—Nina the crazy bitch was the best thing in this whole bar. "Put down the beer and let's go," I said.

He put on the hurt drunk act, batting his eyes around, "C'mon, I'm not hurting anybody," he said. "I'll be a good boy. I'm sorry, okay? So back off."

I stepped back and told him there was no discussion—not only was he cut off, but he had to leave immediately. In a desperate attempt to save face he took a hard line, clutching his beer and declaring that he'd paid for it and he wanted to finish it. I let him take a few grinning sips before I reached out and grabbed the bottle, knowing full well that this would escalate things.

Of course he resisted. The beer foamed and spilled as he gave me an I'm-going-to-do-something-stupid look. And he did—a weak and boozy punch. It was meant for my chin, but it missed and caught me on the shoulder. Sensing what was about to happen, the crowd stepped back. The rest was quick and ugly. Never a puncher, I grabbed his arm and pulled close, snapped his head to the floor, slipped a choke hold on him, and began dragging him toward the back door, making sure his face caught a few walls along the way.

In the alley he got brave again, and, well, let's just say with the help of a few head butts he slumped against the Dumpster, vomited, and passed out.

As I crept back to my post, the usual postfight shame and embarrassment took over as several women looked at me and shook their heads in disgust and a bearded dude in a Guatemalan poncho passed by and said, "Harsh." I was pretty sure that my display of power had confirmed Nina's worst thoughts about me and that after closing time I'd be Lenny to her George—she'd corner and lecture me about how all she'd wanted was for the guy to leave and how she felt bad because I'd hurt him, used a little too much force.

But as ashamed as I felt, and as much as I didn't want to turn off women like Nina, I had to admit that I liked bouncing people. I got off on wading into a mosh pit and dragging violators out with a joint lock, knowing I was one of the few guys in town who could do so easily. For those brief, confusing moments it was like I was back on the football field, hitting and getting hit, and I'd enter some zone of intoxicating calm that comes only with practice and with the knowledge that your job requires you to fight when words fail. The trick was to control the jangle of nerves and focus on the task at hand without worrying about the consequences—a lucky punch, a knife, or even the sudden appearance of a gun. For the moment there was only the two of you, muscle against bone. Primal, cretinous, and violently wrong, sure—but somebody had to do it, and that somebody was me. It was a big part of who I was, and I couldn't deny it. It was, for better or worse, all I knew. I was trying to know more, but I wasn't there yet, and unfortunately, this was the only side of me Nina knew, or so I thought.

For the rest of the night I went about my duties, dreading closing time and Nina's inevitable lecture. And then, sure enough, as I was sipping my after-work drink with the rest of the staff, Nina came up and sat on the stool next to me. But to my surprise, instead of laying into me, she pointed at the Philip Roth book I was carrying and asked if I'd ever read Robertson Davies's *Deptford Trilogy*. The connection was lost on me. I told her I had not, and instead of the usual uncomfortable silence, she said she'd bring me a copy, that it was important I read it. For the next hour the rest of the staff melted away and we talked books—something I'd always been shy about because the few literature courses I'd taken in college had taught me how poorly read I was, a condition I'd worked hard to correct. She'd read Roth and Carver and Cheever and wanted to hear my thoughts on them. She told me about her ex-boyfriend and how he was sort of stalking her and how she kept picking the wrong men. And then she lobbed a big fat clue my way when she told me I was nothing like her stalker ex. I took it as a compliment, and although I did not offer to find and pound him, the thought did cross my mind.

Around 3 A.M. the manager flicked on the ugly lights and said it was time to go home. Nina and I looked at each other and knew something had happened or was about to happen. After witnessing all sorts of drunken and regrettable late-night collisions, we proceeded with caution. I decided to step back and let her call the shots. We could go home friends or we could take it outside; it was her choice.

At the door she asked, "So do you want to get breakfast? I could really use some bacon."

We went to an all-night greasy spoon and kept talking. I began to realize that just as my size and brutish inscrutability sometimes kept people at arm's length, Nina's intense, no-bullshit manner (often mistaken for bitchy) coupled with her heart-on-the-floor beauty made her just as unapproachable. As odd as it seemed, we were a match of sorts.

She went home with me, or more accurately to my friend Napalm's basement apartment where he let me sleep on the floor. After that, Nina and I were inseparable. I read *The Deptford Trilogy*. We moved in together and, like some mixed-up version of *My Fair Lady,* Nina began to civilize me. She weaned me off beer, took away my beloved jar of mayonnaise, and forbade me from making sandwiches out of every meal she cooked. She tossed my polyester coaching shorts and introduced me to intimidating stuff like sushi, Truffaut's *Two English Girls,* and Rilke. Not once did she mention the fight that had brought us together, although later I learned she'd often defended me when other members of the staff said I was nothing more than some meathead ex-jock. The thing is, I made Nina feel safe—she could justify my lumbering demeanor because deep down she felt I was just a soft bookworm trapped inside a lineman's body. Besides, it wasn't like she was asking me to wear Birkenstocks and friendship bracelets (although later I'd be guilty of both), but more that she let me strike a masculine balance and loved me precisely for my sometimes stubborn and aggressive manner in the way a teacher is often charmed by the class pain in the ass. Point being, I wasn't perfect and still had plenty of Neanderthal behavior left to keep her busy and interested for a long time. I still called women "chicks" and things like peach turtlenecks "gay"—an old Cleveland term. I liked guns and beer and thought soccer—or at least the pussy version practiced stateside—was un-American and soft.

·　　　·　　　·

After we were married, I kept bouncing, not only for the extra cash but because I'd grown fond of the bar's scruffy regulars and the chance to hear great bands before they went big-time. And Nina—who, by the way, was raised by vegetarian, peace-loving hippies—was okay with it for a while. She was still waiting tables now and then, and like at the beginning, my presence in the bar reassured her. Whenever some drunk asked her out or demanded her number, she'd point at me and say, "See that guy over there? He's my husband." All I had to do was look big and mean and violently jealous.

Eight years later, when our first daughter was born, I was still picking up shifts at the bar. Having long quit the bar scene herself, Nina urged me to retire. I was too old, she said, and I had responsibilities. She was worried about something happening to me and warned me several times that if I got hurt, she'd kill me. I put her off because we needed the money, and after years of successful extractions and fights I'd gotten a little cocky. But in truth I sensed that bouncing was all that remained of my good old days; Nina had sanded away most of my rough edges. While I was a long way from puddling up over Oprah or understanding the purpose of a dust ruffle, I was, for better or worse, domesticated and housebroken. And I liked it, because I needed the boundaries as much as I needed a wife who wasn't asking me to get in touch with my feminine side by flushing the masculinity from my system. I still worked with my hands, called people pussies, and checked the box scores every morning. And the Pig, for me, played into this because it was like a ringside seat to danger, drunken mistakes, and all of the other immature behavior I'd long since sworn off now that I was married and supposedly knew better.

Then, like a strange bookend, a big fight broke out one night at the bar. Midway through a snarlingly loud show, a pod of roided-up dudes started the trouble they'd come looking for. A waitress ran out of the crowd screaming and pointing, and I plunged once more into the breach, grabbing the first guy I saw, choking him in a neck lock, and dragging him to the door. I felt the rush. I grabbed another and put him away. Then, wrestling a third large guy to the door, I felt a few dull thuds on the back of my skull and all of a sudden things went black.

I'd been knocked out—a first. Later a waitress told me that while I was busy dragging the guy to the door, his buddy had speed-bagged the back of my head with his beer mug. Besides the dried blood and lumps on the back of my head, my ribs hurt and I'd cut my arm on broken glass.

After my shift I watched the younger bouncers recount the fight with grins and high fives, and for the first time I felt old and out of place. I went home to Nina.

A friend had already called and told her about the fight, and she was waiting for me on the couch. I tried to play it off, telling her it was no big deal. But when she hugged me my ribs popped and ached. She felt the lump on the back of my head and examined the cut, shaking her head.

I braced myself for the lecture about how I had to take care of myself and how I was too old to fight. Instead she bit her lip and pointed at the couch where Sophia, my six-month-old daughter, lay sleeping under a blanket. "Take her up to her crib," she said. Then she clicked off the light and went upstairs to bed.

I picked Sophia up. She stirred and I rocked back and forth until she sighed and her body went limp in my arms. And while I paced around the dark house with my daughter sleeping against my chest, something clicked into place—the fight left me and I knew it was time to give up my stool, quit the Pig, and say good-bye to all that glorious violence. I was done with it, retired for more important things like my family.

And so it was. I was still big and menacing—nothing was going to change that. But *I'd* changed—my size and strength were still my most obvious characteristics but no longer my most important ones. I had a whole houseful of wonderfully tough responsibilities that finally had made me into the better man I'd always wanted to be.

I carried Sophia to her crib and covered her with her blanket. Then I turned fully to the brutal work of marriage and fatherhood with the knowledge that on these matters I was soft.

Embracing
the Little Steering Wheel

MANNY HOWARD

nce, years ago, I was engaged in a prolonged game of romantic chicken with an ex-girlfriend. She was married at the time. And she had a child. Not exactly the sport of kings, I'll grant, but sport was what it seemed (at least for a time). Over a period of months we met at the overwrought bar-of-the-moment and passed the time flirting shamelessly, noodling over past liaisons, each waiting for the other to crack under the building sexual tension and make an unambiguous advance.

Not being married, and not having a child, I wasn't aware just how much unhappiness and disappointment must have been compacting within her as she kept washing up into what was clearly—even in the eighties—a pathetically shallow bar scene in order to rekindle long-cold passions.

One evening, though, I was given a peek into the state of her marriage. True to form, I missed the significance of the revelation in her life entirely. Its effects on mine were immediately clear, however. Breaking all the rules we had wordlessly agreed to, about discussing our life outside The Past or The Bar, she began to complain bitterly about her husband. Neither she nor I had ever spoken of her husband or my girlfriend while at The Bar, so naturally I found myself gripped by her tale. If I understood her correctly, her husband (whom I knew and, terrible as it sounds, admired), having found himself on the losing side of a power play at work, was being squeezed mercilessly. The pressure was getting to him, she reported to me; in fact, he had recently started exploding into tears every evening as soon as he returned home. "Before he can take his own tie off," was the way she put it.

I gasped, in naïve horror, imagining what was for me the unimaginable: pressure so intense that it would bring such a proud man so low. She looked at me as though we understood each other completely. "I know," she said, almost yelling now. "I feel like screaming, 'Be a man, would you!'"

My memory of the moment—now a faded victim of the passing time, no question—is that The Bar suddenly fell silent, our conspiracy revealed to all present. The shame of knowing burning my callous heart, I pulled hard on my bottle of beer to hide the resulting rush of emotions and took a quick time-out with the Lord. I entreated, "Lord, I am truly sorry and I humbly repent, but if, in your infinite wisdom, you ever see fit to have me marry, and if my wife ever finds herself in a bar with a puke like me and she shares such intimacies and voices such cruel complaints, please, rather than let me live long enough to discover this betrayal, could you strike me dead where I stand? A stray bullet, maybe, or bad brakes on a mail truck, a lightning bolt, even, I don't care how you do it, just take me, Lord."

The next week I canceled our standing date at The Bar. I did the same the following week. She didn't call to inquire about meeting the third week, and neither did I.

Now, it came to pass that I did marry. Twice. My first marriage was what, these days, is blithely dismissed as a starter marriage. Marred by all manner of conflict, it did not last very long. And although it is entirely unsatisfying to take the unilateral conclusions about any failed marriage seriously, I'll go ahead and suggest that "equality" was the unifying theme around which our most toxic disagreements swirled. We constantly struggled against each other to define ourselves as equal and somehow independent. The marriage itself was, therefore, clumsily distinct from its partners, a wobbly third force around which we were held in a rattling orbit. She felt free to disappear periodically for six weeks at a time, and upon her return I felt justified spending my evenings retaliating in strip clubs and bars. During this time, our wedding vows, never sacrosanct, became merely guidelines—helpful hints. We figured that we were certainly both more sophisticated, more modern, and possibly smarter than whoever had written those optimistic lines. So when the center of our marriage began to collapse, even being unfaithful was merely a symptom of a larger, still unknowable problem.

And for us, the eight-hundred-pound gorilla in the room of our larger, unknowable problem—the issue that neither of us would acknowledge—was the issue of money. Money cleaved us more effectively and efficiently than all other problems either visceral or emotional—and unlike matters of the heart, it split us with an almost instantly recognizable permanence. When it came to sex, when it came to withholding, even when it came to fidelity, we both had the tools necessary to discuss the matter. In fact, we excelled in breathtakingly grisly heart-to-hearts. These conversations (as long as they were not about money) often drew us together, temporarily. When it came to money, though, we each registered (for the purposes of problem solving) as both deaf and dumb. Neither of us, it turned out, trusted me not to fritter away every penny we had, and because this scared us so terribly, we never ever discussed it. The death of love came, then, not so much during the struggle about money, or even about the use of money as a metaphor for equality, but during the relatively humble effort to define (more likely divine) the terms by which our war over money would be waged.

Our own distinct momentum continued to increase as we whirled around our marriage until, one unseasonably warm fall evening, its gravity could no longer hold us.

In my second (and last, if she'll have me) marriage, my wife, Lisa, and I don't war over issues of equality. Granted, we have a new baby daughter (and another child on the way), and at home we struggle, like all new parents, with logistics and other practical matters. But we do not struggle over issues of equality because we are not equal. Lisa is better than I am. Better in what sense? Let me be clear: Lisa makes more money than I do—*much* more money.

I know men who would sooner bitch slap their own mothers than admit that their wives outearn them, especially to the degree that Lisa outearns me. But I don't mind. In fact, most of the time I think our inequality is the best thing that's ever happened to me.

And it would be hard for me to compete with Lisa even if I wanted to. A competitive swimmer from the time she was a child, Lisa had been tapped as Olympic material early on and was expected to win swimming competitions from the ages of five through twenty. She won an athletic scholarship to the University of Georgia, where she swam for the Bulldogs—ranked in the top five at the time. Her events were breaststroke and butterfly—two of the most difficult. It was in this arena that she internalized the competitive ethic and learned to expect success for herself, and—validating all the rosy promises of every booster of children's athletics—Lisa has applied this victorious worldview to business, at which she thrives. In her office her every action is intended to generate more revenue for the company she works for. If she works hard (and she does, always), the company makes more money. The more money Lisa makes for the company, the bigger her bonus. There is a little more nuance to it than this, she assures me. Nonetheless, from my vantage there is a delightful bottom-lineness to her work.

Our marriage would be infinitely more complicated if, like so many people, Lisa hated going to work every morning. But she loves her job. She considers herself lucky to be well compensated for doing what she loves. So do I. That is, I consider myself lucky to do what I love—I just never imagined I'd be well compensated for doing it. Lisa, on the other hand, says she believes that one day I will be the primary breadwinner in the family. I hope to Christ that she is mistaken.

I did try to warn her. When we discovered Lisa was pregnant with our daughter, the first thing I did was to try to talk her out of the idea of marrying me. She was nearly two months pregnant when we took a long walk through the woods in Brooklyn's Prospect Park. As far as I was concerned, it was my responsibility to make plain what she had, for some reason, failed to see. I intended to explain, like any trusted friend would, why I was a very bad person for her to marry.

I make my living, such as it is, writing magazine stories. I explained that I had prospects, sure. I had momentum, or so I thought, on good days. I even believe that there might be a book inside me somewhere. However, during the best year thus far in my career (the one I was afraid to speak about while it was happening for fear that, if I acknowledged it, I would wake up to discover that the year was actually a dream), I had earned exactly 29.6 percent of Lisa's annual take-home pay averaged over the few years we had known each other. I used a calculator to run this equation using her base pay, before her bonus is calculated. I was about to factor in the bonus but thought better of it. No reason to get carried away.

After I explained this to her, we walked through the park in silence for a while. Then we exchanged weak smiles.

"Even if I earned *twice* what I made during that very good year," I continued, "I still wouldn't make *nearly* what you make."

Lisa looked at me. She was sad now, like it was I who had missed something. She said that she didn't care about how little money I made compared with her. She said she'd spent time with men who had reversed the ratio I had just described and that she had never dreamed of marrying them.

"Not even if you were knocked up?" I said with a smirk.

"Not even if I was knocked up," she said, deadly serious.

Standing in the woods, equally elated and terrified, I realized that was it. My careerist caveat emptor, my only argument, gone. Still, I heard myself repeating my litany of fear: Okay, so, just say I'm your husband and you're my wife, and I earn less money than you and that's okay with you—at first. But, eventually you will fantasize about the things we could have, or the experiences we would share if I only made as much money as you do (maybe just half of what you make). Then one day you'll get bored with me.

"Nonsense," she replied.

We were married less than three months later. That was more than a year ago. So far, so good.

Now, in my own defense and in the interest of full disclosure, I should explain here that it's not like she's carrying all the weight in this marriage. No marriage can survive when one person is bringing much more to it than the other, and ours is no different. If Lisa fills the checking account, I stock the fridge.

Yes, I'm that guy. In addition to cooking and shopping (including all diaper runs to the Big Box Store), I regrout the tile work in the bathroom and have been known to install the odd marble mantel piece. I sew buttons. I clean up before the cleaning lady arrives, make sure Debbie, our nanny, has the juice she likes, and I walk the dog. I also gallop off home, up the hill from my office, every afternoon at four-thirty to perform the baby handoff with Debbie. In order to get a full day of work in, I'm usually at my desk each morning by six-thirty.

Even so, not long after our wedding, my position in our marriage became clear to me. One Monday, the one designated day of the week when I stay late at the office—something I had lobbied feverishly for since our girl, Heath, was born—while enthusiastically engaged in a petty squabble over whether I was actually going to get to stay on at the office, I realized Lisa had just negotiated me into a hopeless, losing position. To my horror, in the middle of the heated phone call, I understood that my wife was in the process of rearranging the terms of the entire argument to support her strongly held view that her way, and only her way, would yield what she, somewhat predictably, rejoices in calling a "win-win." I listened in wonder as she decimated the few pockets of resistance that remained of my original argument, and later, as I plodded up the hill in the summer swelter with the dog panting along behind me, I tried to recall how many of our arguments had ended this way. Standing at the curb, waiting for an overly long traffic light to change, I was appalled by the very real possibility that, in all likelihood, every last one had.

In my first marriage, with its core in perpetual meltdown, a peripheral disagreement like this would often appear to be cataclysmic. But now, with Lisa, this squabble could not be reasonably extrapolated to indicate the health or success of our union. Lisa was not probing it for resistance or resilience, to reassure herself that her partner was a worthy adversary. In this moment of clarity I felt free to lose not only this argument but also all of our future arguments, knowing that doing so would have no effect on Lisa's commitment to me or our marriage (might, indeed, strengthen it). What was the point, I concluded, in fighting to maintain the illusion of equality when giving in was such a painless alternative?

In my mind's eye I saw myself as I had always behaved in the past, trying to stay in control—maneuvering furiously to guide the relationship along the course I felt it should follow. But this marriage clearly was not under my control. I could try to maneuver it, but it wouldn't do any good, because my hands were white-knuckling a child-sized steering wheel made of yellow plastic. I had no brakes, no accelerator. I did have a horn, though. It was made of red plastic, and embossed on its center were the words FISHER PRICE.

And thus was inaugurated the parable of the Little Steering

Wheel. It's the best way I know to reveal my identity as husband to Lisa. And it usually doesn't bother me in the least that I'm in this position.

Occasionally, though, I wonder. Recently I confided over coffee to a friend, Maud, that being married to a woman who made more money than I did bothered me much less than I had anticipated. But I did worry that this was, in large part, because I did not sense that Lisa had a problem with being married to a man who did not earn as much, or more, than she did. I told Maud that I understood clearly that this meant I was still taking cues from Lisa, reacting, looking for signs of agitation. Rotating my coffee cup on its chunky saucer, I said, repeating my litany of fear once again, that this means the moment it bothers her it will start to trouble me. "What do you think *that* means?" I whined.

Maud summarily dismissed my concerns. "C'mon," she said. "I know plenty of couples where She makes more than He does." And then she launched into what seemed to me a substantial digression, explaining that one of the main reasons she thought her current boyfriend was The One was because he was not threatened by her substantial professional successes and this was because he was a schoolteacher and therefore not part of her work world. Reason number two, she said, was that because he was a schoolteacher he could pack up and move to Paris or one of a half dozen cities in Italy, or *somewhere,* if that's what she decided she wanted to do, without him worrying—not overly, anyway—about his career.

I flirted with the idea of inquiring whether Maud's boyfriend— or, for that matter, his students—knew of her presumptions about being able to yank him out of class midsemester so that she might have some company on her extended jaunts abroad. But instead I asked her to describe the specific qualities her boyfriend possessed that made him The One, where other men, not a few of whom had been her peers at work, had fallen short.

During her lengthy soliloquy she detailed her boyfriend's finest qualities. She said, first, that he was kind, and that "no one has ever kissed me like he does" (which I, mistakenly, took to be a euphemism). She added that he knew when he was being needlessly mean to her and could stop on a dime. (This is indeed a very impressive quality. After countless years with various therapists, I am only occasionally capable of recognizing when I am about to be needlessly mean, at which point I sometimes am able to jump up and take the dog for a walk. More typically, I am able to offer a sincere apology shortly after the fact without an excuse or a blame-deflecting explanation.)

Even as I was starting to get a pretty good feeling about Maud's boyfriend, the fine hairs in my inner ear detected that the analysis was beginning to shift. The shift started, if not innocently, then certainly banally enough, with her modernist rejection of romantic love, ergo: "I never believed that there is only One Special Man, it's all about Timing."

From there it moved seamlessly and familiarly to a description of how conveniently he fit into Maud's life. And ultimately, her explanation for the synchronicity and efficiency of their relationship fell solidly upon the disparity in their incomes and, more to the point, the *power* that this dynamic imbued her with.

I grinned fiercely. Nodding and blinking in agreement, hoping that, if I could not suppress the nervous tic in my left eye, then all the motion would at least disguise it. Later, much later it seemed, I walked away from the diner, haunted by the image of Maud's boyfriend, The One, a clearly adoring, sensually attuned, respectful, and responsible man crouched inside of her Louis Vuitton carry-on.

Steve, one of the guys I share an office with (whose wife is fabulously wealthy), told me he thinks that, behind my back, people talk about the fact that Lisa makes more money than I do. He says it is probably one of the primary descriptors that even my closest friends, and possibly family, employ while engaged in the most idle, even well-meaning conversations about me. He says it does not matter that, these days, there are many men in my position (here, thinking of his own wealthy wife, I wonder why he does not describe this as "our position"); people still think it's noteworthy, that it affects people's impressions of me and even of my work. In fact, he asserts, the same way people still react to miscegenation when they see it on the street (and he insists that they do), as soon as people discover that your wife earns more than you, you are both implicated as players in some vaguely scandalous subculture.

I stifle the self-protective urge to kick him around the office and, instead, ask him why he thinks this is true. He says he doesn't know the reason, he just knows it's true. He then asks me if, deep down, I don't feel in some way diminished ("you know, as a man") by the fiscal facts of my marriage.

After a considerable pause, I tell him that, since Lisa and I were both many years into our careers when we were married, we just took the income disparity as one of the many differences—distinctions rather—between us and proceeded from there. For good measure I added that Lisa doesn't seem to mind. Steve screwed up his face in disbelief.

Then he smiled and told me that for the first time since he and his wife have been married he will probably make more money than she will this year. Although he admits this added money does nearly nothing to affect their enormous net worth, he believes his wife is even more relieved than he is about him finally becoming the top wage earner between them. And, he adds, he's plenty relieved.

Clearly, Steve is having some trouble embracing the Little Steering Wheel.

And I'm guessing he's not alone. No doubt there are plenty of husbands in my position who will wake up one morning gripped with fear by the realization that they have been given the Little Steering Wheel to play with. Wailing inaudibly, protesting the fading image of themselves as the men they want to be, they'll likely dissolve in a panic, then, turning to their wives and, as though once blind and seeing for the first time, notice that she has the chrome-plated, molded chain steering wheel and is, and always has been, directing the course of their relationship using only her index finger.

For now, I'm at peace with my Little Steering Wheel. Will the time come, someday, when I start to feel more like Steve? When I'll want to be the one driving the big rig while my wife sits in the passenger seat, gazing at me adoringly? Sure, maybe.

But more than that, will the day ever come when Lisa gets fed up with my inferior earning status, gazes at me with contempt, and thinks, *Be a man, would you!*

"Out of the deep have I called unto thee, O Lord, hear my voice. Let thine ears consider well the voice of my complaint . . ."

PART IV

All I Need

I don't need anything except this [ashtray] and that's it, and that's the only thing I need. . . . Just this ashtray. And this paddle game. The ashtray and the paddle game, and that's all I need. And this remote control. The ashtray, the paddle game, and the remote control, and that's all I need.

—*Steve Martin in* The Jerk

It is not good that the man should be alone.

—*Genesis 2.18*

Why Men Lie (and Always Will)

Vince Passaro

efore I pulled my Roberto Duran, before I moved out, before I lost the ability to go forward in what had been a long and rich and difficult and painful and profoundly rewarding marriage with three great children—before I lost the strength and the desire, to put the matter more precisely, to try to be the person I was supposed to be and hide the one I'd become, I asked my wife: "Why do men lie so much?" I can see now that the long pondering I'd been doing on the subject of men and lies was a circling-the-airport approach to where I might land, which was my own conscience.

"Your sperm makes you evil," my wife said. "It does something to your minds."

"No, seriously," I said.

"Because you're all cowards," she said.

"That's a little *too* serious," I said. "Do you have anything in between those two?"

"In between the two," she said, "is just a charred landscape."

・　　　・　　　・

There are things that everyone almost always lies about (cheating, stealing, sex), there are things that women almost always lie about (food, money, orgasms), and then there is the rest of life, which generally comprises what men tend to lie about. A female friend says of the men she's known: "Are its lips moving? Then it's lying."

I'm talking about the issue later at a party with a fellow I've met (during this period I talked about it a lot with many people—friends, acquaintances, and people, like this guy, that I'd just met); he plays poker, sometimes for a living, other times merely competitively—this is very high-stakes poker. Average annual American college-grad salaries frequently rest on the table. Games can go on for more than twenty-four hours. Someday, it's my guess, he'll get close to a woman who doesn't want him to play this kind of poker or, in fact, since this is the only kind of poker that he's interested in, any poker at all. He'll promise not to, and then he'll join the eternal cycle.

"Men pretty much always lie to avoid conflict, argument, the airing of unpleasant truths," he says, in a jovial, unmarried way. "It's been my impression that both parties are pleased with the outcome."

"Kind of like our attitude toward Homeland Security and the Patriot Act," I say.

"Exactly. The less we know the better. The media understand this perfectly, that's why they tell us so little. And we're grateful. Like our girlfriends are."

He's half right: to avoid unpleasantness is one reason we lie, a frequent reason, but not "pretty much always" the reason. Another woman, married, hearing the topic, says, "You have to talk to my husband. He's Italian."

She means native-born, from-Italy Italian. "That's a whole different league," I say. "We can't even begin to compete."

"I know," she says. "Isn't it incredible? I asked him once, why do you lie *all* the time? Always? Why do you feel the need to do that? And he told me, 'Because then it feels like I've gotten away with something. It's a kind of power.'"

That is it, of course, in a nutshell. It is a struggle for power. If we choose to win by brute force, we go to jail. We cannot (some of us) allow ourselves to lose, but our partners frequently are relentless—they will never, ever surrender. Therefore we lie.

•   •   •

"You're a man, you lie because you don't want to get caught," a male friend of mine says. This is my wife's "coward" theory put plain. Questions such as why we have to avoid being "caught," or who the "catcher" is, or, most pressing in the long run, how the hell she got appointed to that position, don't need to be answered. The answer, like Chomsky's syntax, seems to be built structurally into our brains.

My friend is a writer, fairly successful, which, in that field, isn't saying much. "You lie because you don't want the lecture, the dirty look, the new entry in a catalogue of never forgotten betrayals"—he goes into an imitation-girlfriend voice—" 'This is just like when I needed you that time when I was using *your* car and it wouldn't start and they were going to tow me and you were out at *that* bar with your friend . . . or *whoever it was.*' " My friend and I ourselves are in a bar for this conversation. He lights a cigarette, though technically speaking he's "not smoking" right now.

He says, "Now you need a translation. 'Your car' means even though she had it, it was your problem, which is as it should be, and very satisfying too—because one of the underlying struggles that will last until the very final moments of the relationship and even slightly beyond is whether she ever actually ought to face a crisis *alone.* I mean, what's the point of enduring a man in your life if he's not willing to be called in like an EMS driver every time something goes wrong?

"And 'that bar' means a place utterly bereft of value or interest to any *decent* member of the human species except you, an utterly squalid spot on the map of your life, to which only your most depraved and disreputable self is ever drawn.

"Now, the highly nuanced 'whoever'—this part is really ominous.

It means that *if* you were really out at a bar with a friend when you could just as well have been in the apartment and ready to take her call, *when she was going to be towed for God's sake, if* you're actually *that kind of man,* then you might just as well have been with a woman too. Because nothing about you is respectable or trustworthy at that point." He shoots the plume of smoke luxuriously toward the glittering bottles lined before the mirrors. "And you want to say, 'I didn't have to tell you I was at the bar with the friend—and if I had been at a bar with a woman, honey baby, believe me, I wouldn't have told you I was at a bar at all.'"

For my part, I can see the moment precisely in my mind's eye, the scales of justice weighing the two sides of the conversation. I say, "To which she would reply, 'So you want some kind of *credit* for telling the truth?'"

"Exactly," my friend says. "But of course it wasn't credit you wanted; you just wanted her to see the logic behind your telling of the truth, the natural outcome of that narrative. And yeah, you did want slightly to remind her that the truth is just an option: that fact is your final card. Possibly they lie as much as we do: the difference is that most of the time, unless they're sleeping with someone, we don't give a shit what they've been doing, spending, seeing, hearing, being tempted by, when we're not together. Aren't we awful?"

"Are you going to report we had a drink tonight?" I ask him.

"Shit no," he says. On his way to the apartment he's sharing with his girlfriend, he says, he'll pick up some mints, and maybe some flowers or a bottle of wine.

"What happens when you tell the truth," he says, "is that now this incident of you being at the bar, which you sanitized to the point of what you thought would be innocence, just a matter of three beers, some talk, a handshake, a slight buzz, this historic betrayal actually can be called upon at a moment's notice, for *years,* long after you've forgotten about it and long after you would think it had any moral weight whatsoever, simply to wipe out whatever argument you might be making in favor of yourself and your priorities at the present moment. So guess what—you lie. They teach you to lie."

I tell him that not all women are like that; that not all women need to take such a strong position on what their man does with his time or with whom.

"Yeah?" he says. "That's a very interesting theory. That would mean there are some women who don't really care if you have a job or make any money or occasionally have meaningless ego-boosting affairs either. I just haven't met any yet."

Truth be told, some of this man's relationships have been pretty shallow, and he always arranges his life so he's in just this sort of trouble, or worse. We all know from therapy that he is the true architect of his psychic circumstances. But he's lived with this woman for almost two years, and I happen to know that he actually loves her and she actually loves him. I like her, she's nice, and she's fundamentally kind. What he's talking about, essentially, is that word, *power*. And in the power struggles that every relationship goes through, the terrain fought upon is frequently one of moral authority. In each relationship we invest the most significant parts of our lives—sex, money, loyalty, social desirability, affection, humor, kindness—with precise moral values, and when we've come to some fluid agreement about the values assigned to each, we commence adding up. Men know that women almost always are ahead in this valuation; we are, generally speaking, comfortable with the idea. Even back when men were invariably the major earners and were allowed to act like lords of the manor, the women's suffering gave them a certain moral standing. Thus it was the same in our parents' marriages most of the time, to the degree those marriages lasted; and when they didn't it was even more severe an imbalance in the woman's favor—as children, many of us *knew* our fathers were assholes—and so this state of moral disparity seems fairly natural to us. Of course, now most women have jobs; many earn as much or more than their mates; we can't take on the airs of a couple of generations ago; our valuation in the power equation has fallen significantly, even though on the whole our behavior has improved. My friend's point is that, without any special handicap or privileges, in the struggle for moral legitimacy, we have to lie even to stay close.

. . .

The social human being lies about all kinds of things for all kinds of reasons. The phenomenon has been widely studied and analyzed, and books on it are published all the time: I look up books on lies and lying in the database at the bookstore, a search limited to books issued over the prior six months: eighteen titles. The definitive philosophical investigation is by Sisela Bok, called *On Lying,* in its umpteenth edition. She examines lying for every reason but the main one: maintaining a workable sexually intimate relationship with another human being. What interests me, increasingly, is not the relatively clear-cut world of lies we tell for social purposes or political purposes or to protect ourselves from tyranny or even to fend off shame and retribution; I am most intrigued by the seeming necessity of the mild and constant coloration of the world that men do in order to get along with women, in order to make the world as we understand it palatable and understandable to them.

For instance: say you're a man, and you run into an old acquaintance on the street and you end up talking and joking around for twenty-five minutes. This throws off a tight schedule of errands and later commitments, so you cut off one errand and shorten up on another and you're still behind by fifteen minutes, so you make up some reason for it, even though you're not really asked to do so— "You should have seen the line at the produce market!" or "It took them fifteen minutes to find my shirts"—because you'd feel foolish, and you'd probably be chided (hard, should the later commitments be fraught enough with some kind of social tension, or if there are small children that need to change hands) if you simply reported that, guess what, I ran into so-and-so and we ended up talking for twenty-five minutes. So-and-so is relatively insignificant in your life and you won't see him or think of him again in all likelihood for six months, so why did you waste so much valuable time chatting him up? Wouldn't five or seven minutes have done just as well, in the economy of fellowship laid out to acquaintances of that kind? And you peel back the outer skins of your own motives and you find that you were in good spirits and so was the acquaintance and you managed to make each other feel slightly more vital and significant in the flow of world events that day. You were given an opportunity to stage a production, outside the bakery-café, and the play was the current version of the story of your life. It actually interests you to do that. On a given day like the one I've imagined, I doubt any man, put on the spot, could possibly explain such a minor transaction in the economy of his ego in a way that would make it easily comprehensible to a woman.

Given, of course, that when a woman is waiting for a man to run some errands, there is already established a certain moral platform for her expectations: that he will screw up somehow, that he will get the wrong things or come back late or blow some engagement he has promised to go on with her *after* he has run his errands, something that she knows, in the depths of her heart, he doesn't want to do and that he shall try to find some way to get out of, even up to the final moment. She knows that what he wants to do is hang around on the couch and read magazines or watch movies and not even speak for the remainder of the day—that's what he really wants to do, and she doesn't want that to happen. The maneuvering begins. Or it never ends.

•   •   •

My wife and I had a dog, years ago, and we gave the dog to my mother-in-law when a time came in which we couldn't keep it anymore. It was a male dog, a dog whose entire being screamed out "Get me fixed." We didn't fix him, though, seemingly out of laziness but really because we liked him the way he was—sweet but totally out of control. My wife especially loved him; he signified everything she actually likes about men—he was relentlessly exuberant and strong, and in his tremendous eagerness to get to *the next thing* he used literally to pull her over when she was walking him. The crucial point was that she was able to enjoy his generally compulsive, single-minded, uncooperative (and relentlessly horny) nature because she associated him with none of the disappointed social expectations or emotional pain that she associated with actual male humans, such as me. I envied him, frankly.

And in my mother-in-law's house was a large and extremely comfortable feather-cushioned sofa, which was so positioned that you could see it as you came downstairs from the bedrooms toward the living room, reflected in an ornate entryway mirror below you, around a wall that divided the stairway from the living room. Now, the dog, who was not supposed to lie on the sofa, because he shed and he didn't always smell that good, didn't know the sofa could be seen from above and beyond the wall. And my mother-in-law would put folding hors-d'oeuvres tables and other such items on the sofa at night to keep him off it; but during the day, if no one was in the living room, he had free reign. And we used to come down the stairs and watch in that perfectly positioned mirror as the dog, hearing us come, would slide quietly off the soft cushions and get himself swiftly into a resting posture on the floor. By the time we'd get to the bottom of the stairs and turn into the living room, his eyes would be closed and he would be pretending to be asleep. I never knew of another dog that would *pretend* to be asleep. I know just how he felt. When in doubt, when trouble's a-brewin', when you think you might get caught: lie.

•   •   •

I ask another friend, a successful editor, about lying. I tell him, "I'm not talking about the things everyone lies about because you absolutely must lie about them. I'm talking about the daily stuff, painting the sky all pink and blue." 'All those pretty lies,' as the Joni Mitchell song puts it. He's young, and recently wed to his longtime girlfriend.

"Oh, man," he says. "I don't want to talk about that."

"Why not?" I say.

" 'Cause I'm not sure I want to share this stuff with anyone who's not a full-time psychiatrist," he says. Then, after a significant pause, he gets to the real point: "And because I'm not sure I want to give up my trade secrets—if I put them out there, the world might become an imbalanced place."

One of the theories that emerges as I discuss this with other men is that it all begins with Mom. Doesn't everything? A boy loves his mother, but he reaches a certain age, and he becomes, among other things, sexual—chaotically and overwhelmingly so. His father knows well enough to steer clear of any area where this subject might be touched upon; but his mother doesn't, so the boy must start lying to her, lying essentially about who he is, because the world he has come to inhabit is simply not translatable into the terms of the relationship he has with her, or into the terms established by her daily expectations, and none of these terms are negotiable as far as he can see.

"I remember the day I began the lie," an executive friend tells me. "And it really is all the same lie, your whole life long. It was the day my copy of *The Godfather* moved from the bookshelf to under my bed. That was the day I started lying to my mother. It changed the valences. Remember page twenty-seven, with Sonny at the wedding?"

"I think it was page twenty-eight," I say.

This same man reveals that whenever he tells his wife about female colleagues, particularly any female he has had lunch with, his wife eventually will inquire about the woman's age (albeit as subtly as she can). "I always add ten years to the estimate," he says. "It keeps the conversation clear."

·   ·   ·

In Joseph Conrad's *Heart of Darkness* there is a seemingly gratuitous little misogynistic aside, in which the narrator, Marlow, before leaving for the ugly colonial world of the Belgian Congo, visits with his aunt, who lives in "the white, sepulchral city" as he calls Brussels, who goes on at enthusiastic length about what is, essentially, the rape of central Africa for European profit. The aunt believes the hype, that this colonization is a great and civilizing enterprise. Marlow comments dryly, "It's queer how out of touch with truth women are! They live in a world of their own. . . . It is too beautiful altogether, and if they were to set it up it would go to pieces before the first sunset." At the end of the book, when a very damaged Marlow returns to Europe, having looked into the nightmare world of the ivory trader Kurtz, this earlier scene makes full sense. Kurtz had gone off to Africa full of lofty ideals; instead of an agent of civilization he became a brutal tyrant, and now he is dead. Marlow visits Kurtz's fiancée, who remembers Kurtz in rosy and heroic terms; she remembers his magnificent ideas for the civilization of Africa, which he wrote out at length, only later to scrawl across the pages, never seen by her, the rather comprehensive phrase "Exterminate the brutes!" She asks Marlow about Kurtz's last words. Marlow cannot tell her that in actuality they were "The horror! The horror!"—nor can he begin to render the kinds of horror that the words refer to. So he tells her that Kurtz's last words were her name. "It seemed to me," he says, after the lie, "that the house would collapse before I could escape, that the heavens would fall upon my head. But nothing happened. The heavens do not fall for such a trifle."

·   ·   ·

When men cease to be boys, when we pass for the first time beyond the moral circle of our mothers' kingdoms into new worlds of our own making, into what we soon think of as the "real" world, we commence a psychological journey similar to Marlow's; we look into the darkness of our own developing willfulness, our sexuality, our ambition, our egos. In order to succeed as men, in the terms that our particular civilization has established, we have to build these things up and constantly strengthen them. This task feels (and always will feel) in some essential way like an immoral activity, and one that we should undertake largely in secret: from our families, for fear of being identified as alien and repulsive, and to a lesser degree from our friends, for fear of being too sharply cut down to size in what turns out to be a highly competitive mission.

Women wonder, often out loud, about the male ego, about its outlandish size and its callous assumptions. Well, here's an announcement that I'll deny in the morning: it's even worse than you think; that's why we try to hide a lot of it from you. And here's something else, which I'll deny even before the morning: when you discover a man has lied to you about something, what he then "admits" to you as the truth will—at least in a few crucial respects—also be a lie. The full truth, the whole thing, almost never feels to us like a viable option.

On Loneliness, Comfort, and Being a Savage

ANTHONY SWOFFORD

or three nights I slept alone on the hardwood floor in the living room of my new apartment. In a few weeks I'd turn thirty-three. My scant belongings were en route from another state. It was not planned that I would sleep on the hardwood floor for three nights. It was planned that in a perfect ballet movement of interstate transfer I would fly down and meet the movers just as they pulled their truck into my new neighborhood, but such are the exigencies of the open road that my California King bed, couch, dining room table and chairs, two desks, three wardrobe boxes, seven bookshelves, thirty-four boxes of books, and my maternal grandfather's 1939 Zenith radio were in a trailer on the roadside in southern Oregon, waiting for a new S-cam—something, I was told, that had to do with the brakes, something that would be "no big deal if I wasn't driving into fucking California," the driver informed me.

Though I was happy to know that California abided by strict rules concerning the brakes on eighteen-wheelers, vehicles responsible for something like 75 percent of highway fatalities, the accusatory nature of his voice caused me further anxiety over moving to California—a state attempting to get rid of its governor, a state that charged sales tax, a state that had been for many years of my life the place where I failed at both love and work. I considered what I owned in the back of that dusty trailer and decided that I should get rid of it all and live again as I once had during my savage younger years in the Marine Corps, with all of my belongings in a sea bag and a rucksack. I contemplated telling the driver to dump my stuff at the Goodwill in Ashland, that he could take the tax credit and catch a few plays and we'd call it even. But I did not.

The afternoon of my first night on the hardwood floor I'd stolen a worn paperback copy of *The Great Gatsby* from an acquaintance's roommate's bookshelf. It was the copy with the thrilling and apocalyptic cover art by Francis Cugat. I must state that in the past people have stolen books from me, including this same paperback edition of *Gatsby*. The day prior I'd decided that I needed to reread *Gatsby*, which I hadn't read since college. I tried two bookstores, but the first was closed and the second only had one Fitzgerald title on offer, *The Crack-Up*, which I purchased.

I'd once stolen this book from my former parents-in-law. (It is likely that while I write this sentence they are still my parents-in-law and that the Dissolution of Marriage petition I recently filed, amicably, with my wife, has not yet been signed by an honorable judge, but well before publication date she will be my former wife and her parents will be my former parents-in-law. These legal proceedings will not affect my love and fondness for any of those involved.) My wife and I were helping her parents pack their house in Chicago's Hyde Park, a home they'd lived in for over thirty years. Busy at the task of packing the third-floor library, I ran across *The Crack-Up* and read from it. From the title essay I memorized these sentences: "The test of a first-rate intelligence is the ability to hold two opposed ideas in the mind at the same time, and still retain the ability to function. One should, for example, be able to see that things are hopeless and yet be determined to make them otherwise." From the section called "The Note-books" I memorized this: "Women are fragile that way. You do something to them at certain times and literally nothing can ever change what you've done." So there was no real need for me to buy the book; I knew these important sentences by heart, and my stolen copy was in one of the boxes sitting in a trailer alongside the dusty southern Oregon highway. But I had no idea when that truck might arrive, and I had plans to return that copy to my in-laws, just as I intend someday to return my new copy of *Gatsby* to my acquaintance's roommate.

On the hardwood floor of my apartment in Oakland, California, I read *Gatsby*. Jay Gatsby might be one of literature's lonelier men, and so too might Nick Carraway, the man who sings Gatsby's song. Nick is not fond of any of the people he surrounds himself with, the people he allows to surround him in a mob of money and violence. He's a man after a story, sure, but he's also alone in that rented cottage, and the Toms and Daisys and Gatsbys of the world let him be less alone, if only for a while, if only as long as the drink and the story pour from the deep fountains at Gatsby's mansion. Nick is not only a narrator, he is a writer, meaning he is a rascal who will steal from the misery of others and use that cheap-gotten misery for his own work—and if he has worked hard and has written a good enough book, he will receive praise and fame and profit, in small doses. The writer will happily invite people into his life who will perform their misery for him. He will also invite people who will offer the illusion of stopping the loneliness.

I have allowed people into my life for the sole purpose that they might make me feel less alone. Once this person was a fellow student, a young man who wrote poetry and chased women. From here on out I will call him the Hobbyist. The Hobbyist often invited himself to stay at my apartment because, at the age of thirty, he lived with his mother, and in the "chasing women" field living with your mother at the age of thirty rarely counts as points to the good. Probably in the poetry field this odd practice is also a hindrance, but maybe not, considering the numerous poems written about mothers.

The Hobbyist appeared at my apartment one Friday night just as my girlfriend and I were heading out to dinner. I told him we would meet him later, at a bar downtown with jazz after midnight.

My girlfriend and I ate sushi and drank sake, and at the end of the meal we were both rather or very drunk. On the short walk to the jazz bar I pulled her into an alley, where we committed acts that are illegal in public and even in the comfort of your own home in some southern states. But we were not arrested.

The upstairs club was packed with young people whose parents had money. My money was my own, made by hard days of work at a warehouse. Hard nights of work, rather. Or hard *half*-nights of work for an entire night of pay, the warehouse being union. These young people whose parents had money reminded me that my parents did not and had never. My father was and still is the man who owns a few Jaguars or Corvettes because they make him feel good. This does not mean he can afford the cars or that two Jaguars is the wisest use of his money. My father has decided that when he hits retirement age he will attempt to become a patient at one of our country's Old Soldiers Homes. I imagine he hatched this plan after returning home from Vietnam, afflicted with the combat veteran's hopelessness and doom and tendency toward self-destructive behavior. And if you're going to end up in the Old Soldiers Home, fuck all and spend your last ounce of money on cars and pussy.

At the time of which I write I was still young enough, twenty-five, to be attached to a false romantic vision of my family's wealth and carriage. I was also a fantasist, one who lives inside of his fantasies. But there was always the possibility that my father had been hoarding money away that he would deliver to me when I reached the age of thirty, and at every family reunion the Francis Scott Key argument erupted, with an aunt by marriage claiming the relation was a lie and all the Swofford-cum-Key blood ready to remove her scalp with a rusty pair of hedge clippers. I was with them on this, but my interest in the matter had nothing to do with the ever-in-peril "Star-Spangled Banner." For me, this bloodline proved true would link my DNA to Francis Scott Fitzgerald. But I was the only one who gave the writer any purchase on the Swofford genes.

Because of reading novels and Shakespeare I'd been convinced that one sure way to impress a woman was to pretend to come from money or a famous bloodline. Not until I became a writer, perhaps not until I finished my first book and realized that I could create something of value on my own, did I drop this poisonous notion. Now I do not care about the possibility of being related to Francis Scott Key or F. Scott Fitzgerald, and I have some real money and no use for it.

Back at the jazz club, scale is important. The club was in Sacramento, California, and the money and the beauty must be weighed against this locale. Also, it is likely that few of the patrons' parents had any real money, but because mine had none, I assumed theirs did. This is a caustic assumption I learned from my mother, the source of my life but also of much of my past pessimism, God please bless the woman. Her pessimism was the daughter of a frightening hatred of affluence, education, and success. She bypassed these possibilities in her own life in order to marry my father, a poor southern boy in the Air Force, and I sometimes think she secretly hated him because of this. I should state that at around the age of twenty-eight, shortly after my older brother died, I realized what a pessimist my mother was and also her hatred of affluence, education, and success, and I also noted what a waste pessimism is, in the end. I renounced pessimism for life. But anyway, I did not like these strangers I'd decided to surround myself with this certain evening in a jazz club in Sacramento.

My girlfriend was an international student studying ESL. She was Japanese, a butcher's daughter, and her parents had real money. They paid her tuition and her rent, bought her a car, and sent her four thousand dollars a month spending money. Sometimes I disliked her for the ease of her lifestyle. When we met she'd been living with a born-again Christian family in the rural area of Sacramento known as Rio Linda. She was not a virgin, she told me, but she wished she could be again in order to erase that singular greatest sin. But shortly I convinced her that I could born-her-again better, and in bed: no river, no holy water, just some good old-fashioned fucking, and I stole her away from the tyrannical grips of an unforgiving Jesus. I am not proud of this, but I enjoyed it—and the subsequent years of accrued sexual rewards. However many seconds this counts against me in the heaven-versus-hell race, I will accept them.

My girlfriend refused to purchase alcohol with the money her parents sent her. I respected this decision and always paid our bar tabs, and anyway, as a Ugandan friend of mine once offered, using, he said, the Wisdom of the Bush, "Money spent on alcohol and drugs is not money, never was money, it is simply some paper you once held that magically turned to alcohol and drugs." He also shared with me one of the best sex tricks on earth, but I swore silence on the issue.

I found a table for three, left my girlfriend there, and battled my way toward the bar. The amateur quartet tried its best at a Monk composition, "Mysterioso." The Beautiful and the Damned were everywhere. Many of the girls carried augmented breasts on their chests and walked as though they were balancing pails of scalding water rather than closed satchels of flesh. If the breasts weren't augmented, the women had spent the extra money on the type of bra that would create this ten-thousand-dollar illusion while restricting blood flow to the nipples and the toes. It was January, and most of these women had striking and abnormal tans. Their teeth were white and they smiled. The young men were brawny and looked certain of themselves and the likelihood that in the future they would drive large European sedans and own numerous vacation homes. Considering it now, it's possible that my dislike of these people was also based on their youth and the promise that youth owns. I was only twenty-five, but I was an old man. A few years earlier I'd gone to war, I had little money to my name, and the decades in front of me—only a few, I was certain—looked less like a Field of Wonder than a minefield I'd once known in southern Kuwait.

At the bar I ordered three gin and tonics. I'd not yet seen the Hobbyist, but I knew that once I bought him a drink he'd appear posthaste. When it was his turn for a round, he'd disappear just as remarkably.

(From London, where I am revising this essay and working on my novel, I've checked my voice mail to discover that my former wife left me a message letting me know that she is now my former wife. This information arrived at her house via a postcard from the Multnomah County Courthouse in Portland, Oregon. Now her parents are my former parents-in-law. When I return to the States and collect my mail from the Oakland post office I will receive a similar postcard. This news makes me ill. I am alone in London. I vomit into the bathtub. I have left my hotel only to eat [fish and chips, falafel and hummus, chicken vindaloo, for five straight days] and buy the newspapers [*The Guardian* and the *Daily Mirror, The Sunday Times,* and *The Sun* for the pictures of *babes,* as their advert states]. When I return, I will be alone in Oakland. Such are the exigencies of the open road.)

Back at the table in the jazz club the Hobbyist had his arm around my girlfriend. I found this troubling but not actionable. Cigar smoke thickened the air. He spoke into her ear, but I could not hear what he was saying. I'd never really trusted the guy, but I'd never *not* trusted him. He was a hobbyist poet, and he lived on his mother's money, and his talent was minimal at best, as it would remain, but he'd never harmed me. He was lazy, the only truly detestable trait in a writer. Let your writer friends be thieves and cheats and cuckolds and drunks and pill poppers, let them curse God and Devil both, let them hate the masses and the individuals, let them be vain and petty brutes, let them sleep with their neighbors' wives (but never yours)—but never let your writer friends be lazy. If they are lazy, leave them to die on their own scorched islands.

The lazy Hobbyist accepted the drink and removed his arm from my girlfriend's shoulder. I realized she needed water, not gin, so I headed to the bar for a bottle of seltzer. At the bar I ran into an acquaintance from high school. He bought me a drink and we spoke briefly about his lucrative job in technology. When I returned my girlfriend was passed out, and the Hobbyist's hand was down her skirt. At first I did not recognize what I was seeing, and then I figured it out. I broke the bottle of seltzer against the table, and the explosion of glass and carbonated water woke my girlfriend from her deep, boozy sleep. The Hobbyist's hand remained down her skirt. With her eyes she followed the forearm up the arm to the shoulder, to the face, and she looked astonished and confused when she realized that the hand did not belong to me. I realized that his molester's hand was swimming in the detritus of our alley lovemaking session. And then I proceeded to beat him with such violence and precision that not a single onlooker protested, but rather the crowd was in awe of my vigor and care. I beat his face, mainly, and his nose and lips and eye sockets were bleeding. My fists ached with the force of the blows. He cried out my name and asked me to please stop, and my girlfriend pleaded with me to stop, but I continued. Over the shouts of the onlookers, "He's going to kill him!" "That motherfucker is finished up!" I heard the quartet hard at work on Monk's "Epistrophy." I grabbed the jagged, broken neck of the water bottle, and for one quick moment I considered stabbing him with it. I pictured myself in jail and dropped the bottle. I landed one last solid blow against his hobbyist nose. I picked my girlfriend up and threw her over my shoulder and made my way out of the bar. I was a savage, and I knew it, and I was proud.

Back at my apartment I put my girlfriend in a bath and washed my hands in the sink. She cried for a long time, apologizing, and I told her she had nothing to be sorry about. The fact that the Hobbyist had made her suffer mentally after assaulting her made me feel good about how thoroughly I'd beaten him. I was with this woman for a few more years, but we never spoke about the events at the jazz bar. It was not important. What was important was that prior to arriving at the bar we'd eaten good sushi, put on a sake buzz, and then had sex in an alley, and that we loved each other.

I am in London now, for a working holiday. My belongings finally arrived in Oakland, bed included. The night before traveling I slept a good night's sleep alone in my comfortable bed and finished *Gatsby*. On the plane, traveling in business, I slammed three glasses of champagne, swallowed a Valium, and read *The Crack-Up*. Today I will cross the street to Hyde Park and read it again. My hotel room is small and cheap, sixty-five pounds a night, nothing like Fitzgerald would have let. I can afford a room that would cost ten times what I'm paying, but then I would be comfortable. As it is, the room is stuffy, the bed is a single, I am writing on a cramped bureau. Comfort is cheap, I have discovered. And loneliness, while necessary, is horribly expensive.

The Hole in the Window:
A View of Divorce

ROBERT SKATES

y landlord, Francis Lavallee, was a pain in the ass, a little buzz saw of a man with curly salt-and-pepper hair above a meticulously trimmed white mustache. Francis drove a golf cart to his properties along Goose Bay and treated everyone like an employee. One morning in early June he hammered on my door. He was wearing an orange tank top, white tennis shorts, and orange-striped socks, and his eyes were pink and rabbity as he explained he had bad news. I let him in and we sat on my porch overlooking the lake and he began to spill his heart. After thirty some-odd years and a flock of grandchildren, his wife was leaving him for a younger man. It was, to say the least, an awkward half hour. We were in no way friends, but obviously the guy needed to talk to someone. I listened and nodded and made every gesture of sympathy. Finally, when he was done telling me his sorrows, he informed me that I was evicted and that he wanted me out by the end of the month.

It was my guess then and now that Francis himself wanted to move into my camp for the short Vermont summer. But only two weeks earlier he'd offered me a new lease over the phone. So I told him I was sorry about his divorce, but this was business, and I was going to look into my rights. Then I walked him outside and stuck out my hand for him to shake. He glared down at it a long moment, growled *Goddammit,* and then wheeled and marched off to his golf cart and sped down the road.

.   .   .

Vermont law stated that I could not be evicted without two months' written notice. The next day I knocked on Francis's door and stepped back and said I'm sorry man but here's the law you're not gonna like it. And he didn't. He started screaming at me, and he kept it up for months, trying, I assumed, to harass me off the property. I was thirty-eight then, maybe twenty years younger than Francis, who topped out at my chin, but even so I was afraid of getting poisoned or shot. He'd sit on his porch waiting for me to step outside so he could scuttle across the street and light into me. I talked to the police about it twice. But until he killed me, or at least threatened to, it was out of their hands.

Francis's was only the first divorce to infiltrate my summer. Two weeks later I found out that my ex-wife—and the mother of my nine-year-old son—was divorcing her second husband. A mutual friend had told me the news by accident. Then I went home and called my ex-wife. Yes, it was true. Yes, they were divorcing. Yes, they were selling the house. Yes, she was in love with another man.

"Where are you going to live?" I asked her. "After the house sells?"

The answer could have been Juneau, Alaska, and there was nothing I could do about it. One thing about my ex-wife, though—she always had a plan. If she wasn't telling me the plan, that simply meant I wouldn't like the plan. She hesitated, then said she wasn't sure. I said like hell you aren't. And she hung up on me. For a while I stood there staring at the lake. A lake is a good place to live at such moments. The bay was calm and soothing, a few straggling Canada geese herded into the shallows. I took a deep breath, then threw the phone through the porch window.

The hole it made was rather star-shaped and let in a warm breeze filled with cottonwood seedlings. As I stood there I heard a phone ringing. I realized it was my phone, and I scrambled outside down the rickety wooden staircase to the beach, but by the time I found the phone it had stopped ringing. I shoved it into my back pocket and started down the raked beach. Men in Goose Bay prided themselves on primping the beaches in front of their camps, and my landlord was king of the raked beach. Francis was always roaming the shore with his rake and white bucket and picking up shards of glass. The moment he spotted me he dropped his bucket. "Hey," he called out. "Hey, Shithead!" I walked through his barrage toward my little day sailer while he trailed after me like a flock of hungry seagulls. I ripped the cover off the boom, attached the rudder, then raised the mainsail and pushed the boat into the water. As the breeze swung the boat, I dropped the centerboard, trimmed and cleated the sail, and finally turned around sitting backward and watched Francis standing on the shore growing smaller and smaller as he cawed at me.

I wondered if all men went crazy during their first divorce. I certainly had. In one fell swoop I'd lost my son, my home, my wife, and my business. Yes, no doubt there was some first-divorce syndrome at work here. Probably they'd invent a pill for it soon. I sailed morosely around the bay worrying. In my heart I knew that my son would soon be moving in with yet another guy I'd never met, and that this man would greatly influence his life. This man would be able to watch my son sleep; he would advise my son about girls; he would push certain sports over others; and if he was a bad man, he might abuse my son in ways I would never hear about. But my biggest worry was of course that they'd move. And if that happened, then what would I do? Tag along?

"Whoever told you life was fair?" That was my father's mantra. Growing up I'd heard that question a thousand times. And yet out on the sailboat that day it seemed to me as if men were driven crazy, more than anything else, by this notion of fairness. Maybe for women it's obvious early on that life isn't fair, but men cling to the idea. We murder and go to prison over this idea of fairness. Little boys especially worship fairness. My son was nine then, the sweetest kid in Vermont, and he was about to learn firsthand what his grandfather had tried so hard to teach me: life ain't fair.

The next morning I got a call from my ex-wife. She'd had a talk with our son, and he'd taken the news okay, but of course he was confused and sad. There was a bigger problem, though, she warned me. Roger, her current husband, the one on his way out, was behaving "irrationally." The two of them had just adopted a baby girl from Vietnam, a process that had been delayed by the authorities for two years, and apparently it was Roger's belief—rightly or wrongly, I don't know—that my ex-wife had stayed with him only until the adoption became final. She described Roger as being livid, maybe dangerous.

"He's started drinking again," she told me in a hushed voice.

"Well, of course he's started drinking again!" I replied, perhaps too loudly. "What the hell do you expect him to do?"

For someone with a hot temper herself my ex-wife has little patience with other people's tempers. She hung up on me again, and I stared at the lake through the hole in my window. I was still staring at the hole when the phone rang in my hand. This time it was Roger, the man who had been a good and gentle stepdad to my son for four years now. Although we seldom spoke, I had always liked Roger. But his voice on the phone that day was unrecognizable. Half choked, he asked if we could talk. Could he come over and could we talk?

We set up a time for the next day, then I opened a beer and stared out the hole in the window. When I was five a neighborhood kid named Darren had led me to the back bedroom of his house to show me a giant hole smashed into the plaster wall. "My dad did that," he whispered. His parents had recently separated. His dad was a cop. We both stared and stared into that hole.

As to my own marriage, I had known my girlfriend two months when a pregnancy test came up pink positive. We were in love, we figured, and so decided to get married. Pregnant women tend to get what they want, and my new wife wanted to move home to New England. So a week after our son was born, we moved from Arkansas to Vermont and shortly thereafter opened an imported-clothing store. Our dream was to someday travel the world buying our own merchandise. For now, we traded off work every day—one of us minding the store, the other minding the baby. Our baby did not sleep at night. We did not sleep at night. We were both overworked and exhausted. We argued. One night I bounced my wedding ring off the dinner table all the way to the roof. It caromed crazily across the room. I never saw it again. During our divorce, I gave her the store I had invested all my savings in and that she had not invested one penny of her own in. I never tried for custody. I felt a baby belonged with his mother. My ex-wife is a dedicated mom. Under Vermont law we had to go to court to settle child support. She hired a lawyer, I didn't. And because I no longer had a job or an income, having given up my store, her lawyer lit into me and basically described me to the judge as a future deadbeat. Her lawyer was a large and bitter-seeming woman dressed in a black miniskirt, and I will never forget the shocked expression on her face when her client, my soon-to-be-ex-wife, stood up in court and yelled at her, "Stop being mean to Rob!"

Here is an unmanly confession: I both like and admire my ex-wife. She has gumption. There is something there that will stand the weather. But God help any fool caught standing between that woman and what she wants.

Roger was a big guy with a long mane of golden dreads and bright blue eyes who resembled a lion. He and my ex-wife made a stunningly handsome couple. Their home was filled with photographs of them looking beautiful together. But now, at my porch table covered with white seedlings, Roger appeared wounded. He kept shaking his head instead of finishing his sentences. Naturally enough he had some issues with the new man on the scene. We talked about divorce, and I told him how divorce was the hardest thing I'd ever survived.

To illustrate the point I told him a story about something that had happened years before I got married. "One night in Arkansas I came out of this bar and these four guys crossed the street and told me to hand over my wallet," I said. "Now, the bar'd had this margarita special going, and I was lit up enough that I told these guys to fuck off. So they dragged me down the railroad tracks and beat the shit out of me with a crowbar, then one guy jammed a knife against my throat. Turns out they had all been released from the penitentiary in Russellville that afternoon. And when they found out I only had five bucks in my wallet, they formed a circle and starting hacking at me with their boots."

Roger was staring at me as if I had wandered off track.

I shrugged and told him divorce was kind of like that. Except the ass kicking lasted about two years.

Later he told me the story of how they had gone to Vietnam to pick up the baby girl they'd been receiving photographs of for two years, pictures that my son had been showing me of his future baby sister. The baby had been in an orphanage her whole life and had never seen a man, so every time Roger came into the room she started howling. Finally he'd had to take a room next door in the hotel. It took him over a month to win the little girl over. Roger paused, then told me he wanted full custody of the girl they had adopted together. He'd already hired a lawyer. The divorce was going to get ugly, he warned me.

"Full custody," I said, nodding. "That means she'll be paying child support to you, right?"

He shrugged and nodded, as if I were missing the point. I wasn't. The point was that the child support I was paying would now be rerouted directly to Roger. This, I felt, was not fair. I stared through the hole in the window. The lake was filled with whitecaps. After a while I pointed out my landlord to Roger. I said, "See that guy down there raking the beach? He's being divorced too, and it might be the death of me yet." I described my landlord's behavior. "Yeah, that old fuck just might shoot me, he's so heartbroke. I'm not kidding either. He'll bury my ass on the beach, some kid ten years from now will find me with a fucking metal detector."

As we watched my landlord rake the brown sand, I could not think of anything else to say to Roger. Was I supposed to give *advice?* And just what kind of advice was I qualified to give? "Drink," I could tell him. "Yeah, drink a lot. Drink a lot and throw things. Punching doors seems to help. Throwing phones through windows ain't bad either. Oh, yeah, try this: go to bars and explain your side of things to strangers. Watch *Casablanca* obsessively. Seek out the music of Willie Nelson, the poetry of Jim Harrison. And above all, no matter what else you do, don't cut your throat, and always *always* think about the kid first. And while you're at it, remember that divorce is a two-year tunnel. A long, dark, and evil tunnel but a tunnel nonetheless."

I didn't say any of that. Mostly I tried to talk him out of hurting anybody. And I told him one worthwhile thing, the hardest and most important rule of being a divorced dad: you can't hurt your ex-wife without hurting your kid.

"It's true," I said. "Think of them as Siamese twins—you can't hurt one without hurting the other."

But I doubt he was listening. He wanted to beat up the guy he blamed for wrecking his family. It was understandable. I don't know if the visit did him any good, but a week later he came over again, and in a very surreal sense I became his mentor in divorce. One thing I managed to do was to talk him into settling for joint custody. I also talked him through some rowdy bouts of anger, and if I was helpful to him at all it was because I could so easily identify with his anger.

But throughout this ordeal my loyalty was to my ex-wife. Like it or not, we were a team. We had a kid to raise.

My son came over that weekend and we talked about what had happened to his life. He had been blindsided the same way Roger had, the same way my landlord had, the same way I had seven long years ago. My son looked like his mom, especially the big brown eyes he stared at me with now. He didn't want to move. He didn't want his mom to break up with Roger. And he seemed to think I could change things. He seemed to think that I had some power to bear here. I had to tell him the truth, that there was nothing I could do about any of it. Which is the forever plight of the divorced dad—infinite power-lessness.

As it turned out, though, there was one small thing I could do. My son hadn't seen his stepfather since the breakup. Everybody was on bad terms, and because of this he hadn't seen Roger in weeks. I stared at the hole in the window, then picked up the phone and called Roger and invited him over. He couldn't make it that day, but he asked if he could come over the next weekend. The next weekend was the Fourth of July, a big deal here, fireworks over the bay. The Fourth of July was the only holiday I ever got to spend with my son. It was our tradition. I hesitated. I didn't want to share that day with Roger. Then I invited him over anyway.

On the Fourth of July my son and I were on the beach building a fire. Thousands of boats had filled the bay even though the weather was spitting rain. Usually my landlord had his own fireworks display. He'd set off hundreds of dollars' worth of Roman candles and such on the beach in front of his grandkids. But not this year. This year he was sitting alone in his little powerboat moored in the shallows. Roger arrived and my son ran up to him. Roger had brought a camp chair, one of those baggable canvas gadgets that unfolds into a loveseat type of thing with beer-hole armrests. We chatted a bit, then I made myself scarce. My landlord was sipping a beer in the prow of his little boat. The boat was tethered to two giant inflatable tubes his grandchildren usually played on. As it got dark I threw on more firewood, then I sat on the sand with my arms around my knees. The fireworks were late. Maybe they'd been canceled. Dozens of campfires lined the beach. My son and Roger were still on the collapsible loveseat talking with their arms around each other when the first candle soared up.

Whoever told you life was fair? I thought about this while staring at the two of them on the loveseat. Well, certainly not my old man. I wonder what he would've made of this situation. It was certainly nothing I'd ever been prepared for. I opened another beer as the sky exploded with a bright white globe of light. And when I looked up at the fireworks raindrops hit my eyes.

Quarantined Behind Concrete and Steel

BENJAMIN LaGUER

he first thing I see in the morning is the sunlight coming through the bars. The first thing I hear is a whistle signaling five minutes to count. Everybody has to be on his feet at 7:15 A.M. so the guards can check to make sure that nobody's dead.

My cell—number 309—is not much larger than a closet. The walls are regulation beige, and the ceiling is high and white and stained. Bolted to the floor is a steel desk. The bed is bolted to the floor. The toilet and sink are bolted. Opposite those is a cosmetics shelf, where I keep my books. Other than my clothes, my only possessions are a twelve-inch Zenith TV, an Optimus AM/FM radio, and a Smith Corona manual typewriter. In this place, with these things, I spend my days and nights seven days a week. It is where I face reality, the reality of my soul.

After resting for half of my life in prison, quarantined behind concrete and steel, encircled by silhouettes of faceless men in uniform and armed guard towers, I feel not only like I've been on a physical roller coaster but emotionally as if I am suspended in state. The pictures I keep on my wall are of my family from twenty years ago. It's as if they are frozen in time.

But I am not frozen. I am always pacing. When I am not physically pacing, my mind is pacing. At night, long after the voices have fallen silent and the imprisoned garrison is asleep in either its dreams or its nightmares, I lie in bed still awake, wondering what has become of me. It's that ultimate question one asks in search of self-truth: that question that arises in the night, when the human heart pounds its loudest. I ask myself in that way one demands answers from the gods, "How is it possible that 7,394 days could have been stolen from my life's calendar?" I remember when the judge in his black robe ordered my days forfeit. He had spoken with the ease of Pontius Pilate, upholding the letter of the law and the verdict of the crowd. It was not his function to deliver justice, he may have thought, only to carry out the letter of the law. Although I physically reside on this side of the stones, I have tried to convince myself, in a multitude of disguises, that in spirit I must be free.

But try as I might, I can't suppress those first sights and sounds from that day two decades ago—the instant I was arrested, the moment I stood accused, and later that evening when the steel door slammed behind me and I was left alone in a jail cell. Daily I remind myself of that time when my life darkened.

I first spent eight months in the house of correction where all you hear is that pretty little boys like me get raped at the Big House. So I pumped up my masculinity a hundredfold with the idea that the first motherfucker who looks at me with any smile, with any sense of winking at me, I'm taking him out. My masculinity was like Jimi Hendrix's guitar on acid. I dressed in green fatigues. In those years they gave inmates surplus Army fatigues if they wanted them instead of the prison blues they require now. And you could also get cigarettes and cigars at the canteen. So I used to always walk around in my Army fatigues with a big cigar. I wore dark sunglasses, not wanting the fear in my eyes to betray me, and I grew a beard. People called me Fidel.

My father's way of teaching me how to be a man had been to send me off to the Army when I was seventeen. Army life gave me structure, which prepared me for prison life. My father himself had been in the Army. He'd also spent several months in a Puerto Rican prison as a young man. The police had rounded up a bunch of people they thought were subversive. And my father was subversive in his way. He did not like authority. His experience had been abuse at the hands of authority, especially when he got to this country.

Only after I was in prison did I really come to understand my father. He was not one to share his inner life with others. I don't believe there were ever more than a handful of people, including all seven of my sisters and brothers, who asked my father what he thought. My father and I never went to a baseball game. Except for the knowledge that he would leave for work before the streetlights turned off and never return home before the lights were lit again, I had no idea who my father was. Until the last seven years of his life, for me my father had been a thing that, by some cosmic order, just happened to inherit me.

Over many conversations, held at weekly intervals of two hours across a vast row of metal chairs in the prison's visiting room, my father and I became friends. I had never been with him one-on-one before; my little time with him growing up was always with the family around. Spending two and a half hours within two feet of each other provided a space of intimacy in which we were finally free to talk. We told each other our secrets. Curious about who I was, I began asking my father who he was.

The main thing I knew about him was that he'd spent thirty summers laying blacktop in New York City and Westchester County. During winter, the off-season, he went to sea with the merchant marine. But I always associated with my father the smell of black tar. Just seeing him would evoke for me the stench of a road crew. I still sometimes smell it in my sleep.

My father always dressed up when he went to church, when he changed out of the tar stench of his work clothes. And he was a sharp dresser. He was an elder in the Seventh-Day Adventist church. I always saw in my father this aura of respectability. And though there were the things that pierced that aura—he had frailties, he had done things that caused pain—they did not take away from the man he wanted to be and the man he wanted me to be.

I once asked him about our ancestors and if they had been noble or scandalous.

My father replied, in words I will never forget, "All men have more scandal than nobility in their hearts. That's what makes us human. Don't trust a man who says he is noble." My father had never spoken like that before; he spoke as if he had surprised even himself, perhaps having never thought of answering such a question. In the end, I realized I admired the old brown man. He was human like me. And I could tell he admired my spirit of protest, my thirst for justice, my endless attempts to exonerate myself, and my determination not to let this institution rob me of my manhood.

For twenty years I have seen men come in here proud and tall before being reduced to always asking for stuff. I've seen their families leave. Their daughters, their little girls, now have children. Their boys have grown to be men. These once proud men are reduced to having no role, of having to be taken care of by the state. Being at the mercy of the generosity of their families to come visit or to send a letter every now and then.

My sisters do not want to wake up in the morning and think, "Benjie's in the penitentiary and God knows what his day is like." It's too much for them to handle. In the case of inmates, absence makes the heart grow cold, because people just want to forget. When I call my family I don't want them to know all the details of what I'm doing. The most dignified thing I can say to them is, "It's a beautiful day here at the penitentiary."

Prison, if you let it, obliterates your sense of manhood, because you are no longer an individual, you are part of this machinery. They have rules about everything, and if you break a rule, you get a ticket. I haven't had a ticket in well over a decade. Following the rules is my subversive act. It's almost Gandhian.

Three times a day, every day of the week, inmates can be seen walking, like an army of ants, toward the hospital building. The most common prescriptions dispensed in prison are not for physical ailments but are psychotropic pharmaceuticals to keep the inmates from facing reality. It is as if the prison psychiatrist has the power to single-handedly dispense more mercy than the prison chaplain. These inmates return to their cells like children coming home from the corner candy store. They lie in their beds and they do not wake again until it's time for more mercy and more pills.

The prison gave me these pills and they put me to sleep. I woke up one day and it was a week later. And I knew that I couldn't do this. I couldn't spend my days in the penitentiary sleeping. I have a meeting with destiny to attend.

•   •   •

It was a February day almost ten years ago that a uniformed man walked upstairs, stood in front of my cell, and said, "Your father died." The blue uniform then disappeared from sight. I arose from bed, removed a single piece of white paper from the desk's steel drawer, folded it, and covered the window, in need of even greater solitude than that found in a prison dungeon.

I had known for some months that my father's health was deteriorating, and earlier that week I had asked the prison's unit counselor if, upon my father's death, I could be favorably considered for an escorted furlough to attend the funeral. Within hours I was told I would be granted such permission. And so I waited for that moment when I, the son of a LaGuer, would no longer be connected to the LaGuers of the past, for that hour when I would stand alone, linked only to a future.

And what is my future? Someday I will leave here, but what will happen to me then? No matter how much I have tried to convince myself that twenty years in solitude has left me unaffected, I must confront the fact that I am a creature inextricably tied, in both failures and accomplishments, to what has happened to me in prison. It is here, in solitude, that a man attains what is nearest to his nature, where he battles to deliver himself either to his God or his devil. In whatever mold, a man emerges from his battles with scars of honor or wounds of disgrace.

When, nine years ago, I was to step outside the prison for that trip that would take me in front of my father in his final coffined image, despite all my efforts to prove I should be worthy, I felt afraid. I no longer had concrete sights or sounds of what was beyond the stones. Why was I afraid?

I can only figure that whatever had paralyzed me in fright had something to do with how years in solitude can transform even the strongest of human beings. It is my understanding that our lower primate brothers and sisters in captivity are often so traumatized that they suffer extreme physical and cognitive impairment, sometimes to the point of not being able reproduce even when they have access to the opposite sex. And while I claim no unique insight into the natural science that explains such a phenomenon, I suspect that I am not so different in composite. If one were asked to remove one's space suit while standing on the moon, surely the impact would be immediate and profound. That probably is the nearest analogy to bringing a human outside, after spending year upon year in solitude.

Often in flashbacks I remember that summer morning when I was taken outside the prison for an appearance at the Worcester County Superior Court. Usually prisoners from across the state are brought in through an underground shaft under the courthouse building, then brought by elevator up to the courtrooms. For some reason, however, that day was different. The men in uniform parked the transport almost two hundred yards from the granite edifice. I say all this to make a point: I have no recollection, except in flashbacks, of the sound of my shoes striking the pavement across those two hundred yards, or of the façade downtown, or of the many faces that I must have seen that morning. It is still a surreal experience. I remember the events, but only as if I were outside myself, as though I know what happened from watching it through an angelic distance.

My emotional paralysis doesn't seem so profound to me now. Yet I can't dispel the feeling that almost half of those who leave prison return. My question out of this feeling is simple: are these people returning to prison because they are actual deviants, or are they simply unable to adjust?

•   •   •

En route to my father's funeral, riding in the rear seat along the state's freeway system, I said to myself, "You mustn't be afraid." It wasn't that I was scared of having emerged from the abyss. I suddenly had awakened. Not only had I awakened in a metaphysical sense, stroked by systems of physical oppression and perceptive freedom, but a new reality had exploded within me, and there I stood, naked, transient, between two zones. Although I was overwhelmed by the sudden glitter of new images, sounds, and aromas, I was not afraid.

Perhaps that awakening was necessary. I came closest, nearer than ever before, to understanding how easily life can be negated. I had lived not only physically as a prisoner but also trapped in perception. But I have been able to crawl out of the box and to think for myself. Now I stand in front of the window faintly watching the world from afar. I am in exile, but I am in peace.

You attain peace by understanding that you have come as close as you are able to get to the truth of your life. There is a certain peacefulness that comes from not being confused over where it is that you are going.

As I knelt before my father's coffin, I said, as if in conversation with his spirit, "I have brought uniformed men who carry steel to this sacred place, Dad. I hope that I am forgiven. I hope to be a son and a father, like you, of Honor."

Log Man

DAVID GATES

It's the middle of May, and down in Brooklyn, where I live four days a week, the lilacs have gone by. But up here on the border of New York State and Vermont, where I *live*, they're only budding; the radio said it would get down into the thirties tonight. So when it got dark, I closed off the living room—I'm always here alone now—and fired up the woodstove in the kitchen. No, this isn't going to be some shit about the poignantly fading glories of the rural life, though it will have to do with the woodstove. I'm drinking Bombay Sapphire as I type this on a Toshiba Satellite laptop, which is simultaneously playing these mondo obscuro songs I downloaded. Just now it happens to be "Viola Lee Blues" by Cannon's Jug Stompers (vocal by Noah Lewis), a prison song that never gets around to mentioning Viola Lee. As I go along, I'll keep you updated on what's playing, and won't *that* be interesting. Then, when I finish this, I'll get high and burn the CD compilation I've been promising some friends in Brooklyn for a year now. Or at least get high. So: no lowing of obsolescent oxen, no scent of new-mown hay, no PCB-free water from the old enameled dipper. But it would be less than honest not to report that right now, from this window, I can see the full moon, its face netted across with the branches of the trees on my hilltop. And one hates to be less than honest. The radio said there's an eclipse tonight.

Now playing: "My Crime Blues," by Barefoot Bill, whose real name was Ed Bell, born in Alabama around 1905. "My crime, my crime, I really can't understand." Okay, so about the woodstove. I heat this house entirely with wood, partly because it's all I can afford and partly so I can say I heat with wood, but mostly because I'm so in love, if that's the expression, with the whole wood thing. Cutting it. Splitting it. Stacking it. Smelling its different smells; when macular degeneration finally gets me as it's gotten my father, I'll still be able to tell the sourish scent of red oak from the maplelike scent of maple. Owning three chainsaws (a Stihl Wood Boss, a Stihl Farm Boss, and a Sears electric my father gave me when his eyes got too bad to trust himself with it). Owning a splitting maul (like an axe but three times as thick and heavy), a sledgehammer and wedges (for those chunks too big or stubborn to split under a blow of the maul), and a cant hook (to roll those long, heavy tree trunks). Owning a pickup truck. My father likes to say wood warms you twice, which is either an old New England thing or his own thing, but it actually warms you more than that. After you cut and split, you load the wood onto the truck, haul it home, then stack it outside to dry for a couple of seasons, then bring it inside and stack it again. Then, when it's time to burn, you bring wheelbarrow loads to stack on the back porch, where you can get it to both the stove in the kitchen and the stove in the big living room. How many times is that? Six, I think.

Now playing: "Mean Old World," by Little Walter. So we're out of the mondo obscuro for a while, at least to the extent that Chicago blues is not mondo obscuro. "This is a mean old world, try living by yourself." Well, sure, okay, noted. But on the other hand, try living with somebody else. This house has outlasted two of my three marriages—the first predated my buying the house—and since it's over three hundred years old and I'm fifty-six, it bids pretty fair to outlast me too. If I don't sell it eventually, God knows who I'll leave it to. That should be *whom*, but I'd rather cut off a foot with the Farm Boss. Since all those marriages yielded zero children, maybe some younger friend of mine will get a weird surprise. Or should it go to the stepchild who used to come here, whom I haven't seen for two years? And now playing: "Commit a Crime," by Howlin' Wolf. Say, this hooks right up with "My Crime Blues" by Barefoot Bill. So we've definitely got some guilt. I swear I'm not making this up about the songs: the stuff I say is playing as I write this or that really *is* playing, to some extent.

But I was talking about the whole firewood trip—that *is* what this is about, no? So I'd be remiss if I didn't try to evoke for you that satisfied feeling when you look at the wood you stacked outside last fall and you see the little cracks in the ends of the split logs, meaning it's ready to rock and roll. And one hates to be remiss. So does that evoke it for you? Didn't think so. At any rate, after you bring the seasoned wood into the shed, you go back out and cut and split some more— just as if you yourself were going to live on for season after season after season. But of course sooner or later, you know? I always think about how J. D. O'Hara—this is a shout-out to my mentor at the University of Connecticut—taught that Robert Frost poem "The Wood-Pile"—about an old, apparently forgotten stack of cut and split firewood he finds way out in the woods. Frost says that when he saw it, he thought that only someone "who lived in turning to fresh tasks/Could so forget his handiwork"—and back before Wood Bosses and Farm Bosses, those poor sons of bitches *did* have to work. But what O'Hara said was, isn't it more likely that whoever had cut this wood had simply died? That put me away. It wasn't merely a smart way to read the poem but a true observation about what everything eventually adds up to. Shit, is this getting too grim now? Or just too literary?

Now playing: "Death Is Not the End," by Bob Dylan, from his noncanonical *Down in the Groove*, 1988. In 1988 I'd had this place three years, and marriage number two was ending. *Quel* coincidence, huh? I know, not really. "When you're sad and when you're lonely and

you haven't got a friend/Just remember that death is not the end."
This may actually not be a comforting lyric. That *just remember*
sounds like the formula for consolation—*Everything's for shit and
now here comes the silver lining*—but Dylan may in fact mean that if
you think this life is bad, no friends and whatnot, when you go to hell
it's even worse, at least for those of us who are unsaved. That *Hamlet*
thing. I mentioned that I did have friends, right? This whole piece is
starting to sound a little dire, and I don't want you to think, you
know, do we need to do an intervention here.

Too literary, did I say? Fuck it, I'm going to get even *more* literary.
It's four hours from Brooklyn to here, and for the last few years, in
addition to music, I've taken to listening to Shakespeare in the car.
The old Caedmon recordings, which always had Paul Scofield or
John Gielgud, whoever. And while I listened to *The Tempest* for like
the twenty-second time, it leaped out at me what a huge thing firewood is in that play. Look at it: when Prospero first calls for Caliban,
his misshapen, hag-born slave, the first thing out of Caliban's mouth
is "There's wood enough within." We find out a few lines later that
Caliban's got other, unspecified stuff to do, but the task Shakespeare
seems to want us to notice is bringing in firewood to keep Prospero
and his daughter, Miranda, warm—that is, to ensure their very sur-
vival. As Prospero tells her, "We cannot miss him [meaning do without him]; he does make our fire/Fetch in our wood, and serves in
offices/That profit us." And when Stefano and Trinculo temporarily
set him free, his immediate thought is that he'll no longer have to
"fetch in firing/At requiring."

Then look at this. When the shipwrecked young prince Ferdinand
falls in love with Miranda, the trial to which Prospero puts him is
Caliban's principal "office": stacking firewood. "I must remove/Some
thousands of these logs and pile them up,/Upon a sore injunction."
This isn't just an absurdly large chore—some *thousands* of logs?—
but one far beneath a prince's dignity; only for the love of Miranda

does Ferdinand consent to become, as he puts it, "this patient log-man." But the test Prospero has imposed isn't just some random fairy-tale ordeal in which the hero must temporarily endure ritual humiliation: it's specifically about his ability to provide for Prospero's little girl in the most basic way. That is, in the *other* most basic way. Prospero also lays another sore injunction on Ferdinand: that he not break Miranda's "virgin-knot" before they're officially married. And finally, just to tie it all up, no pun intended, look at this: Prospero had enslaved Caliban, *The Tempest*'s impatient log-man, specifically because he'd tried to rape Miranda. Shakespeare, always alive to opportunities for phallic funning and punning, may not have meant his log-men's logs to be anything but logs, but I wouldn't bet against it.

I let fly with all this lit-crit because I was tired of keeping these mondo obscuro insights to myself, but also because *The Tempest* suggests a primal connection (and there's that academic tone *again*) between firewood and sex that long predates the chainsaw, that dangerous, dick-shaped snarler. I suppose it's basically a hunter-gatherer thing, where the man does the muscle work out in the world and the woman waits back home with legs spread. You hear it in those blues songs where the guy who's trying to seduce the woman says he'll cut her kindling and make her fire. The kindling thing is not a double entendre, as far as I can tell—I mean, what would it *mean,* cut your kindling? Cutting kindling used to be woman's work; in other words, I'll do a Ferdinand for you. Or I don't know, maybe it's a *maladroit* double entendre—like Albert King's "Crosscut Saw," which I've puzzled over for years. "I'm a crosscut saw, baby, drag me across your log." Try picturing *that;* you can't. He's not even *splitting* her, but specifically cutting her. You'd think maybe there was some kind of vagina dentata thing happening, except that *he's* the saw and *she's* the log. I don't know, you're probably not supposed to examine it too closely—it's vaguely smutty, and shouldn't that be good enough? At any rate, isn't the stacking of firewood an image of the good marriage? Some thousands of logs all ready to burn on some thousands of cold nights, season after season after season? Hey, I just remembered, I'm missing the eclipse. Oh no you're not. That was supposed to be a grim joke.

Now playing: "Wish I Had My Time Again," by the Hatton Brothers. A fiddle-banjo tune from Kentucky, with square-dance calls. Recorded in 1933. The fiddler, Vertner Hatton, was born in 1883, Jess Hatton in 1895, the caller, Asa Martin, in 1900. Even Martin, who'd now be like 103, could probably tell you now whether or not death is the end. But, as Hamlet says, that's the undiscovered country from whose bourne et cetera.

What this piece is really about is that today's the day I sent the letter saying let's finally get this over with and make the divorce official.

Whoa! Where the fuck did *that* come from, right? Oh, I know it's cheesy writing to withhold crucial information for effect. When I teach writing classes, I always come down hard about this. I also come down hard on those cheap one-sentence paragraphs, like the one just above. This stuff is manipulative, disrespectful to the reader—to *you*—and worst of all, easy to see through. So am I not being inconsistent verging on hypocritical? Am I not, in fact, a lying sack of shit? You know, the kind of person who would end up cheating on his wife? (Let's not try to work up any unearned pathos about this divorce thing.) I mean, today wasn't even the day. I really sent the letter two days ago. Today's just the day it would've gotten there. I thought this piece would read better if I simplified—that is, if I lied—but it's a mess anyway. Now you're supposed to go, *No no it's brilliant, get the fuck outta here.*

Now playing: "Ain't A-Gonna Lay My Armor Down," by McVay and Johnson. Two more dead people from Kentucky. Being dead seems to be a thing in Kentucky. This is a religious song about being vigilant "till He comes." The armor *I* can't or won't lay down is this fucking irony.

Back when she and I were together, I used to lie that I cut the wood and split the wood and stacked the wood and brought in the wood to keep us both warm, as best I could, the way men have done ever since they went scraping their knuckles along the forest floor. But really, it was only about me: performing this obsessive-compulsive impersonation of a man, a freeborn Jacksonian lout of the back woods, complete with chainsaw, myself as audience. Three chain-saws. Now, that *is* excessive. So now that it really *is* only about me, now that I'm warming only myself twice—six times, however many times—I hope I'm satisfied.

The Dog's Life

Thomas Lynch

My sister Brigid's yellow Lab bitch Baxter was put to death last Monday. What can be said of such proceedings? That every dog has its day? The following from my sister's partner, Kathy, tells the tale.

It is with a heavy heart that I write this e-mail to notify family of the death of Baxter Bailey (11½ years old) on Monday, July 14th. Kidney failure. She was buried in a deserved spot, at Mullett Lake. She is survived by her sister, Bogey Bear (who is a little lost as to what has transpired) and her mother/best friend/Companion—Brigid. A brief ceremony will be held the weekend of the 25th on Mullett Lake.

Whether you loved her, feared her or were entertained by her, she will never be forgotten. Long live her memory.

Kathy

In receipt of which I replied:

Dear Kathy and B,

Thanks for the sad and tidy news. I will not pretend to have admired the deceased. She was, however, a walking (more lately hobbled) example of the power of love. She was not bright, not lovely, less communicative than most mum plants, and drugged into a stupor for most of her life. But here is the mystery—the glorious mystery—that a woman as bright and lovely, articulate and sober as our B loved her, loved her unambiguously. For a man of my own limitations (and they are legion) the love B showed to Baxter was a reminder of the lovability of all God's creatures—even me. In that sense she was a constant beacon of faith and hope and love. If this is what they call the Dog's Life, I say more of it is the thing we need.

You and B will be in my prayers for a brief if deserved bereavement.

Love & Blessings,
T

It was a hasty but heartfelt sentiment, managed between the usual mélange of mortuary, literary, and family duties. I meant only comfort by it.

·   ·   ·

Part of the comeuppance for calling our small chain of funeral homes Lynch & Sons is that the daughters—our sisters—control the purse. Three of my father's sons, I among them, went off to mortuary school and got licensed, years ago, to embalm the dead and direct the living through the funerary maze. Before our father died, we bought the enterprise from him. His three daughters—ever his favorites—went to university and business schools and were installed in various key positions. Mary is the bookkeeper and paymistress. Julie Ann is her factotum. Brigid handles trusts and insurance and preneed finance and is the de facto comptroller at my brother Pat's funeral home. We call them the three furies, and they travel between my establishment and Pat's bringing light and joy and accountability. (Our brother Tim, seeing the shape of things to come, quietly dismissed them years ago and installed a clerical staff he could lord it over after he'd bought the place in Walled Lake from our father.)

When I see them together—Mary, Julie, and Brigid—I often think of the headlands on the Dingle Peninsula called "the Three Sisters," which rise in a triad of sweeping, greeny peaks to protect the Irish countryside from the ravages of the North Atlantic. Like those features in the west Kerry topography, they are strikingly beautiful, immovable, and possessed of powers we know nothing of.

Wednesdays Mary and Julie come to my funeral home in Milford for payroll and accounts—receivable and payable. Brigid remains at my brother's office but calls to consult with her sisters three or four times on the day.

Last Wednesday when Mary and Julie read my sympathy note they rolled their eyes and smote me with their disapproval. "How could you say such an awful thing about Baxter to your grieving sister?"

"What awful thing?" I asked. *"A beacon of faith and hope and love?"*

"This bit about the mum plant and stupor. Couldn't you have just said something nice? Something about her loyalty?"

They did not see that stating the obvious about Baxter's life and times was central to the art of condolence and, a fortiori, the construction of the note's kindlier sentiment.

·   ·   ·

Truth told, the dog was a disaster, which had worn out her welcome by eleven years with everyone except, of course, my sister B. A female assigned a fashionably suburban but oddly mannish name, Baxter Bailey never seemed to know whether she was coming or going, whether to hump or be humped, whether she ought to lift a leg or squat. When she had just achieved adult size and indoor continence, she bit my sister—quite literally the hand that was feeding her—thereby missing the only requisite point of Dog 101, to wit: *don't bite the humans*. B. had her neutered. Later she growled and snapped at B.'s infant and toddling nieces and nephews as they approached to pet her. On the strength of these misdemeanors and distempers I once had B. talked into putting her down, citing the liability presented by a dog that might attack neighbors or their pets or children, houseguests or passersby. I reminded her of the One Bite Rule, with roots in the Book of Exodus, near where the ordinances on the seduction of virgins are recorded (alas, the emergent patriarchy!), which held that an owner would be called to account for the second infraction of a domestic animal. I'd gone so far as to set an appointment with the vet for the euthanasia and had Baxter leashed and loaded in the backseat and B. agreeably disposed to the good sense of it all. But when she got there she waffled in her resolve. She asked the vet, instead, for medication, something, she pleaded, "to calm her down"—Baxter, not Brigid. The cocktail of pharmaceuticals thus prescribed amounted to the nonsurgical equivalent of lobotomy. She was given phenobarbital to control her seizures, Lasix as a diuretic, something for her stomach disorders and insomnia, and a giant daily dose of canine Thorazine—enough, I daresay, to dull an orangutan—to quiet her demons, real and imagined. Baxter remained more or less on the edge of a coma for the rest of her life. She never snapped at anyone or anything again. She roamed about, bumping into the landscape and geography and furniture, like an outsized, spongy orb in a game of pinball or bumper pool. At the lake she would sometimes walk into the water, as if some distant memory of her breed still flickered in her. Brigid would have to wade in and lead her ashore. People would toss Frisbees and tennis balls in her direction, hoping to engage her in the usual play. They would bounce off her snout and hindquarters, causing not so much as a flicker in Baxter's glassy eyes. The customary commands—Sit, Fetch, Heel, Come—meant no more to Baxter than a recitation from the Township Zoning Ordinances. To the voice of her mistress or any human directive Baxter was uniformly nonresponsive. The only trick she ever performed was "Breathe, Baxter! Breathe!"

"Where there's life there's hope," Brigid would say, ever the loyal human, as if the dog's damage were reversible. It was a sad thing to witness, this zombified miscreant working her way through a decade and then some of meaningless days. Her end was a mercy to all and sundry.

But what my sisters Mary and Julie seemed to be saying was that no empathy or fellow feeling could be tendered that did not include the ruse that Baxter was Rin Tin Tin done up in drag, or Lassie or Old Yeller—a great dog to be greatly grieved and greatly missed—a loyal, loving, exceptional specimen of Man's (read Woman's too) Best Friend. When I protested that Baxter would not want to be placed on a pedestal, or to be loved for other than the amalgam of distress and misfortune that she was, that authentic feeling could not be based upon a vast denial of reality, they both rolled their eyes in counterclockwise turns and said, one to the other, "He just doesn't get it."

That I just don't "get it" is the conventional wisdom and the conversation's end with the several women in my life. Though I am the son of a good woman, now deceased and lamented, and sibling of three of them; though I am the father, friend, and spouse of females, like most of the men of my generation, I just don't get it and maybe never will.

·　　　·　　　·

Five mornings out of every seven the woman across the street in the gingerbready Queen Anne manse with the Martha Stewart garden emerges with her two snow-white toy poodles to attend to what Victorians called the duties of their toilet. Each is the size of a bowling ball and their tiny feces like wee, green, cat's-eye marbles, about which more, alas, anon. This daft and dainty pair of little sexless things are named for their mistress's favorite libations, Chardonnay and Champagne, which are shortened in the diminutive to "Chardy" and "Champy," as she is heard to call out when they go bouncing about the neighborhood in search of somewhere to take their tiny designer shits. Most mornings the entourage looks a little dazed, as if they all might've gotten into the vodka and tonic late. But who am I to say?

She doesn't like me, the woman across the street. The list and variety of our quarrels and quibbles on civic, cultural, and neighborhood issues is a long and exhaustive one. I'm sure she thinks I just don't get it. Truth told, I'm not that gone on her. Except for the occasional wave or sidelong glance and nod, we make no effort at neighborliness. We knew from the get-go we would not be friends. And though I admire her refusal to maintain any pretense or decorum, it is better to do so from afar. Maybe we remind each other of each other's former spouses.

Still, I uphold her right to her ways as she upholds my right to mine. This is America after all. Though we hold forth from opposite sides of the street, the name of the street is Liberty. So the insipid little dogs, the fellow she's married to (who must on the weekends attend to Chardy and Champy's morning office), the overgrowth of garden—these are situations I accept like variations on the theme of weather. It could be worse is what I tell myself. In the same way she tolerates me and mine: the overflow parking from the funeral home, the mysterious vans arriving at all hours, the bright impatiens we plant every year among the uninspired juniper and yews, and, the dear knows, my manifest personal foibles. Like me, she has much to tolerate.

It's only when she brings Chardy and Champy over to the funeral home to sniff about in search of a proper shitting ground that I take especial umbrage. To give her and her poodles their due, she always comes armed with a plastic bag and a rubber glove—the latter affecting the transfer of the turdlettes from my greensward into the former. She is, in keeping with local and regional custom, fastidious about the fecal matters. I think she uses them with her prized delphinium. But for some reason, I cannot shake the sense that I and my real estate have been shat upon, and that there is a kind of message hidden in the act, that there is some intelligence she intends for me to "get" by the witness of it. Nor can I shake the temptation, so far resisted, to mosey on over and shit on hers.

·　　　　·　　　　·

After my first wife and I divorced, I was the custodial parent of a daughter and three sons from the time they were ten, nine, six, and four until I was married again, some seven years later, to the Woman of My Dreams. It's when I most wanted to be a feminist. The divisions of labor and money, power and parental duties—those good-for-the-goose-and-gander concerns of the third-wave feminism of the day—were themes I found the most intriguing. I read Beauvoir and Friedan, Brownmiller and Millett, Germaine Greer and Gloria Steinem. I read Robin Morgan's man-hating rhetoricals on "cock privilege" and castration and Doris Lessing's *Golden Notebook* and Andrea Dworkin's sad and incomprehensible screed and wondered if there were miseries out of which such people could really never be put. I was a card-carrying, contributing member of NOW. I vetted my personal lexicon for sexist terms. "Postman" became "mail carrier," "chairman" became "chairperson," "ladies" became "women." I never said "girl." I made my sons wash dishes and my daughter take out the trash and filed for child support from my former spouse, in keeping with the equal-rights amends I was trying to make. I was encouraged by the caseworker from the Friend of the Court's office—a fetching woman with green eyes and a by-the-bookish style—who said the children should get 50 percent of their noncustodial parent's income. This, she assured, was a gender indifferent directive. The state-prescribed formula called for 20 percent for the first child and 10 percent for every one after that. "It's what you'd be paying," she said matter-of-factly, "if the shoe were on the other foot." I figured I could save it for their higher educations.

The judge, however, overruled the caseworker's recommenda-tion. Her honor conceded that while in theory our sons and daugh-ter deserved the benefits of both of their parents' gainful labors, she could not bring herself to order a mother to pay child support, even one that saw her children but every other weekend. It was enough that the erstwhile missus was making her own way in a difficult world. Supplemental payments for the support of her children were more of an indenture than the judge was prepared to order. During the brief hearing I was advised by her pinstriped counsel to leave well enough alone. I just didn't get it after all.

Back in those days I kept a lovely cur, free of any registered pedi-gree or jittery habits. She had a small head, a large body, and lovely temperament. We called her Heidi. When she was a puppy I walked her round our little city lot at the corner of Liberty and East streets and the half block next-door occupied by the funeral home and its parking lot and told her that she could come and go as she pleased but that if she showed up at home, more nights than not, she'd be fed and petted and sheltered well; she'd be loved and cuddled, bathed and brushed. In short, if she would do her part, we'd do ours. Such was the nature of our covenant.

And though Heidi traveled widely, she never strayed. She would follow the mail carriers on their rounds, forefending them from more vicious dogs. She'd find her way to the corner butcher shop and beg for bones and to the bakery on Main Street to beg for day-old doughnuts. She was particularly fond of custard-filleds. She would stare balefully into the doorway of the delicatessen for hours until someone proffered some Polish ham or Havarti cheese or some other succulent morsel or delicacy. Later in the day she would make her way to the school yard to accompany my younger sons home from their day's studies. Evenings she'd position her repose in the driveway of the funeral-home parking lot, acting the speed bump and sentinel whilst the children practiced their skateboarding or Frisbee or whiffle ball. On weekends she'd be in Milford's Central Park, fishing with my oldest son or accompanying my daughter and her friends on their rounds through town, field-testing their ever-changing figures and fashions. She died old and fat and happy and was buried under the mock-orange bush where she used to shade herself against the summer heat. Near two decades since she is still remembered with reverence; her exploits and loyalties are legendary.

Which is all I ever wanted out of love and husbanding, family and parenting—to be fondly regarded by the ones I loved; to be known for how I came home at night, minded the borders, kept an eye out for impending dangers, paid the piper, did my job, loved them all fiercely to the end. It was the dream I inherited from my mother and father, for whom a division of labor did not mean a disproportion of power.

•   •   •

I was, in those times, a casualty of the gender wars that the men and women of my generation waged over duties and identities. It was, I suppose, a necessary battle, which we did not choose and were powerless to avoid, damned if we did and if we didn't fight. We all took too seriously the carping and dyspepsia of a generation for whom sexism was a sin only men could commit, and only and always against women. Power and money were zero-sum games. Sex and love were often trophies. Women of the day kept their litany of injustices—

the glass ceilings, the hostile work environments, the sixty-three-cents-on-the-dollar deal, the who-does-the-most-work-in-the-house debate. The little tally of inconsistencies I maintained kept driving me crazier and crazier. That *Roe* v. *Wade* gave legal reproductive options to women but not to men (there was no clinic to which men could repair to terminate, with Supreme Court approval, their impending paternity) was a bother. If "choice" were such a fine thing, it occurred to me, oughtn't one and all, not one half, of the population have it? That my daughter might "choose" a career in the military but only my sons had to register for the draft struck me as odd. No less the victim-chic status of the feminist intelligentsia who were always ranting about "women and other minorities" whilst quietly ignoring the fact that women had been the majority for years. That women not only outnumbered men, they outlived them—by years, not months, in every culture—seemed a thing that ought to be addressed. Never mind the incessant sloganeering, or the women who blamed Ted Hughes for Sylvia Plath's suicide or who blamed their husbands for the history of the world or who turned men into the tackling dummies for their chronic discontents. Maybe it was all that "every intercourse is an act of rape" hysteria or "a woman needs a man like a fish needs a bicycle," or the way they joked about the man who had his penis cut off by his angry wife. I used to wonder what late-night talk-show host would survive any less than reverential comment about a woman's genitalia if the roles had been reversed. Violence against women was quite rightly abhorred, whilst violence against men was generally ignored. Nothing in the literature rang more true to me than something I had overheard in a conversation between pathologists who were autopsying a fatal domestic case: "A man will kill his wife, then kill himself," one said grimly; "a woman kills her husband, then does her nails." Whatever else I did not get, I got that one loud and clear: the higher ground of entitlement that victims, self-proclaimed, could occupy. I'm certain there were additional grievances, like so much else, I've forgotten now.

That women have been oppressed is not a secret. Nor is it news that men have been betrayed. But we are members of an evolving species, victims and beneficiaries of history and herstory. The blaming of fathers for the trouble with sons, like the blaming of women for the trouble with men or the blaming of husbands for the trouble with wives can be defended or debunked by the arrangement of facts. But the rebuke keeps us from the deeper meaning of our lives. Justice, liberation, equal rights, reproduction, morality, security, the costs of war, the future of the species, education, the environment, sexual respect—these are neither men's nor women's issues. They belong to humankind.

In ways that were not so for my parents' generation and, please God, will not be so for my sons' and daughter's, the men and women of my generation suffered a kind of disconnect that left them each wary of the other's intentions, each ignorant of the other's changing, each speaking a dialect the other could not cipher, each wondering why the other just didn't get it. Such are the accidents of history and hers—that we make aliens of our intimates, enemies of friends, strange bedfellows entirely who crave the common ground but rarely find it.

I still don't get it. And I've quit trying to. I've been humming a tune I heard on a country station called "The Truth About Men." The chorus goes: "We ain't wrong, we ain't sorry and it's prob'ly gonna happen again." After a while, it's the truth about women too. Years of living with and among women have convinced me I just don't have a dog in that fight. My daughter, my sisters, my beloved wife (in the associative, not possessive sense), and no few women that I count as lifelong friends, the memory of my mother, aunts, and grandmothers—they've all been and remain powerful and courageous and selfless humans, gifted with a dignity and calm that has made me wish I knew them better. Most days I recite a litany of gratitudes for the pleasures of their company, the beauty and beatitudes of their intellections. Mine and I have been saved and comforted, challenged and loved and mightily improved by the knowledge of them.

Young neighbor couples and their designer dogs go walking with leashes now on weekend mornings. Their puppies and their babies are all pedigreed. Everyone is better trained and behaved. At every corner there are dangers and warnings, at every intersection, flashing lights and signs. The lesson, of course, is to mind the traffic. They learn to speak and heel and fetch and to return. The men, as is their custom, bark out wisdoms. They pose and sniff, they howl and growl and whine. Their wives and pets grow weary of listening. Some things only the dogs hear, some the women.

I ordered a mum plant for Baxter's obsequies scheduled for later this month at Mullett Lake. I asked the florist to write "Sorry" on the card.

I hope they get it.

Father of the Year

TREY ELLIS

Sure, I get some pity, but not nearly as much as I deserve. You might think that all those moms in my daughter's elementary school would be lining up with casseroles for a newly single dad like me, but no. After I put Ava and her little brother, Chet, to bed, I either microwave a Healthy Choice hospital-quality frozen dinner, or I nuke whatever is left over from what Lucia, Chet's nanny, fixed him for lunch that day. More often than not I wash it all down with a few juice boxes (they're so small!) on the couch in front of HBO. *Taxicab Confessions* is one of my favorite shows, cameras hidden all over the back of a taxi giving us a glimpse into the real lives of drunken visitors to Las Vegas. I want cameras installed all over my home so people can see how I live, see what an attentive father I am. Over the course of the season, viewers would also discover the other hurdles I'll have vaulted: my health problems, my near bankruptcy, the deaths of my parents . . . it would become the breakout reality show of the season. (Re)marriage proposals would soon be flooding my e-mail.

One of my favorite episodes would be the one where I'm awakened at 4:15 A.M. by my five-year-old daughter shouting into the monitor, "Daddy! Daddy! Come quick!" As fast as a fireman, and not yet fully conscious, I scamper to their room while trying to hop into the legs of my sweatpants. The bathroom looks like Aerosmith just stayed there: wet, unspooled toilet paper hanging from the medicine cabinet, an entire bottle of deliriously overpriced Mustela baby shampoo puddled over the toilet-seat cover. My almost-two-year-old son stands in the middle of the wreckage looking confusedly at me. I learn later, after interrogation, that his sister had to pee in the night and forgot to shut the bathroom door with the childproof plastic bulb over the knob. She then went back to bed only to be awakened a little later by her brother's celebration. Why Chet was out of bed at four in the morning I don't know and never will. He still holds the pot of hair gel that he has applied to all parts of his face and much of his hair to a thickness of about one adult knuckle. Devo had less product in their hair. Trying to wipe away the goop only applies it more evenly, so I give him a warm bath. By a little after five I am back in my bed, ready to be up at seven again to get Ava to preschool.

Another episode sure to please my viewers would be the morning I find both kids naked and scampering happily around their room. I smile. They look like rare, almost mythical little forest mammals that I feel privileged to have glimpsed in the wild. Then I start to wonder what has become of Chet's diaper and notice two little brown stains on his tiny bed. Not too disgusting. I've seen worse. A quick wipe, a spritz with the Spray 'n Wash, and I pitch the sheets into the dirty clothes. The diaper itself I discover under his bed and miraculously not too stained.

I give the kids a bath. Their naked splashings, Ava's queries— "Daddy, why can't I marry Chetty when I grow up?"—all make me feel like the luckiest parent in the world. In those boring, ordinary, two-parent households you have to share indelible moments like this. I get to greedily hoard them for myself. And I don't have to com-promise with a significant other who might feel that maybe kids shouldn't be encouraged to slurp the rest of the cereal milk right from the bowl. In my house I am the tsar. Trey the Terrible.

I am smiling at these happy thoughts while walking back into their bedroom. Suddenly I stop. Just next to my foot, on the carpet between an overturned baby stroller and a naked, black Ken doll with amazingly ripped abs, looms a mountain of turd nearly as large as my son.

I pull Chet out of the bathtub and bring him to the cairn of shit. I don't think he has ever looked more cute.

"Do NOT take your diaper off. Do NOT leave piles of crap all over the . . ." It is getting too complicated, so mid course I correct and get back on message. "Do NOT take your diaper off." I haven't had a dog since I was five, but I have seen people training them, so I model my tone of voice on theirs.

Chet just smiles and nods, his thumb as always plugged into his mouth, his index finger hooking his nose.

"Mommy-daddy," he says. That's what he calls me when he's excited.

I loved it. I loved it in the moment and I loved the anecdote it instantly became. I imagined, thanks to my show, that all the world had watched me clean up the crap and spray carpet cleaner on the carpet, and all the world had seen that I hadn't strangled my son, raised my voice, or even just slapped him around a little. I imagined that I would be a shoo-in for Father of the Year. Being black wouldn't hurt my chances either, since the unfair cliché about men of my race is so much the opposite.

Often I fantasize an elaborate and televised ceremony, warm and funny speeches, my pleasant embarrassment at all the attention. I imagine my kids at my side, spit-shined and radiating the pure joy of the well-parented child. Bill Clinton on behalf of the Children's Defense Fund would give me the award, as golden and as weighty as an Oscar.

The award would mark the end of the loneliest period of my entire life, easily the hardest time in a pretty hard forty-one years. My married friends, who had been so supportive immediately after Sybil left me, would be reminded of my parental valor and so guilt-ridden at having forgotten about me that I'd be invited to fascinating dinner parties every week, well stocked with lovely and eligible future step-moms. My bachelor friends would so envy my newfound celebrity that they would put up with me bringing my kids along to the auto show. I'd finally be able to look back at this time in my life and say, "*Phew.*"

In my speech I would explain how I got here; how it was not at all the life I was aiming for. Sybil and I started living together almost as soon as we met. I was twenty-eight, she was twenty-five, and we were married four years later. For eight years we felt like a celebrated supercouple, profiled in *People* and the *Los Angeles Times*. I was a successful novelist and screenwriter, and Sybil had published her first novel. We were convinced that we were on our way to becoming the greatest literary marriage since Dashiell Hammett and Lillian Hellman.

We'd been together seven years when Ava was born. Since we were both working artists we divided child-care duties right down the middle, scrupulously so. I watched Ava until ten, when Lucia, the nanny, arrived and stayed until two, at which point my wife took over. Then in the late afternoons my wife and I would alternate days playing with our daughter and putting her to bed. Saturday was my wife's responsibility, and Sunday was mine. I was pretty goddamn smug about our seemingly civilized division of labor until I realized that I was seeing less and less of my wife. On Saturday I would try to stay close and do some sort of family outing, but on Sundays, her day off, she would disappear like a rabbit in the woods.

A few months later, while I was slogging through the first draft of an already overdue script, I would hear her across the hall in her office, the door closed, cackling to herself. To add insult to my injury she was typing almost bionically fast. By then I should have been used to her superhuman feats. Before Ava was born she was in the Ph.D. program in American Studies at UCLA by day but would write and rewrite her first novel till dawn every night. Weeks went by when I don't believe she slept more than two or three hours a night. Finally, however, she finished the book, sold it for a bundle, and slept.

This time when she showed me what she had written my heart stopped. "Fjeikcim mmmieim jmdskaij jkjakop aalkkmmie" for more than one hundred pages. My mom had MS and shot herself in the heart when I was sixteen. My dad died of AIDS complications when I was twenty-two. All I had left in this world was this woman and our little girl. If I lost Sybil I knew that I could not survive. Our Dashiell and Lillian lifestyle had suddenly devolved into something more akin to F. Scott and Zelda.

At UCLA she had studied the First Great Awakening, the outbreak of religious piety in the American Colonies right before the revolution. She told me that *this* was her Great Awakening, her first step from the run-of-the-mill Buppie into a conscious, spiritual being, and that she'd never felt more fulfilled in all her life. I didn't know what to do. Yet on her own she started writing in English again and I thought the crisis had passed. In fact, great times returned. Sure, I had a kooky wife and she had a straight-laced husband, but we still held hands in the house and made up love ditties to whisper to each other before going to bed.

One day, about a year later, I noticed that my feet had swollen. After a few days I finally told a doctor friend of mine who ordered me to the emergency room that night. It turned out the urine sample I gave them was awash in protein. A biopsy later confirmed that I had focal segmental glomerulosclerosis, the same serious kidney disease that affects former San Antonio Spur Sean Elliott and recently retired New Jersey Net Alonzo Mourning. I started taking thirty pills a day, and still the lower half of my body was flooded with an extra twenty pounds of fluid. My dick looked like a water balloon, and I used to just stare at it whenever I wanted to wallow in abject panic. The immunosuppressants I gobbled three times a day made me so susceptible to the tiniest bug that every few weeks I would find myself doubled over the toilet bowl facefirst, and then I'd have to jump to my feet to try to get my ass around to the bowl before the onset of an unspeakably messy catastrophe.

Throughout all of this Sybil was amazingly supportive. She held me when I cried, lit candles, and saged the house to bring "white light" to help protect me. I didn't complain. There was no cure for what I had (and there still isn't), so I was open to anything.

About a year and a half later the swelling mysteriously disappeared and I thought the most difficult chapter of my life was just behind me. Instead, as soon as I stopped needing Sybil's constant comforting, we started living more and more separate lives, the center of hers being a hippie dance class every Sunday morning. She got me to go once, and as I walked in I saw a hundred of them, from now-old original-issue hippies to young wannabes, all twirling, undulating, and hooting. She had gotten me to open up to many New Age practices that otherwise I would have ridiculed, but flailing my arms next to overweight tie-dyed grandmas named Serenity was a path that I just could not bring myself to take.

Then one night she went to a party for some of her dance friends without me, wearing red-sequined devil horns and her red Kenzo shearling coat I had bought her one summer in Saint-Tropez (the single-most expensive article of clothing I have ever bought anyone). The next morning I could tell something had changed. We were in Ava's room, cooing over our then two-year-old napping in her crib, when Sybil told me that at the party she had made out with a raw vegan, a white guy who'd changed his name to something Indian, a jumble of vowels, and now she was convinced that he was her "soul mate." I had to force myself to keep breathing. I went downstairs and Sybil followed me and I lay down on the floor and suddenly my entire body started trembling. My legs, my arms, my chest all quivered as if somebody had put a quarter in the slot of some cheap motel's Magic Fingers mattress. Sybil held me and told me that she still loved me too but that the "new" her needed to be free to love the world, not just her husband.

Before Ava was born I'd volunteered at the Suicide Prevention Center, manning the hot line, and I now found myself so devastated that I was contemplating a technique a very depressed old woman had once described to me over the phone (duct-taping a plastic bag over your head). For weeks I couldn't write, I couldn't do anything except drive in my car up and down Wilshire Boulevard wondering if I was going to survive. But eventually I would come home and play with Ava and I knew that I could never rob from her what my mom had robbed from me.

Sybil found us a New Age couples' counseling team whose theory was based on absolute and complete honesty between partners. It was exactly what both of us needed to try to clear the undergrowth of mistrust that had been growing between us. I had been trying to morph her into Shirley Jones on *The Partridge Family*, while she had wanted me to shapeshift into Lenny Kravitz.

She swore the "soul mate" was now just a friend, and I gradually began to hope of being able to rebuild a life together again. Then I went off to a weekend yoga retreat in Santa Barbara and Sybil told me that I could make love with someone there if I found a true "heart connection." I told her that wasn't why I was going.

Her "free love" pass did not come totally out of the blue. Living in Southern California, we were practically ordered by the state to practice tantric sex, and once there was this lovely Italian *tantrika* that I had discovered on the Internet who came over and gave us both an extremely hands-on, simultaneous lesson. I had not been a saint during our twelve years together. I was addicted to porn, had gotten a few hand jobs from a few strippers, and slept with two Heidi Fleiss–type girls at my bachelor party in Las Vegas. When I had confessed to these misdeeds years ago, even before couples' counseling, my friends thought that Sybil and I deserved each other, two nutcases under one roof. Maybe they were right. Though she always said she loved my (retroactive) honesty, looking back on it now I know that she never really fully trusted me again and at least part of the reason for her making out with the white boy with the Indian name was old-fashioned payback.

As luck would have it, when I got to the retreat I found myself surrounded by gorgeous actresses (including my tent mate—a then-unknown Naomi Watts), but I didn't try anything with anybody. I didn't want to, and our marriage was already so fragile that I knew it would not withstand a fling, no matter how much New Age tolerance Sybil spouted.

When I got home, Sybil sat me down and told me about the incredible adventure she had while I was gone. She showed me her new butterfly tattoo, then went on to tell me how she had flirted with dozens of guys all over the Westside. At first I thought she was kidding. She is a great storyteller, and I thought this was some sort of test. But as it started to sink in that she was telling me the truth, that the tattoo was as real as the phone numbers she'd given out, it suddenly felt as if my heart had disappeared and all that was left was a construction site.

Somewhere inside of me I must have finally understood that our once storybook romance was now terminally ill, but just like when my dad had said he had AIDS-related complex, not full-blown AIDS, I again deluded myself into thinking that somehow our love could survive.

We went back to the counselors. We even went to an intensive weekend seminar taught by Gay and Kathlyn Hendricks, the inventors of the relationship technique our counselors were trained in.

Sybil and I ended up crying in each other's arms, vowing our undying, ever-expanding love for each other.

Ava was now three years old. Sybil and I had been together ten years and had already weathered a lifetime's marital conflict. We thought we'd come out on the other side with a marriage that was tempered and now invincible. So we decided to have another child. I thought that having two kids might ground Sybil through her wilder episodes, and for the first few months after Chet was born everything seemed perfect. Then, when Chet was six months old, I noticed that she seemed consumed with sadness. I assumed it was post-partum depression and would disappear with time but it just seemed to get worse. One day she asked me to help fix something on her computer, and I was so worried about her that I took advantage of the opportunity to spy at her diary. In it she talked about how trapped and depressed she felt. I confronted her and she agreed to see a therapist. But after only a few months she stopped.

One night she insisted on stripping at a local gentlemen's club's amateur night. Then she insisted I take a lover and tell her all about it—"Something," she said, "to shake up our boring lives." I refused, but of course almost all of me finally realized that our marriage was dead. Then she at last told me what she had been itching to tell me: that she wanted to sleep with other people, to have a totally open marriage. I told her that if she wanted to take a female lover (and not even allow me to watch), I could stomach that because I knew that eventually she would come back to me. But—and here I drew a last-ditch line in the sand—I said she would have to choose between being with only me and being with anybody else but me. I was about 80 percent sure that she would back down, come to her senses, and choose the love of her life. After all, we were made for each other. Everybody said so. Hell, we even have the same birthday.

She just looked at me with a smile of sweet pity and told me that we would always be friends.

Nothing in my life has ever so emptied me. I would drive and cry and the tears would streak back toward my ears and feel cool in the breeze. Even though she had decided to leave me, I was the one who moved out. I was the man, and isn't that what men are supposed to do? The kids need their mother more. The father scrounges for weekends.

For a week I slept on friends' floors, then got up at six in the morning to get back to the house by seven when the kids woke up. I had had breakfast with them almost every morning of their lives and Sybil only watched them in the afternoons, and she said she didn't want to shock them by such a big change in routine. I thought it was crazy that she wouldn't get up with them while I was out of the house, but I was too destroyed at the time to protest. Everything in my life, it seemed, was collapsing simultaneously. I hadn't had a writing assignment in over a year and was $100,000 in debt; the credit cards were all maxed out so I couldn't even charge a hotel room. To make things worse, horrible songs like "Just When I Needed You Most" and "If You Leave Me Now" played over and over in my head. Yet that was exactly what it felt like, as if she was abandoning me at my lowest point, as if most of me had suddenly been scooped away and all that was left was one eye, half a nose, maybe an arm.

I remember very clearly the night all the credit cards were frozen and I was trying to sleep on a piece of foam on the floor of my friends' apartment in a rough section of Venice. A police helicopter was circling the neighborhood, its forceful floodlights illuminating the curtains and the backyard. I looked at my 1965 Rolex and wondered where the nearest all-night pawnshop was. I thought about giddy summers Sybil and I had spent in Saint-Tropez, Santorini, and Martha's Vineyard; our months living in Paris, the vacations to Rio, Saint Bart's, and Mallorca.

"So this is the bottom," I said to myself. "I always wondered what it would feel like."

I was right. The next day was already better. I received a $120 check for something and it was drawn on the same bank that I use, so I got the cash on the spot. The money, and the prodding of my friends, knocked some sense back into me, and I went back to Sybil and demanded that she move out. She was the one who craved freedom. I just craved my family. A few days later I freed up some money and paid for a little studio she'd found on Venice Beach.

Oh, how I appreciated my king-sized bed! We sold the house in Santa Monica, which put enough money in my pocket to move myself and the kids to our current architecturally significant but dilapidated house in Venice, a five-minute walk from their mother's studio.

Settling into single life is the hardest thing I've ever done—harder than the death of my mother when I was a teenager, harder than nursing my father to his death when I was twenty-two. Taking care of the kids distracts me, but then we say our "I love yous" and I turn off the light, close the door, and a cavern of loneliness opens up and swallows me whole. I might read, watch cable, or surf Internet porn, but nothing fills the emptiness. Every night I slip into my kids' room and readjust their blankets. Sometimes I lie on the carpet and flirt with the idea of sleeping there all night. In this way they're luckier than I am. When they close their eyes, they've at least got each other.

Usually I don't resent Sybil. I no longer recognize or understand her, but I don't resent her. Family life overwhelmed her, and I understand that. She needed to get out of it, and she did. Since leaving me she's changed her name and opted out of accepting alimony. The kids love her, of course, and she still keeps the hours with them that we carved out when we lived together. Every afternoon Monday through Saturday she comes over for four or five hours and takes them to play dates or the park or cooks with them. Yet unlike me, every night she's free as the wind.

So she'll never be Shirley Jones on *The Partridge Family*, but *The Courtship of Eddie's Father* was one of my favorite shows. This is what I was made to do, apparently, and except for the loneliness, I'm not complaining. I'm proud of my NASCAR-emblazoned child seats strapped into the back of my 1973 electric-blue Mach I convertible. At stoplights I love the way folks in their SUVs look down, stare, and smile. Then the light turns green, I gun my engine, and the three of us race away. We're free too.

Contributors

Eric Bartels is a feature writer for the twice-weekly *Portland Tribune* in Portland, Oregon, where he lives with his wife, Nancy, and children, Léna and Errol.

Kevin Canty is the award-winning author of the short-story collections *Honeymoon* and *A Stranger in This World* and the novels *Into the Great Wide Open* and *Nine Below Zero*. His work has been published in *The New Yorker, Esquire, GQ, Details, Story, The New York Times Magazine,* and *Glimmer Train*. He lives in Missoula, Montana.

Ron Carlson is the author of eight books of fiction, most recently his selected stories *A Kind of Flying*. His novel *The Speed of Light* and the paperback edition of his short-story collection *At the Jim Bridger* were published in 2003. His short stories have appeared in *Esquire, Harper's, The New Yorker, GQ,* and other journals, as well as dozens of anthologies including *The Best American Short Stories, The O'Henry Prize Series, The Pushcart Prize Anthology,* and *The Norton Anthology of Short Fiction*. He has taught writing at Arizona State University since 1986 and was named the first Foundation Professor there in 2003. Among his awards are a National Endowment for the

Arts fellowship in fiction, the Cohen Prize at *Ploughshares,* and a National Society of Arts and Letters Literature Award.

Sean Elder has written about men, marriage, divorce, and raising children for a number of publications including *California, Parenting* (where he was also an editor), *Men's Health, Men's Journal,* and *The New York Times Magazine.* He was the film and music editor at *Elle* magazine in the early nineties and has continued to write about show business for a host of magazines including *Entertainment Weekly, Harper's Bazaar, Premiere,* and *Vogue.* He covered the web for *The New Yorker,* where he wrote the "Only Connect" column for several years. More recently he wrote a media column for *Salon,* where he is still a regular contributor, and is a contributing editor at *Details.* His essay "On Ecstasy" appeared in Chronicle Books' psychedelic reader, *White Rabbit* (1995), and working with designer Roger Black he wrote *Web Sites That Work* (Adobe Press, 1997). He lives in Brooklyn with his wife and two children.

Stephen Elliott's most recent novel, *Happy Baby,* was copublished by MacAdam/Cage and McSweeney's in February 2004. He lives in San Francisco and teaches at Stanford University.

Trey Ellis is a novelist, screenwriter and essayist. His acclaimed first novel, *Platitudes,* was recently reissued by Northeastern University Press along with his influential essay, "The New Black Aesthetic." He is also the author of *Home Repairs* and *Right Here, Right Now* which was a recipient of the American Book Award. His work for the screen includes the Emmy nominated *Tuskegee Airmen* and *Good Fences* starring Danny Glover and Whoopi Goldberg. He lives in Venice, California, and in Paris.

Steve Friedman is a correspondent for *Outside* magazine and has also written for *Esquire, GQ, Men's Journal, Details,* and *The Wash-*

ington Post. He is the author of *The Gentleman's Guide to Life* (Clarkson-Potter) and coauthor of *Loose Balls: Easy Money, Hard Fouls, Cheap Laughs & True Love in the NBA* (Doubleday). Many of his stories have been included in *The Best American Sports Writing.* He lives in New York City.

David Gates is the author of the novels *Jernigan* and *Preston Falls* and the short-story collection *The Wonders of the Invisible World.* A finalist for the Pulitzer Prize in fiction and the National Book Critics Circle Award, he writes about arts and culture for *Newsweek* and lives in New York City and in a small town in upstate New York.

Panio Gianopoulos has published essays, stories, and articles in *Tin House, Nerve, The Hartford Courant, Northwest Review, The Brooklyn Rail,* and *The Journal News.* He is a recipient of a 2003 fellowship in nonfiction literature from the New York Foundation for the Arts. He lives in Manhattan.

Anthony Giardina is the author of the novels *Men with Debts, A Boy's Pretensions,* and *Recent History* and the short-story collection *The Country of Marriage.* His short fiction has appeared in *Harper's, Esquire,* and *GQ* and his essays in *GQ, Harper's,* and *The New York Times Magazine.* His plays, which include *Living at Home, The Child, Scenes from La Vie de Boheme, The Beach,* and *Black Forest,* have been produced in New York at Playwrights Horizons and the Manhattan Theatre Club, and regionally at Arena Stage in Washington, D.C., Yale Rep, and the Long Wharf Theater in New Haven. He has taught fiction and playwriting at the Michener Center of the University of Texas at Austin, Colorado College, and Mount Holyoke College. He lives with his family in Northampton, Massachusetts.

Manny Howard is a food-and-travel writer whose work has appeared in *The New York Times Magazine* as well as *The New York*

Times "Dining" section, *GQ*, the *New York Observer, Elle, Travel & Leisure,* and *Food & Wine,* among others. He grew up in Brooklyn, where he lives with his family.

Rob Jackson lives in Deerfield, Massachusetts, where, in addition to running the household, he writes, coaches, and occasionally teaches.

Benjamin LaGuer is a writer at the Norfolk State Penitentiary in Norfolk, Massachusetts. He graduated magna cum laude from Boston University. His writing has appeared in *Boston* magazine, *Boston Poet, Worcester* magazine, and the *Columbia Review.* In 1998 he won a PEN Award for his memoir, *A Man Who Loves His Mother Loves Women.*

Fred Leebron, a creative-writing professor at Gettysburg College, has received a Pushcart Prize, an O. Henry Award, and two fellowships from the Pennsylvania Council on the Arts. His stories have appeared in numerous publications, including *Grand Street, Triquarterly, Threepenny Review, Ploughshares,* and *DoubleTake.* His novels include *Out West, Six Figures,* and *In the Middle of All This.* Currently director of the M.F.A. program in creative writing at Queens University of Charlotte, he has also coedited *Postmodern American Fiction: A Norton Anthology,* and coauthored *Creating Fiction: A Writer's Companion.*

Thomas Lynch is a poet, essayist, and funeral director. He is the author of three collections of poems, *Skating with Heather Grace* (Knopf, 1987), *Grimalkin & Other Poems* (Jonathan Cape, 1994), *and Still Life in Milford* (Norton, 1998). His collection of essays, *The Undertaking: Life Studies from the Dismal Trade* (Norton, 1997) won the American Book Award, the Heartland Prize, and the Society of Midland Authors Award and was a finalist for the National Book

Award. A second book of essays, *Bodies in Motion and at Rest* (Norton, 2000), won the Great Lakes Book Award and the Michigan Library Association Author of the Year Award. His work has appeared in *Harper's, The New Yorker, Esquire, Oprah,* the *Los Angeles Times,* the *New York Times,* the *Irish Times,* and *The Times* (London) and has been broadcast on NPR, RTE (Ireland), and the BBC. He lives and works in Milford, Michigan, and in West Clare, Ireland, where he keeps an ancestral cottage.

Lewis Nordan is the author of the memoir *Boy with Loaded Gun* and seven books of fiction, including the acclaimed novels *Wolf Whistle, The Sharpshooter Blues,* and *Lightning Song,* for which he has received many awards, including the Southern Book Critics Circle Award in fiction and three American Library Association Notable Book citations. Born and raised in the Mississippi Delta, he lives now in Pittsburgh, where he serves as professor of creative writing at the University of Pittsburgh.

Vince Passaro is the author of the novel *Violence, Nudity, Adult Content.* A second novel is due out from Simon and Schuster in 2005. His essays, fiction, and criticism have appeared in many national magazines and journals, including *Esquire, GQ, The New York Times Magazine,* and *Harper's,* where he is a contributing editor. He lives in New York City.

Jim Paul is a poet and writer who lives in the Rincon Mountains, east of Tucson, Arizona. His most recent book is a novel, *Elsewhere in the Land of Parrots,* published in 2003 by Harcourt. He is also the author of *Catapult: Harry and I Build a Siege Weapon* and *Medieval in L.A.* (both Harvest Books) and of *The Rune Poem,* a translation of the tenth-century naming verse for the English rune set. His poems have appeared in *The New Yorker, The Paris Review, Poetry,* and elsewhere.

He was a Wallace Stegner Fellow in creative writing at Stanford University and a Guggenheim Fellow. He holds a Ph.D. in English literature from the University of Michigan and has taught on the M.F.A. faculty at Antioch University, Los Angeles, and at the Bread Loaf Writers' Conference.

Hank Pine is a pseudonym for a lawyer and writer living in the Northeast.

Elwood Reid is the author of the short-story collection *What Salmon Know* and two novels, *If I Don't Six* and *Midnight Sun.* His new novel, *D.B.,* will be published by Doubleday in 2004. He lives in Livingston, Montana, with his wife and daughters.

Steven Rinehart lives in New York City with his wife and three children. He is a software executive and the author of the short-story collection *Kick in the Head* and the novel *Built in a Day,* both from Doubleday.

Christopher Russell lives in New York City with his wife, Gina, and son, Jacob. He is a ceramicist whose work can be seen at www.russellproject.com.

Robert Skates is a pseudonym for a writer living in New England.

Rob Spillman is the editor of the literary magazine *Tin House* and editor at Tin House/Bloomsbury Books. He has previously worked at Random House, *SPY* magazine, *The New Yorker,* and *Vanity Fair.* His essays and reviews have appeared in *Bookforum, GQ, The New York Times Book Review, Rolling Stone, Salon, Spin,* and *Vogue,* among other magazines, newspapers, and anthologies. He lives in Brooklyn with his wife and children.

Anthony Swofford is the author of *Jarhead: A Marine's Chronicle of the Gulf War and Other Battles* (Scribner, 2003). His writing has appeared in *The New York Times, The New York Times Magazine, The Guardian, Harper's, The Iowa Review,* and other publications, and he writes the column "The Ink" for *Details* magazine. He teaches in the M.F.A. program at Saint Mary's College in Moraga, California, and lives in Oakland. He's currently writing a novel.

Touré is the author of *The Portable Promised Land,* a collection of short stories published by Little, Brown. He is also a contributing editor at *Rolling Stone.* His work has also appeared in *The New Yorker, The New York Times Magazine, Tennis Magazine, The Best American Essays of 1999, The Best American Sportswriting of 2001, The Best American Erotica of 2004,* and *Zoetrope: All Story,* where he won the Sam Adams Short Story Contest. He is a contributor to NPR's *All Things Considered* and CNN's *American Morning* and the host of MTV2's *Spoke N' Heard.* He studied at Columbia University's graduate school of creative writing and lives in Fort Greene, Brooklyn. His novel *Soul City* will be published in September 2004. His website address is www.toure.com.

Acknowledgments

I find it somehow appropriate that three women deserve the most credit for getting this project off the ground. The first two are my wife, Cathi Hanauer, and her friend (and mine) Kate Christensen, who caused enough trouble when they dreamed up the idea for *The Bitch in the House* one evening at our kitchen table and then made matters worse by corralling me into doing a men's version. Once they saddled me up and put the bit in my mouth, I headed straight to my agent, Amanda Urban, who steered me in the right direction, dispensed her usual bulletproof advice, championed the book as only she can, and promptly brought into the effort another man, my editor, Henry Ferris. Henry helped me make this book as good as it could be, just as he did three years earlier with my last book.

And I've been privileged to be in the company of men ever since—namely, these twenty-six brave and talented souls who've written so honestly, skillfully, and humorously about their lives in ways that amuse and enrich. It's been an honor to work with them. In particular, I am grateful to David Gates, Kevin Canty, and Ron Carlson for their early commitment and enthusiasm. Once things got rolling, contributors Rob Spillman, Elwood Reid, Stephen Elliott, and Fred Leebron were especially generous with their time and ideas.

For friendship, brainstorming, time, test marketing, and general assistance and support I'd like to thank Roberta Myers, Frank Michielli, David Handelman, Margo Rabb, Christine Preston, Rory Evans, Ted Conover, Margot Guralnick, Chris Russell, Gina Russell, Elinor Lipman, Eric Goldscheider, Denise Shannon, Jen Marshall, Amy Hanauer, Bette and Lonnie Hanauer, Judy Spring, Fred and Lois Feldman, Elizabeth Feldman, Helen Schulman, Bruce Handy, Elissa Schappell, Stan Yarbro, Betsy Jones, Pam Friedman, and Keith Ulrich. At ICM I owe big thanks to Sloan Harris, Christina Capone, Dylan Kletter, Liz Farrell, James Gregorio, and John DeLaney. At William Morrow, many thanks to Michael Morrison, Debbie Stier, Kristen Green, and Lisa Nager.

To my parents and my brother, thanks for your lifelong support of my creative endeavors. To Phoebe and Nathaniel, thanks for being so patient and funny—you are the best and I love you. To Cathi— your ideas, support, energy, and enthusiasm are what saw me through. This one's for you, with all my love and gratitude.